A Guide to LOCAL
ENVIRONMENTAL
AUDITING

Hugh Barton • Noel Bruder

Ruth Allen • David Dickerson • Richard Guise • Bob Keen • Helmut
Lusser • Dominic Stead • Jane Stephenson • Richard St George

EARTHSCAN
Earthscan Publications Ltd, London

Cover photo © The Environmental Picture Library
Picture research by Brooks Krikler

First Published in 1995 by
Earthscan Publications Limited
120 Pentonville Road, London N1 9JN

ISBN: 1 85383 234 0

Typeset by DP Photosetting, Aylesbury, Bucks
Printed and bound by Biddles Ltd, Guildford and King's Lynn
Cover design by Dominic Banner

Earthscan Publications Limited is an editorially independent subsidiary of Kogan
Page Limited and publishes in association with the International Institute for
Environment and Development and WWF, UK

CONTENTS

List of Illustrations

FIGURES

BOXES

TABLES

GLOSSARY

AIDA   Analysis of Interconnected Decision Areas: a tool used in environmental auditing to determine a framework for policy evaluation.

biodiversity   A global term referred to in the Concise Oxford Dictionary of Ecology (1994) as '...all aspects of biological diversity especially including species richness, ecosystem complexity and genetic variation'.

biosphere   The part of the earth that includes living organisms

BPEO   Best Practicable Environmental Option: A concept established by the Royal Commission on Environmental Pollution that seeks to establish a safe disposal method (by air, water or land) for pollutants that takes account of the environment and utilizes all available technological options.

BREEAM   Building Research Establishment Environmental Assessment Method. A system of certification for housing established by the Building Research Establishment that combines the measurement of energy efficiency and environmental acceptability as well as incorporating an energy efficiency analysis called BREDEM.

CAD   Computer Aided Design

CAP   Common Agricultural Policy

CFCs   Chlorofluorocarbons

Cercla   Comprehensive Environmental Response, Compensation and Liability Act

COD   chemical oxygen demand

CSD   Commission for Sustainable Development

CSO   Central Statistical Office

CORINE   A European Union Network of environmental information that seeks to coordinate the collection of standardized data in member states of the Union

COSHH	Control Of Substances Hazardous to Health
CREATE	Community Recycling, Environmental Action, Training and Education project
DoE	Department of the Environment
DTI	Department of Trade and Industry
DTp	Department of Transport
EA	Environmental Audit: A review of environmental conditions and the environmental impact of the activities of a particular enterprise or institution. At the local authority level, they may be divided into the external audit (State of the Environment Report) and the internal audit (Review of Policies and Practices).
EAP	Environmental Appraisal of Development Plans: A term used when evaluating the environmental implications of policies and proposals set out in District Wide Local Plans and Unitary Development Plans
EIA	Environmental Impact Assessment. A widely used term, especially abroad, generally referring to project appraisal, that is evaluating the environmental impact of particular development policies
EMAS	Eco-Management and Audit Scheme. An EU initiative, designed for the private sector but now adapted for use by UK local authorities, consisting of a set of formalized procedures for addressing the environmental impacts of an organization's policies and practices.
EPA	Environmental Protection Act, 1990
ESAs	Environmentally Sensitive Areas
GIS	Geographic Information System
GNP	Gross National Product
IA	Internal Auditing
ICLEI	International Council for Local Environmental Initiatives
IPCC	Intergovernmental Panel on Climatic Change
IULA	International Union of Local Authorities
LAWDCs	Local Authority Waste Disposal Companies
LCA	Life Cycle Analysis. A 'cradle to grave' assessment of the environmental impact of a particular product or service
LGMB	Local Government Management Board
MA	Management Audit
MAFF	Ministry of Agriculture, Fisheries and Food
NFU	National Farmers Union
NIMBYism	'Not in my back yard' syndrome
NIMTO	'Not in my term of office'
NRA	National Rivers Authority
PIA	Policy Impact Assessment. Evaluation of the environmental

	impact of an agency's regulatory, policy and service activities
PPG	Planning Policy Guidance
RCRA	Resources Conservation and Recovery Act
RIP	Review of Internal Practices. An evaluation of the environmental impact of an agency's own operations and practices
SAP	Standard Assessment Procedure
SEA	Strategic Environmental Assessment
SoE	State of the Environment. Report sometimes known as the external audit, which involves the regular monitoring and review of the quality of the environment in the area concerned, and of implications for global sustainability
SSSI	Site of Special Scientific Interest
TPO	Tree Preservation Order
TPP	Transport Policies and Programmes
VOCs	Volatile Organic Compounds
WHO	World Health Organization

FOREWORD

This new book by a team from the University of the West of England provides a distinctive perspective on current practice within local authorities. Use of the term 'environmental auditing' within local authorities is broader than in the industrial and manufacturing sectors, and this book will certainly help to clarify the different ways in which it is applied in this context.

The case studies the authors present and the methodologies they describe reflect the range of current practices. Those considering the use of environmental audits as a spur to enhanced environmental performance, particularly in relation to the application of Local Agenda 21 towards sustainable development, or the implementation of the Eco-Management and Audit Regulation within local government, will find the book a very serviceable reference and guide.

It remains to be seen how environmental auditing develops within local government, and particularly whether there will be further convergence with the approaches taken in the corporate sector. The area is evolving quickly, and I welcome a book which will encourage the flow of ideas across the sectors involved.

Dr Suzie J Baverstock
Director of the Institute of Environmental Assessment, and
Secretary to the Environmental Auditors Registration Association

ACKNOWLEDGEMENTS

Hugh Barton and Noel Bruder would like to thank the following:

Martin Large, of Hawthorn Press, who commissioned the book in the first instance and helped shape its character, and without whose enthusiasm and friendship it would never have seen the light of day.

Bob Keen, for stimulating the original interest in Environmental Auditing at Bristol Polytechnic (as was) and subsequently giving his unstinting support to this project.

All the contributors, for their commitment, knowledge, patience and tolerance in the face of our reasonable and unreasonable demands; and for their useful comments on the text as it emerged. In addition to those credited with chapters, thanks are due to Brian Price and Mark Letcher.

Finally, a wide range of people across the country, in local authorities, universities and environmental organisations, who have directly or indirectly contributed to the contents of this book through comment or discourse.

Julie Triggle, for ever helpful and efficient typing and retyping of the drafts, putting together the final disc.

Tony Hathway and Jim Claydon for supporting and facilitating the writing of the book in the Faculty at a time of financial squeeze.

Isobel Daniels and (earlier) Suzanne Pauli for assistance with editing, referencing, signposts and index.

PREFACE

The central challenge of the 1990s, enunciated by the Earth Summit at Rio, is to work for sustainability. Local Agenda 21, European moves and UK governmental guidance all stress the growing importance of local authorities as stewards of the environment. Yet few local authorities have a clear picture of the environmental quality of their own area, let alone knowledge of how their policies are affecting global sustainability.

Environmental auditing in this context is a process for establishing what sustainable development means in practice – how to interpret it locally, how to test whether you are achieving it.

The purpose of this book is to show how environmental auditing can be tackled by local authorities. It provides guidance on monitoring the state of the environment in the local area, and establishing the impact of local action on global issues. It shows how the policies and practices of the local authority can be modified to recognize environmental priorities.

The book is both a *guide* and an *analysis*. On the one hand it provides specific help on how to do audits, with checklists, standards and processes spelt out. On the other hand it does not treat auditing as a mechanical procedure. It explores the issues and choices which local authorities may face in developing their audit towards sustainable goals. The process is not easy. Current good practice is examined in order to throw light on the problems. Awkward policy issues where good auditing will threaten established goals or interests – for example in relation to transport and planning – are recognized and dealt with.

HOW TO USE THIS BOOK

The three parts of the book have distinct functions, and may be consulted independently. The reader should pick the starting point suited to his or her needs.

PART I introduces the auditing process, sets it in context, examines the *who*, *what*, *why*, *when* and *how* of auditing, and relates auditing to central questions of sustainability. It is intended to be accessible to those who know little about auditing at the start, but also to give a fresh perspective for those who do know something.

PART II looks at auditing topic by topic. Experts in the field give their own commentary and in many cases make radical suggestions on how auditing should be improved. Where appropriate, chapters cover both 'state of the environment' monitoring and the assessment of local policies and practices.

PART III builds on Parts I and II, taking a certain level of auditing knowledge for granted. It is a more reflective evaluation of current practice, based on extensive surveys and case studies that are reported here for the first time. The main focus is on questions of environmental management within local authorities.

QUICK REFERENCE

The guide is designed for ease of reference, allowing users to pick up the key points quickly. At the end of each chapter in Parts I and III there are specific recommendations for auditors. Part II chapters give extensive checklists which allow rapid review of current practice in your community.

The first three Appendices pull these checklists together in summary, to indicate the scope of each element of an audit. Appendix 4 provides essential background information on the European/UK legislative context. Finally, there are signposts for further reading, and contacts for those wishing to pursue issues in greater depth, organized by topic.

Hugh Barton, Noel Bruder, April 1995

Part I

AUDITING AND SUSTAINABILITY

INTRODUCTION

A main purpose of Part I is to make explicit the link between local authority environmental auditing and the principle of sustainable development. The other main purpose is to set out the *process* of auditing clearly, providing a map which identifies the nature of auditing, and the way in which it may be organized.

This Introduction sets the scene by looking at the background to the concept of sustainable development. In that context Chapter 1 examines the historical and institutional context of auditing. It sets out the different main elements of auditing, the reasons for doing them, and the basic approach to doing them. It makes clear that auditing is not a one-off event but an ongoing process.

Chapter 2 then examines that process in more detail. In particular State of the Environment monitoring (SoE) is set alongside Policy Impact Analysis (PIA) and the importance of the link between them demonstrated. Key issues of who should do the audit, and how councillors, the public and other agencies should be involved, are explored. Some useful auditing techniques, trying to make sense of complexity, are explained.

Chapter 3 returns to the question of sustainability. It suggests the appropriate scope of environmental concern, sheds some light on the concepts of environmental capacity and environmental indicators. It also provides a view on two important aspects of sustainability – climate change, and non-renewable resources.

Chapter 4 then integrates theory with practice. Two case studies, one urban, one rural, are examined. In both cases the authors are prime movers of the auditing process and thus uniquely placed to explain the thinking and experience of the authorities concerned.

THE CONCEPT OF SUSTAINABLE DEVELOPMENT

The holy grail of contemporary environmentalism is 'sustainable development' – devoutly wished by everyone from Porritt to Major, hallowed by the Earth Summit in Rio 1992, invoked by pundits, planners and politicians to lend credibility to argument, and yet – a strangely ineffable concept, hard to pin down, harder still to achieve.

In the modern era the initial focus of concern for global sustainability was population level. At the start of the nineteenth century Malthus was arguing that the Earth had limited carrying capacity, and pointing to the impossibility of exponential population growth.

The fact that he underestimated the potential of technological innovation in agriculture and industry to increase effective carrying capacity has lulled successive generations into a sense of false security. It was only in 1972 that the intellectual battle was fully joined with the publication in quick succession of the *Ecologist* magazine's 'Blueprint for Survival'[1] and the Club of Rome's 'Limits to Growth'.[2] While the former could be dismissed by cynics as a utopian tract (as in part it was) the latter was commissioned by respected European industrialists and posed a real threat to conventional economic wisdom. It demonstrated that the prevailing pattern of exponential growth in population and resource use could not be sustained, and would lead to global economic and environmental crisis early next century. It called for radical reorientation of political priorities and the adoption of sustainable policies.

The weakness in the *Limits to Growth* model was that it worked with absolutes (such as the level of oil resources) which could subsequently prove to be misconceived. Opponents argued that the economic system would allow progressive adaption to scarcity: high prices would force greater efficiency, substitution and an intensified search for raw materials. And indeed this has proved to be the case. Following the energy price rises of 1973 and 1979 we now have a glut of oil supplies again, energy efficiency has to some extent become institutionalized (at least in the first world), and new fuels are substituting for old (eg natural gas for coal) (Flavin, 1984).

But this is only part of the story. While the world is awash with oil now, some of the key resources have limited time horizons (eg North Sea oil). Britain's dependence on imported oil and gas will increase dramatically as we move into the next century and competition for reserves that are increasingly concentrated in the Middle East will lead to renewed geopolitical instability. Current Government policies are failing to husband irreplaceable resources.

Probably of greater significance, however, is that the pollution problems anticipated by the *Limits to Growth* are fast becoming manifest. The evidence about the reality of acid rain, ozone-thinning and global warming now convinces the vast majority of scientists. Equally serious, problems of soil erosion, land degradation, and water quality deterioration are alarmingly evident in many countries. There is recognition of this at the highest level. Al Gore's recent book (1992) sets out the growing severity of the situation with remorseless logic. At the same time the loss of habitat and of species diversity is impoverishing the planet.

So we have moved from an emphasis purely on population and mineral resources to a broader view of resource limits and a recognition that the capacity of the human habitat to absorb our wastes and bounce back is already being exceeded in many areas.

---

1 Goldsmith et al, 1972.
2 Meadows et al, 1972.

In the face of this, governments are beginning to do more than mere environmental window-dressing. The Montreal accord on the phasing out of CFCs (1987), and the Earth Summit agreements on climate change, bio-diversity and forests bear witness to changing priorities.

DEFINING SUSTAINABLE DEVELOPMENT

While 'sustainability' is taken to refer to the long-term health of global ecology, 'sustainable development' is about the long-term enhancement of human social and economic well-being, currently threatened by our own poisoning of our habitat.

The standard shorthand definition of sustainable development comes from the 'Brundtland Report' of 1987. The UN-sponsored World Commission on Environment and Development, chaired by Mrs Gro Harlem Brundtland, PM of Norway, defined it as: 'development that meets the needs of the present without compromising the ability of future generations to meet their own needs'. This definition is incorporated into official DoE green-speak, for example in the 1990 White Paper *This Common Inheritance* and the *1994 UK Strategy for Sustainable Development* (DoE, 1990, 1994).

By marrying the concept of environmental sustainability with that of economic development this term neatly sidesteps the central question as to whether growth is sustainable. Probably the most fascinating exploration of that question occurs in the so-called sequel to the *Limits to Growth: Beyond the Limits* (Meadows, Meadows and Randers, 1992). The conclusion they reach (as many others have done) is that it depends on the *kind* of growth. The current pattern of growth *cannot* be sustained, but a new pattern might be. The notion of 'development' is taken to be much broader than merely economic growth, or gross domestic product (GNP), embracing:

- the quality of life
- levels of basic freedom: association, speech, democracy
- health and nutritional status
- educational and cultural services
- access to resources and distribution of resources
- per capita income.

It is clearly desirable that economic growth should be sustained, providing the opportunity for employment and the support of high quality health/education/cultural services, but this growth needs to be achieved with *reduced* consumption of resources. *Materialistic* growth – expansion of the production of material wealth – cannot be sustained. Measures of wealth and well-being premised on the benefits of material consumption will need replacing with measures of resource sustainability and quality of life.

Sustainable development relies on ensuring that the local and global environmental resources on which communities depend are maintained (or in some spheres, enhanced) so they can be passed on intact to the next generations indefinitely. It means moving from an economy of *flow*, where success is measured in terms of financial transaction, to an economy of *stock*, where success is measured by the quality of basic resources. Those resources can be grouped in elemental categories, reminding us of medieval times when the interdependence of humans and the environment was more immediately understood:

EARTH: soils, minerals, land-forms, land
AIR: atmosphere, climate
FIRE: sun, energy supply
WATER: rain, water courses and water supply, sea
LIFE: trees, wildlife, biological diversity.

Also important, complementing the natural environmental stock, is the artificial or human-made stock, the built environment.

The key aim of sustainable development is to try to ensure intergenerational equity. That is generally recognized to depend on four subsidiary goals:

1) that of economic efficiency in the use of scarce resources;
2) that of intragenerational equity – particularly equity of treatment between the developed and the developing world, fairness in the terms of trade and other resource allocation systems;
3) fairness to nature, treating other species as far as possible as partners in the shared biosphere, rather than as resources to be exploited; and
4) resilience and robustness – survivability.

Chapter 3 elaborates on the different categories of environmental stock that may provide a set of criteria for Environmental Audit (EA), and examines the assessment of environmental impact.

LESSONS FROM THE PAST

Unsustainability is not a new problem. Plato provides evidence of the unsustainable practices in ancient Greece which contributed to the decline and eventual eclipse of the country. It makes salutary reading. Plato demonstrates a level of understanding of earth science and human ecology that we have only recently regained.

Box P.I.1   Plato's theory of unsustainability

All other lands were surpassed by ours in goodness of soil, so that it was actually able at that period to support a large host which was exempt from the labours of husbandry....... And, just as happens in small islands, what now remains compared with what then existed is like the skeleton of a sick man, all the fat and soft earth having wasted away, and only the bare framework of the land being left. But at that epoch the country was unimpaired, and for its mountains it had high arable hills, and in place of the swamps as they are now called, it contained plains full of rich soil; and it had much forest-land in its mountains, of which there are visible signs even to this day. Moreover, it was enriched by the yearly rains from Zeus, which were not lost to it, as now, by flowing from the bare land into the sea; but the soil it had was deep, and therein it received the water, storing it up in the retentive loamy soil; and by drawing off into the hollows from the heights the water that was there absorbed, it provided all the various districts with abundant supplies of springwater and streams, where shrines still remain even now, at the spots where the fountains formerly existed.

Such, then, was the natural condition of the rest of the country, and it was ornamented as you would expect from genuine husbandmen who made husbandry their sole task, and possessed of most excellent land and a great abundance of water, and also, above the land, a climate of most happily tempered seasons.

Plato, 5th Century BC (1929 trans. Bury)

REFERENCES

Department of Environment (1994) White Paper *This Common Inheritance: Britain's Environmental Strategy* HMSO, London

Department of Environment et al (1994) *Sustainable Development: The UK Strategy* HMSO, London

Flavin, C (1989) *Electricity's Future: The Shift to Efficiency and Small-Scale Power* Worldwatch Paper 61, Worldwatch Institute, Washington DC

Goldsmith et al (1972) 'Blueprint for Survival' *Ecologist Magazine*, January, reprinted in Penguin

Gore, A (1992), *Earth in the Balance: Forging a New Common Purpose* Earthscan, London

Meadows, D et al (1972) *The Limits to Growth* Pan, London.

Meadows, D H; Meadows, D L and Randers, J (1992) *Beyond the Limits: Global Collapse or a Sustainable Future* Earthscan, London.

Plato (5th Century BC) *Critias* in 1929 translation by Bury, R G, Heinemann, London.

Report of the 1987 World Commission on Environment and Development (1987) *Our Common Future* (The Bruntland Report) Oxford University Press, Oxford

The Nature of Environmental Auditing

Hugh Barton

INTRODUCTION

Local authority environmental audits are the means by which communities systematically and regularly monitor the quality of their environment and review the impact of public policy on the environment. According to recent surveys (detailed later) environmental auditing is spreading contagiously through the local authority sector; an idea whose time has come. The pace of innovation is impressive. Where only a few years ago audits were often seen as freestanding discrete activities, justified as political window dressing, they are now increasingly seen as an integral part of local authority policy-making, tied into management systems, and the means of 'delivering' the key goal of sustainable development.

The central section in this chapter explains the changing context of auditing and the implications for its role in policy-making and review. This is preceded by a short historical outline, and followed by discussion of the benefits to be derived from auditing, and the goals that should guide the implementation of auditing.

ORIGINS

Environmental auditing began in the US. The early environmental audits stemmed not from the local authorities but from commercial response to national requirements.

They arose as a result of legislation which made companies responsible for environmental damage they were causing. The US formally adopted 'the polluter pays' principle in the 1970s. In order to avoid liability companies took on board 'performance reviews' and 'compliance audits' which evaluated how the company stood with regard to the legislation. Throughout the 1970s and 80s the number of anti-pollution laws and regulations grew. The most significant were the 'Resources Conservation and Recovery Act' (RCRA), the 'Comprehensive Environmental Response, Compensation and Liability Act' (CERCLA), and the 'Clean Air Act'. These had the effect of making environmental auditing obligatory for many US companies. Other enterprises adopted auditing voluntarily as a sign of their environmental probity. In the UK there were a few larger companies (eg British Petroleum) who introduced a measure of environmental auditing early on, but more widespread dissemination occurred as US subsidiaries working here began mirroring the practices of their parent companies.

In the years since its inception the concept of commercial environmental auditing has broadened so that now it has become – for some companies – a major tool for promoting good environmental management. A typical commercial audit involves analysis of inputs and outputs and asks what are the environmental impacts of the raw materials and products brought into the factory? What are the impacts of the products and wastes that emerge from the factory as a result of production and administrative processes?

The move across to the local authority sector began in this country with the publication of the Friends of the Earth 'Environmental Charter for Local Government' in 1989, and the parallel production of an audit for Kirklees MBC in West Yorkshire (1989). Subsequently audits have been produced for areas as diverse as Lancashire, the London borough of Sutton (1991), and North Devon (1990). By 1992 nearly half of all English and Welsh local authorities had attempted an audit, complete or in part (see Part III Introduction).

Given the long-standing environmental concern of local authorities it is perhaps difficult to explain why environmental auditing has come so tardily. Partly it reflects the 'agency' role of local government, responding to government instruction in various discrete environmental spheres – waste disposal, pest control, building preservation, and so on – rather than formulating policy *ab initio*. Recently, however, government itself has expected local authorities to take a broader environmental perspective, and burgeoning public concern for green issues has triggered local political response. Environmental 'statements' and 'charters' have been produced by many authorities. These take a much more synoptic view of the environment than the traditional segmented delivery of environmental services; but they also tend to rely on vague and generalized statements of aspiration. Environmental auditing is coming to be seen as a vital means of converting aspiration to effective action.

Paradoxically the pace of innovation may in some ways be a problem itself. There is a suspicion around that such audits may just be the current 'flavour of the month', that environmental questions are being hyped by the media and cynically exploited by politicians. Local authorities seem to be competing to promote a 'green' image, using an environmental audit to dress up old policies in new clothes, symbols of green virility.

But progressively, as experience of auditing is gained and shared, it is becoming clear that they do have a valuable role to play, encouraging the systematic incorporation of environmental perspectives into many aspects of policy, helping to trigger new awareness and new priorities both within and without the authorities.

THE CHANGING CONTEXT

The pressure for change is coming both bottom-up, from people as voters and consumers, and top-down, from the international community. Government, business and local authorities are caught in a pincer movement between these two forces. Of the top-down influences perhaps the most potent is the aftermath of the much denigrated 1992 Earth Summit in Rio. In anticipation of this event the UK Government began upgrading its own environmental legislation. The White Paper 'This Common Inheritance' (DoE,1990) set the context and made policy commitments which are gradually being realized – particularly in relation to pollution control (The Environmental Protection Act), recycling, and planning policy (DoE, 1990). In the aftermath of Rio, the Government has produced a national strategy for Sustainable Development, including policy programmes aimed at promoting biodiversity and stabilizing greenhouse emissions (DoE et al, 1994).

Not all government departments are getting in the Rio spirit with equal enthusiasm. Indeed the approach is almost schizophrenic, with Transport and DTI (including Energy) fighting a rearguard action to protect their traditional policies. Nonetheless, there is very significant progress, with the DoE in the vanguard and committed to change.

At the local level every authority is now invited to begin work on a 'Local Agenda 21', which will be an action programme for sustainability involving all sections of the local community in partnership (optimism springs eternal!) to fulfil commitments entered into at Rio (LGMB, 1990). Some authorities, such as Leicester, are already well advanced. Others are inventing new means of public/private partnership for implementation: for example, the Bristol Environment and Energy Trust (BEET), set up in 1993, is a partnership of major Bristol firms, fuel boards, transport agencies, environmental groups and local authorities, with participation of higher educational establishments. BEET has, at least ostensibly, the full-hearted support of these influential bodies for a radical programme of environmental research and action, involving all the agencies in their own spheres (Barton and Stead, 1993).

Another catalyst for change is the European Community, now Union. Its varied initiatives in the pollution, energy and development fields have shaped UK thinking. Particularly relevant here is the Eco-Management and Audit Scheme (EMAS) approved in June 1993 (EEC, 1993). While the purpose of EMAS is to help industrial companies improve their environmental performance, the scheme has been adapted by the DoE , the Scottish Office and the Local Government Management Board (LGMB) for use by British local authorities – the first of its kind. In so doing the DoE, SO and LGMB have gone a stage further than the EU, and extended the scope to include not only the internal practices of authorities but their public services and policies as well (DoE et al, 1993). EMAS requires a similar environmental management system to that specified in BS 7750, however EMAS also requires that an independently validated environmental statement is produced. EMAS is widely considered to be more useful in the local authority context.

At present, of course, EMAS is advisory not obligatory. It has tremendous significance for auditing. The main benefits of EMAS are that it provides:

- **A formal management framework for auditing.** For the last four years or so, authorities have spent much of their time trying to develop workable approaches, methods and management structures. Much of this effort has been duplicated throughout the country because of lack of knowledge of what was going on elsewhere and because there were few objective standards against which to judge the relative merit of individual processes. EMAS could overcome these problems by offering non-prescriptive guidelines and a system which allows comparison.
- **External validation.** To date, there has been very little formal recognition of the effort put into and the benefits derived from EA. EMAS will provide independent verification of good practice which will raise the profile of auditing. This should result in both more political 'kudos' for the authority and (hopefully) more awareness and pride amongst members of the community.

The emphasis in EMAS is on effective management systems for 'internal' auditing. The issue of the quality of the *external* environment is largely ignored, however, even to the extent that the benefits of monitoring the environment as a test of policy effectiveness are not specifically addressed.

The complexity of the EMAS system is also very great. There is a danger that resources will be directed to establishing systematic management processes at the expense of devising creative solutions to environmental problems and implementing real actions. This guide tackles the view that maintaining an action orientation is the only way to ensure that tangible benefits are achieved.

Further detailed information on EMAS can be found in Appendix 5. It is important to note that EMAS uses the term 'environmental audit' in a quite specific and limited way, to refer to one stage in the EMAS process. In this book, following widespread practice, we use the term more broadly.

A third area of innovation which impacts on audits is 'Strategic

Environmental Assessment' (SEA). European moves to introduce SEA for all plans, policies and programmes are slowly progressing, but meanwhile the DoE has stolen a march by introducing compulsory 'environmental appraisal of development plans'. The DoE report of November 1993 elaborates the requirement originally stated in Planning Policy Guidance Note 12 (1992) and sets out how local planning authorities should submit their planning policies to rigorous and systematic environmental assessment as a means of moving towards more sustainable development (DoE, 1993). This new procedure, if properly followed, obliges local authorities to introduce State of the Environment (SoE) reports, and encourages the definition of environmental thresholds and capacities.

Local Agenda 21, EMAS, and the Environmental Appraisal of Plans, together set a clear pattern for environmental auditing. It is no longer a question whether audits are necessary. Increasingly it is becoming impossible to avoid them. Yet many authorities have not started, and most of those who have had experienced difficulties in completing them. The next section therefore goes back to the beginning and asks a number of quite basic questions.

WHAT DOES ENVIRONMENTAL AUDITING INVOLVE?

The concept of auditing may at the outset appear rather intimidating, with alarming cost implications. It is therefore important to recognize that the task may be approached in different ways, and at various levels. On the one hand it is true that some audits have been very ambitious and costly. Lancashire County Council has invested £300,000, representing the time-cost of dedicated internal staff, the cost of specialist consultants, and the setting up costs of a comprehensive computerized database system. Most audits, conversely, have been undertaken for anything between £10,000 and £40,000, with many authorities beginning the process without any specific budget at all. It depends on what you want. One of the key conclusions of the Local Government Management Board study on auditing is that:

> an environmental audit does not have to cover every aspect of the environment or of the authorities' operations. Nor does it have to be undertaken all at once. Auditing is a process; it can be conducted on whatever scale is appropriate to the needs and resources of the authority concerned. Moreover it does not require the extensive use of consultants. Some training and assistance may be necessary, but in most cases it may actually be more appropriate if auditing is carried out by the authorities' own staff. Environmental auditing is therefore just as open to and useful for small districts as it is for county and city authorities.
>
> LGMB, 1990

This guide takes the same view. The detailed implications of seeing environmental auditing as a process not a product are spelt out in the next chapter.

WHAT ARE THE MAIN PARTS OF AN AUDIT?

The two principle elements of an environmental audit are the **external** and the **internal** audits.

The external audit

This is commonly referred to as a State of the Environment (SoE) report. It involves studying the environmental conditions prevalent in the borough, district or county. It might be feared that the information requirements for such a report would be formidable. Much of the data, though, is regularly gathered already as a matter of course, by the local authority itself or by outside agencies. Levels of lead, SO_2 and CO, in the atmosphere, for instance, may be collected by the Environmental Health department. Congestion levels and traffic noise may be monitored by Transport departments. Water quality information is available from the National Rivers Authority (NRA). The state of the environment audit is therefore more about systematically collating existing sources of information and identifying gaps than necessarily about undertaking major new surveys. Gaps can sometimes be plugged by collaboration with local community groups, parish councils or other agencies, for example a review of pedestrian rights of way could be undertaken by the parish.

The internal audit

While the State of the Environment report sets the scene, assessing the actual quality of the local human environment, the internal audit assesses the policies and practices of the authority. There are three facets to an internal audit, and it is worth distinguishing very clearly between them:

1) **The review of internal practices (RIP):** this assesses the direct environmental impact of the activities of the organization; the energy-efficiency of its buildings, and vehicles, the impact of its purchasing, the recycling or disposal of its wastes. The review of practices is an aspect of the audit appropriate to *any* organization or enterprise, from hospital to household to house-builder.

2) **The policy impact assessment (PIA):** this concerns the environmental impacts of the local authority in its role as regulator, enforcer, enabler, educator and service provider. Some of the policies are expressly intended to influence the environment, eg pollution control and land-

scape policies. Others may be primarily social or economic in their impact but have important environmental side-effects, eg housing policy and economic development. The policy impact assessment may therefore mean asking questions which have not been asked before, and examining the environmental interactions of policies that previously were put in quite discrete categories.

3) **The management audit (MA):** this is where the auditors assess whether the organizational structures, job descriptions, patterns of responsibility and communication help or hinder environmental effectiveness. Since local authorities tend to be hierarchical and departmentalized, but the environment is an interactive web, the management audit can present a particular challenge. How far, for example, do consultations between Environmental Health and Planning departments deal properly with the noise and pollution impacts of industrial development?

Table 1.1 sets out and defines the main elements of the audit, relating them to the EMAS equivalent where appropriate.

The various elements of the audit need not be tackled at the same time or at the same frequency. The management audit could be a one-off exercise which leads to a more effective management structure, or more ambitiously institutes an on-going system of environmental management to fulfil CEMAS and BS7750 requirements. The RIP and PIA will probably be progressive, and regularly reviewed to see if programmes of improvement have been followed. The SoE is a continuous monitoring process, and provides vital information on the success or failure of policy. The question of where to start is explored further in Chapter 2.

The elements given prominence in Part II of this guide are the Review of Internal Practices (RIP) and the Policy Impact Assessment (PIA), and the relationship of policy appraisal to the SoE. The management issues are a main focus of Part III.

WHERE DO AUDITS FIT INTO THE POLICY PROCESS?

It was common for early audits to be produced as one-off reports, attempting an overview. That approach has the advantage of abruptly raising the profile of environmental issues within the authority, and can result in an impressive and definite product. But increasingly it is being recognized as inappropriate. The aims of auditing discussed above emphasize that environmental auditing is more a *process* than a product. It is to do with on-going monitoring of the state of the environment and progressive review of local authority practices and policies. People at all levels need to be involved and feel commitment to the process. So the audit

Table 1.1 Key elements of environmental auditing

Common usage, as in the Guide	EMAS equivalent	Definition
Environmental Statement or Environmental Charter	Environmental policy	Statement of the authorities' environmental aims and commitment
External audit or State of the Environment report (SoE)	None	Regular monitoring and review of the quality of the environment in the area concerned, and of implications for global sustainability
Internal Audit (IA) — Review of Internal Practices (RIP)	Environmental review (or audit) of direct effects	Evaluation of the environmental impact of the agencies' own operations and practices
Internal Audit (IA) — Policy Impact Assessment (PIA)	Environmental review (or audit) of service effects	Evaluation of the environmental impact of the agencies' regulatory, policy and service activities
Internal Audit (IA) — Management Audit (MA)	Review of the environmental management system	Assesses the effectiveness of the agencies' organization and procedures in tackling environmental problems
Environmental action plan Plans and programmes in related areas	The environmental programme	Policies, plans and programmes with environmental content or implications

needs rather to be seen as part and parcel of normal local authority policy-making, giving an environmental dimension to all facets of policy.

Figure 1.1 shows the elements of environmental auditing tied into a strategic process which involves interlinked activities and feedback.

The audit may lead to a specific action plan with its own budget attached. But the other vital means of implementing recommendations emerging from the auditing process are the established plans and programmes of the agency: for example 'Recycling plans', Development Plans, Countryside or Wildlife Strategies, Housing Investment Strategies, or the annual 'Transport Policy and Programme' (TPP). If the audit is not tied into these procedures it is liable to be just so much well-intentioned hot air. It can be argued that

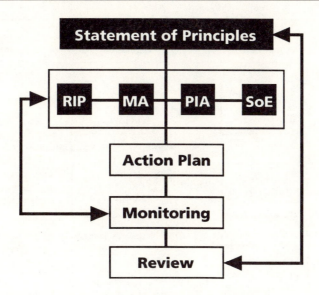

Figure 1.1   The basic auditing process

many audits so far have been just that: pious statements of intent, rather unrelated to the authority's ability to deliver. This is particularly liable to be the case if it is a 'one horse' audit, with one department taking a lead, but others not getting off the starting blocks.

The requirement now is that the environmental audit should come to be seen as a regular corporate review, mirroring the financial audit, where every department of the authority notes progress (both SoE and IA) towards agreed targets. These targets are incorporated in the action plans of the different sections. The authority could also produce a brief annual statement, summarizing the agency's environmental performance, which informs the public and political debate on future environmental priorities. The audit becomes, therefore, an institutionalized process of gaining and maintaining high environmental awareness amongst decision-makers and implementors. Officers, members and public are regularly triggered into an environmental focus. There is the chance for cross-departmental inter-actions to be properly examined. There is the possibility of rhetoric being converted into action.

Figure 1.2 illustrates how elements of the environmental audit should be regularly and systematically tied into the local authority's decision-making procedures. The key procedures are probably those concerned with annual budgeting, and three- to five-year policy reviews (eg development plans and waste disposal plans). The RIP needs to link to the budgeting process. The PIA should dovetail with appropriate policy reviews. The SoE, which can

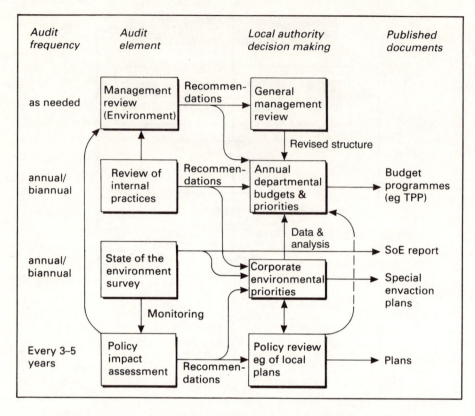

Audit frequency	Audit element	Local authority decision making	Published documents

Figure 1.2 Structure of auditing in relation to other policy processes

provide a time-series database for many organizations in the area, is essentially an ongoing survey with annual or perhaps biannual stock-taking.

A central question to be addressed at the outset is whether the audit is for the authority or the whole community.

- An authority or agency-based audit limits its concern to the express practices and powers of the agency. The audit process is essentially interdepartmental, though, in relation to the SoE, reliant on other agencies as well. Within the authority there needs to be a corporate decision-making process, mediating between different interests, establishing overall priorities, taking responsibility for the environmental action plan.
- A community audit is broader than that. While the local authority takes the lead, it does so in collaboration with other agencies, public, private and voluntary. Possibly the local Environmental Forum, or Local Agenda 21 committee provide appropriate mechanisms. The community audit

allows the consideration of policies and implementation outside the local authority's own remit. For example in relation to energy: the energy supply industries, big industrial users, house-developers and voluntary sector energy groups could be involved. The audit thus becomes a means for gaining the support and drawing on the strengths of a range of agencies.

The agency-based audit has the advantage of clear boundaries and simpler (though scarcely simple) organization; the inter-agency aspires higher, and fits more easily with the need to share SoE data between agencies. In practice it is likely that an authority will try to set its own house in order before moving on to the wider forum.[1]

WHY ARE ENVIRONMENTAL AUDITS NEEDED?

There are both heroic and humdrum reasons for environmental auditing. Local authorities may, idealistically, attempt to adopt a holistic approach to environmental issues, seeing themselves as responsible agents in promoting sustainable development. This implies a shift from the traditional view where local authorities are simply providers of specific services (schools, parks, roads, waste collection, pest control) to one where they are 'stewards' of the environment, co-ordinating the responses of a wide range of agencies. They do this in the interests of both local and global constituencies: locally they are trying to ensure a high quality of environment for people living and working in the area; globally they are attempting to moderate the impact of local decisions on terrestrial ecology and resources.

To aspire so high may seem fairly heroic, and many currently balk at the task. It may also be perceived as unrealistic, raising expectations that can never be fulfilled. At worst it may be criticized as so much sanctimonious humbug!

But there are very practical reasons why this vaulting ambition is becoming the order of the day. Local authorities are increasingly being held to account for their impact on the environment. Government sees them as key players in 'delivering' sustainable development. The moves towards strategic environmental assessment and environmental management systems at a European and national level are forceful (see page 9). Local authorities will soon find that without an SoE and without an IA their credibility with funding bodies (eg the European Commission) and at Inquiries (eg in local plans) will be thin.

The humbug factor, in other words, is on the other foot. Reliance on

---

1 The issues raised are discussed further, in relation to transport, in Chapter 8.

political green-speak and professional green-hunch is no longer good enough. Greater objectivity and honesty is being demanded by government, by the environmental groups, and by the public. Most local authorities are ill-equipped to respond to such challenges. An environmental audit could assist them greatly in making a start. It is argued later in this chapter that the audit need not, and should not, be seen as separate from other environmental policy making in local authorities. In the light of EU and government thinking, doing an audit *now* is simply a sound precaution, a pre-emptive strike, being ahead of the game, not dragged along by the scruff.

There are of course more local and humdrum reasons for adopting environmental auditing, relating to political image, public pressure, and the public purse. These and others are listed in Table 1.2. The financial issues deserve some elaboration here.

Table 1.2 Potential costs and benefits of environmental auditing

Potential costs	Potential benefits: heroic (and needed)	Potential benefits: humdrum
1) Commitment of resources to undertake the audit, including possible disruption of normal work	1) Pinpoints actions to reduce contribution to global pollution eg the greenhouse effect	6) Enables compliance with national and European laws and standards, and a consistent/structured response to new requirements
2) Extra costs of actions recommended by the audit	2) Reduced consumption of non-renewable raw materials eg fossil fuels	7) Reduction in some expenditure, for example for heating and lighting
3) Increased liability, or public disappointment, if action is not taken	3) Improved quality of local air, water, soils, and wildlife habitats	8) Reduction in surprises, identifying matters needing attention, avoiding legal suits and/or public approbation
4) Threat to established patterns of work, priorities, personal empires (can be a benefit)	4) Improved quality of the visual, aural and olfactory environment for local residents/workers/visitors	9) Improved public image and environmental accountability
5) The unveiling of embarrassing actions or inactions (clearly a benefit).	5) Promotes, by example and publicity, environmental awareness amongst businesses and residents	10) Enhanced profile with business and government bodies
		11) Independent verification of policies and procedures
		12) Improves motivation amongst employees by giving an outlet to 'green' impulses and increasing clarity of purpose
		13) Increased information transfer and better channels of communication between sections
		14) Improved environmental awareness amongst staff and councillors

The overt costs of the exercise depend largely on the degree to which new appointments are made or consultants retained, as well as how broad or narrow the initial remit. Some aspects of the audit may also imply on-going expenditure – say to monitor wildlife habitats, or appoint a recycling officer. This has deterred some authorities from embarking on an audit at all. But there are also cost savings to be made. Review of building energy management, of officer transport arrangements, or of parks/verges maintenance regimes, could for example accrue substantial savings. While cost reduction is not the prime concern of the audit it could legitimately be one motivating factor.

WHAT ARE THE AIMS OF AUDITING?

This section examines some of the main aims of environmental auditing, and the problems likely to be experienced in trying to achieve them.

Applying a holistic view of the environment

One of the key justifications for undertaking an EA is that the audit is not confined by the remit of a particular department, but examines environmental problems in the round. This holistic view necessarily means breaking down barriers between different departments and different professions, adopting a corporate approach. There are possible problems of professional jealousies or, more prosaically, of language. The word *environment* for instance means different things to a heating engineer, a town planner, an ecologist. So merely getting people on the same wavelength can pose a real challenge.

The holistic view encompasses dimensions of space and time. On the local to global dimension it is difficult to know where exactly to stop auditing. Macro issues (like global warming, ozone depletion, acid rain) are relevant insofar as local actions impact on them. Micro issues (specific product purchase, building management, or species survival) cannot all be explored comprehensively within a limited budget, and there is also the sensitive question of individual autonomy/responsibility. If an individual employee feels their work unduly under the microscope then resentment and paranoia can undermine the value of the audit. For financial and human reasons, therefore, it is important to involve staff closely in the process of defining priorities for auditing.

The same kind of arguments apply to the time dimension. The holistic view emphasizes the 'conception to resurrection' approach, where the whole life cycle of a product, from extraction to manufacture to use to reuse or disposal, is placed under the environmental microscope. This approach is required by the Environment Protection Act for certain industrial processes, but clearly there are limits to how far back in the cycle it is realistic to go. Local authority audits will normally have to rely on standard national formulations – for example in relation to the choice of building materials there are various studies of energy intensity and pollution implications which can be used.

Achieving an honest, objective and open audit

The audit will have little value if bureaucratic defensiveness or departmental power games impair the truthfulness of the results. In one audit for a rural district chief officers were active in suppressing the clear evidence from lower-tier officers that the planning and health departments did not communicate properly on environmental issues. It is therefore vital that high level support for the audit is established at the outset from all relevant departments and committees, together with a commitment to act appropriately on the results.

Openness is another key goal: audit information should be freely available and used to raise debate about environmental issues more widely in the community. The active involvement of the public and of local environmental groups in the audit helps validate the exercise and raise the profile of the authority.

Providing a normative picture of the situation

Facts are of little value of themselves unless they are seen in context and their significance can be appreciated. It is no use knowing the level of SO_2 emissions if there is nothing to compare it with. So part of the purpose of the audit is to evaluate variables against some kind of standard or criteria. The question arises, then, whose criteria should be used? Should it be those of the Government, or a local politician's, or Friends of the Earth? Whose interests are really being served?

Local Agenda 21 says that 'the community's' interests should be served. The public should be involved in selecting the criteria which reflect the community's values (see page 32 and Chapter 13).

In some cases, particularly in the SoE survey, official standards can be readily identified. The World Health Organization, the European Union and the UK Government have specified 'acceptable' levels of pollutants (though they do not always agree). In other cases, particularly in the PIA, it can be much more difficult. Often (for example, in the field of land use policy) there is no easy indicator of success or failure. Indeed any specific policy is likely to have both environmental costs and benefits. Take the example of the 'green belt': the preservation of open countryside near a town may be taken as an environmental 'good' in its own right, but at the same time housing development may have leapfrogged the belt resulting in longer, car-reliant journeys to work, which is probably 'bad'. There is a danger in applying knee-jerk reactions ('the green belt is inherently good') rather than actually studying the broader environmental consequences of the policy.

Techniques for grappling with policy conflicts and uncertainties are presented in Chapter 2

Being action-orientated

From the outset environmental audits have been seen not just as monitoring exercises but as means of achieving change. Policies and practices are changed when people change. The organization of the audit needs, therefore, to motivate people, to look freshly at their activities. It should try to inculcate new awareness, new values. Out of new awareness will come improved on-going decision taking.

This is so critical to the audit's effectiveness it is worth illustrating the point. Bristol Energy Centre do energy audits of buildings for businesses and local authorities and their experience tells them that while the technology (of energy conservation) is important, the attitude of the people operating and using buildings is still more important. An energy-awareness programme for one major Bristol firm, costing several thousand pounds, paid for itself in one month because room allocation procedures started taking energy costs into account.

A good process, that involves the relevant actors and effective training, may therefore be more important than extensive monitoring exercises or a lavish final audit report. Chapter 15 takes this as a major theme.

CONCLUSION

By way of summary, the different roles performed by the local authority which impact on the environment can be listed as follows:

- Local authorities influence the environment through their own internal actions: purchasing, in-house transport, maintenance regimes, energy management etc.
- Local authorities have long been involved in environmental control and management in their role as planners, monitors, regulators and enforcers.
- Local authorities can influence public opinion by publicizing and making information available on a wide range of environmental issues. They also act as leaders or 'trend-setters' for a local community.
- As providers of services and as major contractors local authorities can influence environmental practices.
- Through their role as a major property owner and landowner local authorities can undertake positive environmental actions.

- By financial actions, such as provision of grants and investment of its funds, local authorities can promote and support environmental improvements.
- Local authorities can work locally and intervene where market forces are promoting damaging activities. It is this action at a local level that is needed to bring about lasting and sustainable improvements in environmental quality. Local authority involvement with the environment is evident at a number of levels. All are important in environmental auditing.

The auditing process is designed to ensure that these varied facets of work are environmentally positive. In the longer run the process will become just a normal part of the working practices of the authority. In the initial period, however, resource constraints will limit the range of the audit. Pragmatism suggests tackling those elements of the audit first which can achieve clear and high profile results, preparing the ground for later stages. A progressive and incremental approach may have learning as well as financial benefits. Given the broad scope of environmental concern the key question is: how are priorities established and dealt with, so that limited resources can be put to good use? (see page 29 and Chapter 14).

RECOMMENDATIONS

1) All local authorities should be undertaking environmental auditing as a matter of course.
2) The auditing process should aim to be as inclusive as possible, including where appropriate external agencies and the wider community, ensuring that ownership of the audit is shared.
3) The audit should not be seen as a one-off exercise but as a recurrent review process tied into the main spending programmes and policy plans of the local authority, enabling a regular coherent view of overall environmental impact.
4) The audit needs to link in quite specifically to strategic environmental appraisal procedures within the authority, and contribute directly to the preparation of Local Agenda 21 strategies.
5) The audit needs to be managed corporately, with the authoritative representation from all departments on any steering group that is set up, and full backing from relevant committees and chief officers. The SoE could well be managed by an inter-agency committee.
6) Authorities should carefully consider the merits of installing environmental management procedures as recommended by the DoE/SO/LGMB report, and subsequently achieving the CEMAS and BS7750 standards.

7) If starting from scratch, authorities should start with those elements of the audit that are easiest to demonstrate progress on and get momentum going – frequently this means the Review of Internal Practices.

8) As soon as possible, authorities should aim to move from just an agency audit to a broader community audit, and have this aspiration in mind from the outset. Only in that way will their potential role as leaders and coordinators in the drive towards sustainable development at the local level be realized.

REFERENCES

Barton, H and Stead, D (1993) *Sustainable Transport for Bristol* Bristol Environmental and Energy Trust, University of the West of England Working Paper no 33, Faculty of the Built Environment, Bristol

Department of the Environment (1990) *This Common Inheritance: Britain's Environmental Strategy* HMSO, London

Department of the Environment (1990) *The Environmental Protection Act* HMSO, London

Department of the Environment and the Welsh Office (1992) *Planning Policy Guidance Note 12: Development Plans and Regional Planning Guidance* HMSO, London

Department of the Environment (1993) *Environmental Appraisal of Development Plans: A Good Practice Guide* HMSO, London

Department of the Environment, Scottish Office and Local Government Management Board (1993) *A Guide to the Eco-Management and Audit Scheme for UK and Local Government* HMSO, London

Department of the Environment et al (1994) *Sustainable Development: The UK Strategy* HMSO, London

EEC Council Regulation (1993) *EMAS No 1836/93* Council of the European Communities, Luxembourg

Friends of the Earth (1989) *Environmental Charter for Local Government* FoE, London

Kirklees Metropolitan Borough Council (1989) *Kirklees State of the Environment Report* KMBC, Huddersfield

Lancashire County Council (1990) *Lancashire: A Green Audit: a First State of the Environment Report* LCC, Lancashire

Local Government Management Board (1990) *Environmental Auditing for Local Authorities* LGMB, Luton

Local Government Management Board (1992) *Local Agenda 21 – Agenda 21: a guide for local authorities in the UK* LGMB, Luton

London Borough of Sutton (1991) *Environmental Statement: Fourth Annual Report* LBS, Sutton

North Devon District Council, ed Keen, R C (1990) *North Devon District Council Corporate Environmental Audit* Bristol Environmental Audit Unit (BEAU), Bristol Polytechnic (now UWE), Bristol

Raemakers, J; Cowie, L and Wilson, E (1991) *An Index of Local Authority Green Plans* Research Paper no 37, Department of Planning and Housing, Edinburgh College of Art, Heriot Watt University

SHAPING THE PROCESS OF AUDITING

Hugh Barton

INTRODUCTION

This chapter takes as given that environmental auditing is a process not an event, and a process that is about people and attitudes as much as it is about objective facts or technical procedures. While Chapter 1 focused more on the **why** and the **what** of auditing, we now examine the **who** and the **how**.

This chapter also makes the presumption that the agenda of auditing – the substantial issues addressed – is set largely by the need to plan for sustainable development. Auditing is the means of assessing progress towards – or regress away from – sustainability.

In Chapter 1 the four main elements of a comprehensive audit were distinguished, ie the State of the Environment (SoE) report, the review of internal practices (RIP), the policy impact assessment (PIA) and the management review. Ideally the local authority should attempt to agree a programme covering all aspects. In practice that may mean establishing priorities. Many authorities have chosen to embark first on the RIP as the most obviously fruitful area, reviewing purchasing policy, recycling, building management, and in-house transport. Others have launched into SoE reporting. Sometimes a partial review of management structures, and the consequent appointment of an 'environmental coordinator', has preceded either.

However, before getting deeply into one element of the audit, it is essential to grasp the way the elements interrelate. The link between internal and external auditing is the central issue, often not recognized in practice. The next section therefore examines the reasons for doing the SoE study, followed by an assessment of how the PIA is to be done, and leads on to the presentation of an integrated framework for both elements in tandem.

The SoE and PIA are the most problematical aspects of the audit – least adequately treated in existing literature. So the general emphasis of the chapter is on these two, rather than on RIP and MA.

In setting up the technical and administrative framework for the audit it could be argued that there are four interlocking decisions:

1) What is the scope of the audit?
2) Who should do the audit?
3) How far should the wider community be involved?
4) What tools are employed in assessing environmental impact?

Each of these needs to be considered explicitly, and consistent decisions taken, for the auditing process to fulfil aspirations. If the audit is partly about motivating people to take environmental factors more fully into account, then the choice of scope and timescale, the choice of technique, auditor and management structure will be critical. The rest of the chapter attempts to shed light on these questions in turn.

THE SCOPE AND PURPOSE OF THE SOE

There are two logical standpoints here. Either the survey can attempt a synoptic review of environmental quality, or it can concentrate on just those aspects which are amenable to policy. The former position reflects the belief that the local authority is the guardian or steward of the whole local environment and has a general monitoring and educational role in relation to it. A synoptic survey looks at fundamentals, identifying the key indicators of environmental quality for each of the elements of stock (see Table 2.1). Thus for example in relation to the land it examines the quality of land and soil – the stability, fertility, problems of erosion, contamination and exhaustion. In relation to wildlife and biodiversity it examines the level of endangered or locally rare species, the extent and quality of different habitats, and pressures leading to change. In relation to aesthetic quality, it might study residents' perceptions of the general quality of townscape and landscape.

All this is, of course, easier said than done. Some information in some spheres may be accessible – eg on water quality from the National Rivers Authority, wildlife from nature conservation groups – but in others is notorious for its inaccessibility. Data on the quality of soils are patchy, and on the use of energy may be protected by unnecessary conventions of commercial confidentiality. So a synoptic SoE report has to recognize severe limits on its comprehensiveness, and may often recommend how information gaps could be plugged, with resource implications, rather than fully satisfy our thirst for knowledge.

A policy-orientated SoE study takes a much more limited and pragmatic view. Basically it aims to collect information which allows the auditors to

Table 2.1 Framework of audit elements and tasks

Main elements	Audit tasks		Examples
SoE	1)	**Primary indicators** Monitor the basic quality of environmental stock	■ Air quality ■ Water quality ■ Mineral reserves (local) ■ Townscape quality
SoE/PIA	2)	**Secondary indicators** Measure basic quality by proxy and assess the *general* effectiveness of policy	■ Preservation of SSSIs ■ Traffic levels (proxy for transport energy use and CO_2 emissions) ■ Rate of recycling in the community
SoE/PIA	3)	**Tertiary indicators** Assess the *direct* effects or effectiveness of policy	■ Have out-of-town retail proposals been blocked successfully? ■ Have planned cycle routes been constructed?
PIA	4)	**Policy impact guesstimating** Evaluating current/proposed policies' likely impact on every element of environmental stock	■ Use of a matrix approach – reliant on informed judgement
PIA	5)	**Comparison with good practice** Assess scope and content of policy against external yardstick	■ cf English Nature recommended policies ■ cf DoE PPGs
PIA/RIP	6.	**Management audit** Assess the effectiveness of the environmental management systems and service delivery	■ Review objectives, programmes, means of implementation, monitoring systems etc
RIP	7)	**In-house indicators** Monitor actual progress towards in house objectives	■ Proportion of paper recycled ■ Energy used in the buildings ■ Water consumption of LA

assess the success or failure of policy to achieve specified goals. If there are policies concerned with reducing fly-tipping, then has fly-tipping actually reduced? If there are policies to safeguard trees and woodlands, then has the rate of tree loss slowed and have losses been more than compensated for by new planting? If there is a goal of reduced congestion, then has congestion decreased? This approach, in which the SoE report monitors the effectiveness of policy, has the advantage that particular sections in the local authority can see the direct relevance of the exercise, contribute ideas for indicators and maybe supply the data. But it has the disadvantage that the aspects surveyed may be so functionally defined that broader issues escape attention. In the third example, congestion in a given town may have decreased because a new bypass has been built, but extra traffic may thereby have been generated which is increasing congestion elsewhere.

The bypass may be encouraging the dispersal of urban development on to car-based sites, access by foot to local services may be deteriorating, and the overall level of greenhouse emissions increased. In other words, the auditors in this case may not see the wood for the trees.

Clearly some kind of balance can be struck between the opposing views. What balance depends heavily on the approach adopted to assessing the impact of policies and practices.

APPROACHES TO POLICY ASSESSMENT

There are four basic ways of evaluating the policies and practices of the authority, each having very different implications for the auditing process and for the level of resources needed:

1) Measure the actual impact of policies 'on the ground' (via the SoE)
2) Estimate the impact of policy on every element of the environment
3) Compare the policy with best practice elsewhere
4) Assess the effectiveness of the management systems that deliver policy.

Reliance on measuring the real impact links back the policy-oriented version of the SoE survey, and the identification of indicators which provide a measure of policy success or failure. The task of assessment is made much easier if the objective or *target* for each indicator is explicit (see discussion in Chapter 3). For example in external environments a target in relation to access to public transport might be that all dwellings should be within 400m of a bus-stop; in the internal environment a target might be that 30 per cent of work-related trips should be made by bus or train.

Clearly it is desirable to evaluate performance in this way, examining actual outcomes. In the long run it is essential, and careful monitoring and review procedures need building in to all spheres of policy. But in the short run it may not be practicable. The cost and time implications can be prohibitive. The reality is that only a limited number of key variables can be systematically monitored. For the rest, authorities rely on professional judgement, outside watchdogs, and the political process, to bring forward issues. The professionals, for example, can systematically estimate the impacts of policies through the use of a matrix. These checks and balances are valuable. They should be used carefully as contributions to the monitoring process. But they are also liable to be rather 'hit and miss'. It is all too easy for potentially critical impacts to escape attention because they are not currently high on the political agenda. An example, discussed in Chapter 1, is green belts: there is little awareness, at the official level, of their environmental and social externalities such as the reduction of locational choice and increase in the length of trips. Audits cannot be dependent on such processes.

In this situation the other two approaches become important. The commonest way of assessing the content of practices and policies is to compare them with some arbiter of quality. Checklists of model policies are produced by environmental bodies (such as English Nature, RSPB, FoE) for just this purpose. Academic studies of innovative authorities here and abroad provide another source. Government itself provides guidelines such as the Planning Policy Guidance notes (PPGs) of the DoE. All these can be used very productively to assess where the authority lies in relation to good practice, and to provide at the same time a strong lead on where they should be. Checklists of this kind are given at the end of each topic chapter in Part II.

The great advantage of a straightforward comparison with good practice is that it is quick. It is also directional, pointing the way forward. The limitation is that it does not assess how far the policy is being converted into action. In many situations the content of the policy may be less significant than the ability of the authority to successfully implement it.

Assessing the management system and its ability to deliver links back to the principles of eco-management promoted by EMAS and BS 7750 (see Chapter 1). The focus in this approach is on human behaviour and organizational structures rather than policy content or direct environmental impact. The questions asked by the auditor include 'Are there explicit environmental objectives? Are there programmes or strategies for achieving them? Are the responsibilities for implementing the programme clear? Are there effective monitoring and review procedures in place?'

The assumption behind this approach is that what matters most is the people involved. Whether they have appropriate goals and values, and whether the institutional framework allows them to be effective. The key to improved performance then is the organizational culture, and trained awareness amongst staff. Retraining can be a critical step. For example transport engineers who for years have striven religiously to provide greater personal mobility need to adopt the new goals of maximum accessibility with minimum use of scarce resources. Once the attitudes and the framework are right, then it is hoped the right decisions will flow.

This approach has much to commend it, but demands a root and branch review of practices. Its slight danger is that all the emphasis is on 'process' and very little on 'substance'. An excessive concern for satisfying procedural requirements could draw attention away from the real issues.

FRAMEWORK FOR A COMPREHENSIVE AUDIT

Having examined the key choices to be made in shaping both the internal and the external audit, we can now establish a framework of thinking which links the two. Table 2.1 sets out the interdependent functions of the SoE, the PIA and the RIP. It is self-evident that elements of the audit cannot be tackled in isolation but must be considered in relation to each other.

Three levels of SoE material are identified. The level or quality of primary stock represents a base-line measure of sustainability – and the audit here needs to assess how far the current pattern *is* sustainable. This is particularly important in relation to air and water and earth quality, the level of greenhouse emissions, and the maintenance of biodiversity. It also provides a measure of the general quality of environment actually enjoyed by people in the area.

Secondary indicators provide in some situations more tangible or available means of assessing progress. For example the level of traffic is not itself a measure of absolute sustainability or quality but does act as a useful proxy for transport energy consumption and CO_2 emissions.

Both primary and secondary indicators are of general interest. They are relevant to Local Agenda 21 and should be therefore agreed in the wider community forum if possible, spreading ownership of the SoE process and increasing its scope.

Tertiary indicators are specific to the particular agency, providing a direct measure of policy achievement (with the reservation about cumulative or indirect impacts that we noted before). These specific assessments are central to the PIA – the acid test of successful policy implementation. Selected indicators should be identified when the policies are devised and approved. Too often at present policies are window dressing or wishful thinking. Insistence on tertiary indicators can lead to a little more honesty on what is achievable.

So, in summary, the potential range of information that could be collected as part of the SoE survey is vast. The cost and time involved in collection can be prohibitive unless there is selectivity. Priority should be given to information which directly evaluates progress towards environmental policy objectives. More generally indicators should be selected which *either*:

■ have global significance, as defined by official bodies such as HMG, EU or WHO

or

■ are locally important, as defined by local politicians, pressure groups and the public.

The indicators of course require standards or criteria to make measurement meaningful. These are normally defined in the policy documents. So the SoE is kept within bounds, and the information given significance. The vexed issues of environmental capacities and targets (which are types of criteria) are discussed in Chapter 3.

Which part first?

Initiating the new system, though, can be difficult and expensive. A comprehensive approach from the outset is ideal, but many demand too much change too quickly, and require heavy investment of time and money. A phased approach may often be more practical. Phasing can be helpful, in that there is more time to experiment and persuade. The instigation of one part can 'trail-blaze' and give the doubters an opportunity to acclimatize. Another point is that the comprehensive approach can easily result in too much information to handle, and the audit sinking under its own weight.

Each authority will have its own priorities. But the easiest and cheapest element to tackle first is probably the review of internal practices. On the political level this makes sense because it is good to be seen to be putting 'your own house in order' before lecturing others on what *they* should be doing. On the organizational level it is useful because the RIP is corporate and will effect all departments, raising environmental awareness across the authority. In addition there are tangible results from the RIP: low energy light bulbs; changed stationery; more recycling; altered travel allowance schemes ... giving some credibility to the process.

It is less easy to specify whether SoE or PIA should come first. As already explained, they are closely related in scope. Logically, the information provided by the SoE report is subsequently used in the PIA; however it could be premature to identify what information is required without first considering the PIA. It may be better therefore to tackle both in tandem by topic (as arranged in Part II of this book), allowing the complete SoE and PIA to be built up over a number of years.

Even then there is a problem, precisely because there is no overview of the issues and their interrelationships. There is a temptation for policy impact to be tackled discretely, department by department. Apart from the obvious dangers of self-validation, such a procedure falls into the trap of assuming the environment, too, is departmentalized. But the statutory requirements that tend to define departments can get in the way of environment-conscious policies, or even the recognition of an environmental problem. From the vantage point of European best practice in the fields of energy, transport, land use and pollution, conventional British divisions of responsibility can look remarkably arbitrary. At the very least, then, the PIA/SoE should be interdepartmental, and where possible interagency, to allow innovatory collaborative solutions to emerge. And that means there are considerable benefits from a comprehensive approach, across all topics.

There is, therefore, no one 'right' answer. It will depend on local circumstances. The most vital thing is to embark on the process, in a carefully considered way, as soon as possible.

WHO SHOULD *DO* ENVIRONMENTAL AUDITS?

The issue of a comprehensive or incremental approach is strongly influenced by the question, who are the auditors?

There are three basic answers to this question. The audit could be tackled by outside consultants, with only modest assistance from internal staff. It could be done internally, with external specialists consulted only on limited and specific issues. Or it could be done by internal staff and consultants working in tandem, the former providing the main impetus and work input, the latter providing guidance, training and validation of the process.

Which of them fits the bill will depend in part on the capability and ambitions of the authority concerned, but there are points of common experience.

Consultants

The use of consultants is increasingly attractive in an age of privatization and 'contracting out', and has the advantage of relative objectivity, mirroring back council operations in an impartial way, providing new perspectives on issues and opportunities. It also has the benefit – presuming the right consultants are chosen – of buying in expertise. For small authorities where staff are stretched the use of consultants may be the only practical way of doing an audit.

But reliance on outsiders can have the disadvantage that they are perceived as such. The audit can become something which is imposed upon staff rather than being a process they own, and as a result their motivation to implement the audit's recommendations is undermined. There may too be disappointment in the content of the audit, since much of it will be material that has been provided to the consultants (in documentary and verbal form) by staff. The results may therefore be rather predictable. Perhaps most seriously, assessors will come and go, but the environmental issues remain. There is a risk of simply using consultants to defuse political pressures, and make an empty environmental gesture, rather than enabling the follow through of the issues in an on-going auditing process.

In-house

If auditing is carried out in-house the obverse is likely to be true. In-house staff will themselves have to confront the issues and make proposals for improvements. Active involvement should enhance their feeling of ownership of the process, and their motivation. The means of implementation and subsequent monitoring are under their control. But the risk is that existing staff will not think radically. They may see the audit as a means of validating current practice. Lack of wider experience, and lack of time specifically allocated for the audit, could conspire to make the exercise low key, even tokenistic.

There may be a temptation for each department, trying to avoid the prying eye, to do its own review. This should be resisted. Not only can it lead to unnecessary duplication, but it may result in differential standards across the authority. The review should be corporate, with every department contributing.

In this context the status of the auditors becomes crucial. If they derive from one department or are relatively junior they will not have sufficient authority and their conclusions may be treated with disdain or scepticism. Ideally, therefore, an in-house audit involves the appointment of a new officer in a key position, and unanimous backing for the audit from chief officers is a prerequisite.

Combining the two

Obviously a weakness of relying on internal staff is the question of credibility. One way round this is to have a combined operation, with consultants employed for specific tasks: guidance on scope and management of the audit; training on assessment techniques and best practices; and verification of the process. In-house staff would remain in control, and carry out most of the audit tasks. If the right consultants were chosen this approach could draw on the strong points of both the partners.

There is real value in employing consultants but not as the prime movers of the process. Whatever role they are asked to play it is vital that following discussion with them a brief is prepared which closely specifies task and management. The consultants should not only have auditing experience but good knowledge of 'best environmental practice' and the ability to communicate their knowledge.

Table 2.2 summarizes these points and covers the relative costs and the question of whether to make a new appointment or rely on existing staff. Some indication of likely effectiveness is given.

HOW FAR SHOULD THE WIDER COMMUNITY BE INVOLVED?

The public

Another critical factor is the degree to which the wider community and other organizations are involved in the process. The choice is between a private process and a public one. The former can be controlled more readily, can be kept more easily on a technical rather than political level and

Table 2.2 Mechanisms for conducting an audit

	In-house team (existing staff)	*In-house team (new specialist staff)*	*External consultant*	*Combined in-house and consultants*
Cost	Cheapest	Most expensive but could be the most cost-effective long term	More expensive than in-house team	More expensive than in-house team
Overall environmental expertise	May not be comprehensive	Excellent and LA controls what it gets	Excellent (if right consultant selected)	Excellent (if right consultant selected)
Knowledge of authority	Excellent	Limited at first but will grow	Likely to be nil or very limited	Good
Knowledge of area	Excellent	Limited at first but will grow	Depends on firm's experience but could be nil or limited	Good
Objectivity	Bound to be affected by LA culture	Good to excellent	Excellent	Good
Ease of management and control	Good	Good	Not as easy as using in-house team	Not as easy as using in-house team
Commitment to long-term implementation	Depends on other duties and priorities	Excellent	Non-existent	Mixed
Continuous involvement in monitoring and review	Depends on other duties and priorities	Excellent	Non-existent	Mixed

Source: Association of District Councils (1990)

is more predictable because the players (chief officers, for example) know each other well. In the early stage of auditing it may well be easier – and less threatening – to keep the process in-house. But eventually such a cosy audit misses the point. The public cannot help but be concerned. It is after all their environment being audited.

From the authority's viewpoint, the public have several roles:

■ Source of information on attitudes, values, and priorities, eg how important an issue is litter, or graffiti, or dog-fouling, in the public's perception?

34

- Source of information on the state of the environment, eg specific local problems, the condition of footpaths, litter survey
- Means of implementing change, eg by improved environmental awareness, altered behaviour, pressure put on organizations which pollute.

Public attitudes, values and priorities are normally reflected to the employed professionals by the elected representatives of the people. The role of politicians in auditing is crucial (see later), but inevitably the views that they hear are those of a small minority, (normally those who are both vociferous and articulate). Responses gained through leafleting and meetings are similarly self-selected and liable to bias. So if a fair representation of community attitudes is desired, then a carefully identified sample survey is essential. As suggested in Table 2.3, this survey could be undertaken by the local university or college.

Table 2.3 Mechanisms of public involvement

Techniques	Purpose	Resource implication
1) Sample survey of residents (door to door, or phone)	Discover general attitudes and environmental priorities	Costs significant, but could be marginal if organized/ carried out by local college or university, using students (as in the North Devon audit)
2) Specific manned contact point in the authority	Giving opportunities for individual issues to be raised, and giving a public face to the process	Given the need for at least one dedicated staff member on the audit, the *extra* costs would be marginal
3) Local press, radio and TV	Publicizing the issues, increase awareness	Marginal, especially if councillors not staff are interviewed
4) Leaflets/questionnaires distributed through libraries etc	Discover general attitudes (but not accurately), and allow issues to be raised	Marginal extra cost
5) Meetings in each area	Publicity and increased sense of political pressures	Time-intensive for staff. Not justified unless there are specific issues on which to hang the meeting
6) Request of parish councils for assistance	Specific information; mechanism for getting people involved in the survey work itself	Could extend the scope and value of the audit, at some organizational cost
7) Invite comments/help from selected list of voluntary groups	Gain extra information, deflect possible suspicion	Very cost effective in terms of increased data and agents of change

Public involvement may well highlight areas of environmental concern given low priority by the auditors. For example problems of litter and pavement fouling can loom large in a local community. The auditors would leave themselves wide open to criticism of elitism if such apparently mundane issues were ignored. On the other hand it would be unwise to simply follow the public's judgement in everything. Some issues (eg global warming) may seem only marginally relevant to many, yet are central to the audit.

The need to communicate with the public puts obligations on the auditors to make material accessible. The key documents are not likely to be erudite technical papers but short, well-illustrated reports that set out the issues clearly. If material is put on a computer database and given public access, then another more detailed level of information is available to those who want it.

Politicians' role

It is difficult to over-emphasize the importance of active participation by councillors in the auditing process. Their commitment is critical to real progress. Where politicians and officers do not see eye to eye over the need for an audit then the audit could well sink without trace. The councillors should be drawn into the process in at least six places:

1) **Principle:** deciding that the exercise is to be undertaken, and deciding the general level of resourcing.
2) **Scope:** agreeing how narrow or broad the audit should be, the time-scale, the relationship in detail to other policy review processes, etc.
3) **Publicity:** giving the process high public profile as key issues are explored, explaining, encouraging participation.
4) **Digesting reports:** reviewing the emerging results of the audit, both in council as a whole (because of corporate nature) and in individual committees as appropriate.
5) **Action:** deciding to implement recommendations and allocate funds accordingly.
6) **Follow on:** subsequently maintaining support and resources necessary to monitor progress and sustaining ongoing auditing.

Involving other interests

The SoE is of value not only to the local authority but also other organizations with a statutory role in environmental monitoring and control. These include HM Inspectorate of Pollution, The National Rivers Authority, MAFF, The Countryside Commission, English (Welsh or Scottish) Heritage, English (Welsh or Scottish) Nature. They have much to gain from seeing their particular concerns in context, and opening up the prospect of collaboration to tackle complex environmental problems. At the same time, of course, the value of the SoE is undermined if information from these sources is not available. If shared ownership of the process can be managed, then much is gained. Most of the statutory consultees are keen in principle to participate in the SoE, and in the evaluation of policy impact relevant to their interests.

Beyond the official bodies are the voluntary groups, and the private sector. Many local voluntary groups (eg civic societies, wildlife trusts, FoE groups) have members expert in their fields, knowing the local area well, able to contribute much data to SoE surveys. They may also have points of criticism of the authority, giving a different slant on a problem, which can help reveal issues which otherwise might get ignored. In rural areas Parish Councils offer another fertile source of assistance, able to organize for example footpath or open space surveys.

If all these varied interests are involved, maybe in the context of a Local Agenda 21 programme of action, then the role of the local authority becomes not so much providing an environmental service as triggering and coordinating a community strategy for sustainability.

TOOLS FOR AUDITING

We now turn from the public and political process of auditing to the techniques that might be employed. Conventionally a *technical* approach to a problem is often seen as being in tension with a *political* approach. Complex techniques can create communication barriers between the initiates and the outsiders – the experts and the public. Clearly the intention needs to be the opposite. The technical procedures should be designed to facilitate effective communication and exchange of information between different groups and interests.

Returning to the aims put forward in Chapter 1, the method needs to encourage the auditors to take a holistic view of the environment; it needs to be honest and open, not in pawn to sectoral interests; it needs to provide a normative, action-orientated approach; and to be practicable within the means available. A critical factor is the degree to which the techniques encourage active involvement of relevant agencies and groups, or by their complexity inhibit involvement and thus reduce the value of the outcome. The method needs to be simple enough to be understood by different professions and agencies, and related by them to their own interests.

The following sections deal with specific tools that might be employed:

■ the geographical database
■ the policy impact matrix

- good practice checklists
- consistency analysis.

The geographical database

The SoE information provides a baseline against which progress can be judged, and it is desirable to be able to update that baseline to a common format as new data become available. A computerized database, capable of manipulating spatial patterns, and accessible to the public as well as to staff, is helpful. It may be achieved using a Computer Aided Design (CAD) package in conjunction with a digitized Ordnance Survey base and a standard database; recent innovations such as 'Mapbase' show considerable promise at very modest cost;[1] or more ambitiously (and expensively) using Geographic Information Systems (GIS). The latter can, of course, be valuable for other local authority tasks as well, like development control. Both these systems have considerable potential, but put up the cost and training requirements of the audit.

Whether or not a computerized system is employed, the SoE report itself is likely to be widely used and widely quoted. It is a saleable commodity for developers and other enterprises. It is essential it communicates accurately and effectively, in a style that is accessible to lay people. Since the data will be regularly updated and extended a loose leaf system could be considered, allowing the inclusion of annual supplements.

The policy impact matrix

The matrix approach (see Table 2.4) is one way of trying to bridge the gap between departments, and to ensure consistency. It is designed to systematize the process of estimating impact, providing a framework for recording professional judgement. The format is straightforward – policy areas are listed down one axis, while aspects of environmental quality are listed across the other axis. It is possible to break down both these sets into much more specific and numerous elements, in order to differentiate environmental effects more precisely. The matrix encourages a systematic and comprehensive approach. Every possible impact is at least briefly considered. The technique allows the auditors to establish priorities from a fair set of comparisons.

But from several angles the matrix approach does not match up to the brief. There are three problems. In the first place it runs the risk of being unduly onerous and long winded, because in order to reflect the real complexity of policy/environmental interactions the size of the matrix has

---

1 'Mapbase' is a planning tool for the PC that links databases with detailed maps. Produced by NextBase Ltd, Headline House, Chaucer Road, Ashford, Middlesex TW15 2QT.

Table 2.4 Matrix recommended by the DoE for plan appraisal

Criteria	Global sustainability						Natural resources				Local environmental quality				
	1	2	3	4	5	6	7	8	9	10	11	12	13	14	15
Policies	Transport energy: Efficiency: trips	Transport energy: Efficiency: models	Built environment Energy: efficiency	Renewable energy potential	Rate of CO₂ 'fixing'	Wildlife habitats	Air quality	Water conservation and quality	Land and soil quality	Minerals conservation	Landscape and open land	Urban environmental 'liveability'	Cultural heritage	Public access open space	Building quality

Suggested impact symbols

●	No relationship or insignificant impact
✕	Significant adverse impact
✓?	Likely, but unpredictable impact
?	Uncertainty of prediction or knowledge
✓	Significant beneficial impact

Source: DoE (1993) Environmental appraisal of development plans, HMSO

to be large: recording the reasons for particular judgements (the nature of an effect, criteria for assessing significance, and the *estimate* of significance) then becomes a difficult and potentially confusing task – the auditors may become drawn into the game of completing the matrix rather than the game of achieving better policies. The second problem springs from the first: it is difficult to achieve consistency in the matrix unless the same small group of people tackle the whole exercise. But that excludes others from ownership of the process. The results can easily appear arbitrary, even contentious, to those outside the magic circle.

The third problem is the most fundamental: the matrix does not allow for the effect of *combining* policies. There are two important ways in which this has significance:

1) by cumulative impact, where the overall effect is greater than the sum of the parts. A typical example of this might be a series of road improvements that individually have modest impact but together add up to a new major route which will generate a lot of extra traffic.

2) interactive impact, where a particular policy has different effects depending on which other policies it is combined with. For example 'free-flow' traffic management measures aimed at reducing congestion have positive environmental benefits if combined with effective measures to curtail traffic growth. But if traffic is allowed to grow, then the free-flow measures will be largely counterproductive, generating extra traffic and emissions, undermining public transport, and failing to solve the problems.

So, the matrix is not a panacea for the harassed auditor. If relied on too heavily it is likely to lead to significant inaccuracies, and may sometimes be dangerously misleading.

Used more casually, however, as a prompt not a straitjacket, the matrix idea has merit. It can provide a standard impact checklist for use by different groups. It should be kept broad and generalized, so that it can be tackled quickly, and used as a scoping exercise to help set priorities. It may point out matters previously overlooked.

Good practice checklists

The matrix approach is about estimating the actual impact of policies on each element of environmental stock. An alternative approach is to look at the nature of the policies themselves. This can be done by comparing them with model policies derived from external sources such as:

■ statutory environmental bodies (Countryside Commission, National Rivers Authority, Pollution Inspectorate, English Heritage, English Nature, etc);

- non-governmental environmental organizations (RSPB, FoE, Town and Country Planning Association, etc);
- government departments, notably the Planning Policy Guidance notes of the DoE;
- other local authorities who are known to be at the forefront in a particular sphere (eg Leicester in urban wildlife, Newcastle in energy-efficiency, Berkshire in sustainable strategic planning, Mendip in corporate environmental management);
- other European countries (eg Netherlands in integrated pollution and land-use planning; Germany in urban transport and environment; Denmark in CHP and renewable energy);
- relevant literature, especially where practical recommendations result (eg Barton, H, Davis, G and Guise, R *Sustainable Settlements: a guide for planners, designers and developers*, published by the University of the West of England and the Local Government Management Board, May 1995).

Arguably it is part of professionals' duty to keep up-to-date with emerging good practice from such sources in their own sphere of interest. Lists of model policies can then be used as templates against which to judge the current performance of the local authority. An attempt has been made in this book to provide a comprehensive checklist which could act as a starting point for auditing. Appendices 2 and 3 contrast common practice with presumed good practice, allowing a local authority to identify where it lies on a performance spectrum.

The great advantages of this approach are that it is simple, direct, and points the way forward. To be effective, though, it does rely on ruthless honesty. The auditor has to distinguish carefully between stated objectives of policy (which may often be sound) and the policy actually being implemented (which may not). For example, the general policy in a transport plan may suggest giving high priority to public transport, but study of the transport budget reveal that in fact little money is being spent or action taken to achieve it.

Another problem that checklists (in common with the matrix approach) fail to address is policy interaction. The presumption of excellence may be too simplistic in situations where the environmental effects of a policy are dependent on what happens in *another* sphere of activity. For example, the promotion of 'car-sharing' is probably on many people's list of approved eco-friendly policies. Yet if the effect of such promotion is to encourage more lift-giving at the expense of the bus services (and it often is), then car-sharing may be counterproductive for the overall emissions standpoint, as non-viable buses are withdrawn and car dependence increases. Such double-bind situations are difficult to cope with using a straightforward policy checklist.

In some spheres of policy at least, then, we are looking for a more sophisticated technique preferably without sacrificing the ease of handling and the action-orientation of a best practice list.

NETWORK ANALYSIS AND CONSISTENCY ANALYSIS

The problems of complex systems are central when dealing with strategic land use/transport policies, such as residential and commercial location policies, education provision, density issues, traffic planning, transport policies, green belts, urban form, rural settlement policies and economic regeneration strategies. A consistent strategy ensures these diverse interests are mutually reinforcing – not undermining – each other in relation to environmental goals.

Consistency is also vital across the whole spectrum of the audit. There is growing recognition that the superficially separate areas of pollution control, waste collection and disposal, sewage treatment, water supply and drainage, energy production, mineral exploitation and recycling all have profound implications for each other, and relate also to issues of urban form and development patterns. Figure 2.1 illustrates the use of network analysis to identify the linkages; each link representing a potential problem and/or opportunity.

Few audits have even tried to grapple with these complex questions. To that extent most PIA's so far have been less than adequate. One approach to the task, used more overseas than in the UK, is called AIDA – the Analysis of Interconnected Decision Areas. AIDA provides a kit of simple tools – linkages diagrams, matrices and flow charts – capable of shaping the complexities and providing a framework for policy evaluation (Hickling, 1976).

The process of analysing connections should be tackled systematically, linking policy areas where there are common environmental impacts. Suggested stages in this analysis are set out below in relation to a transport and land use example.

Stage 1 – Identify a cluster of linked decision areas

Where action in one sphere can reinforce or undermine action in another sphere. Figures 2.1 and 2.2 illustrate graphical presentation of linkage. Such graphs, used quickly, are useful as learning devices. They oblige consideration of all types of connections between policies. They may be useful in gaining the acceptance of different departments and agencies that policies *are* linked, and need collaborative evaluation.

Stage 2 – Identify relevant linking issues or goals

In the case of the present example one key linking principle is the desire to

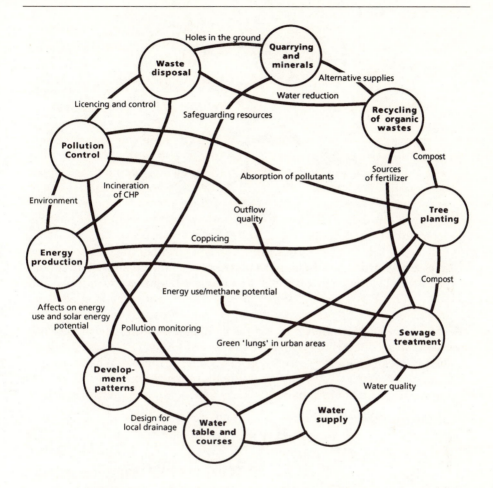

Figure 2.1 Network analysis of diverse decision areas

reduce transport energy use. The identification of the key goal or goals helps to focus the debate on the nature of policy interaction.

Stage 3 – Prepare a compatibility matrix

The matrix should consist of the key policies in each decision area along with the relevant goal(s). It is important at this stage to express the *real* policies, ie those that are being implemented, rather than any bland general statements of policy that may really be no more than aspirations. Clearly such clarity can be an important step in itself.

The matrix is liable to include factors at different levels of generality – ranging from goals and objectives to specific proposals. If the resulting

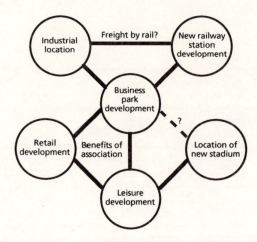

Figure 2.2 Identifying linkage or interdependence between decision areas – a selected group of linked land use decisions

chart looks uncomfortably large – say over 15 factors – then it may be easier to create several interlinked matrices.

The policies shown in Figure 2.3 are extracted from a real case study.

Stage 4 – Analyse compatibility

Using the matrix, consider the compatibility of each policy with each other. When combined will they have a positive or negative effect on the key environmental goal(s)? In relation to the example: will they, when coupled, reduce the need to travel and reduce the level of car dependence ... or will they increase them?

Where possible it is desirable to identify different *degrees* of compatibility and also the main *reasons* for reaching the judgement.

Stage 5 – Drawing conclusions, making recommendations

One useful way of working towards conclusions from the matrix is to identify clusters of policies that are compatible (see Figure 2.4). These sets could then form the basis of a revised package of policies. The illustration in Chapter 8, however, shows a high level of *incompatibility*. A simple chart is used (Table 8.2, page 139) to state conclusions and initial recommendations in relation to each of the policies.

Conclusion

The set of broad planning policies used in the example is similar to sets that

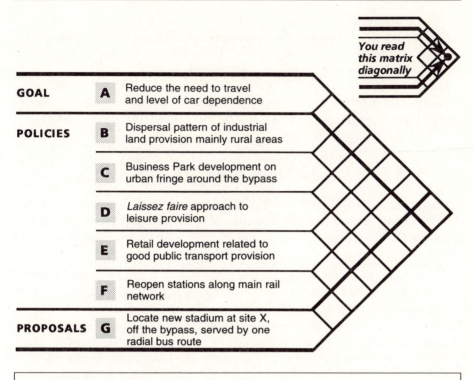

You read this matrix diagonally

GOAL	**A**	Reduce the need to travel and level of car dependence
POLICIES	**B**	Dispersal pattern of industrial land provision mainly rural areas
	C	Business Park development on urban fringe around the bypass
	D	*Laissez faire* approach to leisure provision
	E	Retail development related to good public transport provision
	F	Reopen stations along main rail network
PROPOSALS	**G**	Locate new stadium at site X, off the bypass, served by one radial bus route

Degrees of compatibility and certainty

✓	Policies are mutually reinforcing
●	Policies have little or no mutual effect (neutral)
×	Policies tend to undermine each other
?	Uncertain or unknown effects (may be applied with any of the other symbols)

Explanatory code: reasons for the assessment

B	Behavioural factors, ie related to people's behaviour
M	Market factors, ie related to the response of businesses
D	Design factors, ie related to engineering or architectural design
S	Space factors, ie related to the availability of land or built space
F	Financial factors, ie related to budgetary issues
O	Organizational factors, ie related to roles and remits

Figure 2.3   Compatibility matrix (derived from Figure 2.2)

Note: This matrix is shown completed in Chapter 8, Figure 8.1. The reader may therefore test out the technique here, then check the results against the later analysis.

are enshrined in many plans. Yet when analysed in relation to the environmental goal of reducing the need to travel, the set can be seen to be inconsistent. Some policies undermine others. The audit needs to pick out the inconsistencies and challenge current thinking.

Such techniques are not a substitute for detailed impact assessment. What they do is provide a context allowing the auditor a coherent overview prioritizing areas of critical impact or conflict that merit deeper study.

RECOMMENDATIONS

What this chapter has tried to do is present the key choices which need to be made in order to progress an audit. There is no single right way; there are several, depending on the context and purpose the audit is intended to serve.

1) Consider the relationship between the SoE and the PIA very carefully and ensure that the scope and orientation of the SoE is such as to give answers on policy impact.

2) The choice of SoE indicators reflects the priorities and values of the community and the authority. Public involvement in the process of choice is therefore desirable, especially in the context of Local Agenda 21.

3) Use comparison with a comprehensive checklist of good practice to 'scope' the PIA and identify aspects which need more detailed attention. Appendices 2 and 3 may be useful in this respect.

4) Normally it is best to tackle the RIP as the first audit element, so that the authority can be seen to be 'putting its own house in order'.

5) The audit should ideally be undertaken 'in-house', so officers and councillors feel ownership of process and learn through it. However external consultants (or joint working arrangements with other experienced agencies) are needed to provide training, specialist knowledge where it is missing, and objective validation of the process.

6) The style and presentation of audit material should be accessible and transparent, to encourage the effective involvement in the process of politicians, the public, and different departments and agencies.

7) Use of a computer-based geographical information system to record and monitor spatial and environmental information is desirable, subject to the caveat that it is very 'user-friendly', and can be accessed by a wide range of interested agencies/people.

8) Detailed infrastructure and environmental data should be available (at a price) to developers to facilitate their involvement in planning for sustainability.

9) Where policies interact with each other or have cumulative impacts

consistency analysis should be used. This is particularly important where several different semi-autonomous sections or agencies are involved, each with their own agenda. Collaborative exercises are essential to recognize and act on shared issues.

Note: Part III of the book expands very considerably on the management and organizational aspects of auditing, on the basis of empirical study of auditing in practice. More detailed recommendations can be found there.

REFERENCES

Barton, Hugh (1987) *Evaluating the Potential for Increasing Energy Efficiency Through Local Planning* MPhil Thesis, Faculty of the Built Environment, University of the West of England, Bristol

Department of the Environment (1993) *The Environmental Appraisal of Development Plans: A Good Practice Guide* HMSO, London

Hickling A (1976) Managing Decisions: *The Strategic Choice Approach* Tavistock Institute of Human Relations, Mantec Publishing, Lutterworth

QUEST FOR THE GLOBAL GRAIL

Hugh Barton

Chapters 1 and 2 have set out the nature and the process of environmental auditing. This chapter now links auditing to the goal of sustainable development that was introduced and defined at the outset of Part I. It attempts to work towards criteria of sustainability that could be used in environmental auditing, putting particular emphasis on the concept of environmental capacity. The final part of the chapter takes two key elements of environmental stock – climate and minerals – and examines them in more detail.

CATEGORIES OF ENVIRONMENTAL STOCK

In economic terms the basic condition that has to be satisfied in order to achieve sustainability is constant capital stock. Capital stock is measured in terms of the amount and quality of resources, eg the quality of the soils, the purity of the air, the level of energy resources, the quality of water or the existence of diverse habitats. Local authorities monitor stock quality through the SoE reports. They can assess the impact of policy on the environmental stock. If the authority aspires towards a synoptic view of the environment, then the elemental categories listed above provide a starting point for a checklist, which can be extended to incorporate man-made stock as well as natural stock.

In Table 3.1 three distinct categories of stock are distinguished.

1) **Global ecology:** which is concerned primarily with atmospheric and climatic stability and with the conservation of biodiversity. Key variables amenable to influence by local authorities are CO_2 emissions and wildlife habitats.
2) **Husbanding of natural resources:** which is concerned with appropriate use and conservation of our resources of air, water, the land and its minerals.

Table 3.1 Elements of environmental stock

Elements	*Key objectives for local authorities*
A *Global ecology*	
1) Atmosphere and Climate	Reduce CO_2 emissions: — reduce energy use in buildings — reduce energy use in transport — substitute renewables for fossil fuels
	Increase CO_2 absorption
2) Biodiversity	Conserve extent and variety of wildlife habitats
	Protect rare or vulnerable species
B *Natural resources*	
3) Air	Maintain/enhance local air quality
4) Water	Improve quality of water courses and bodies Protect water supplies
5) Land	Maintain/enhance soil fertility Protect from erosion and contamination
6) Mineral and energy resources	Reduce consumption of non-renewables Protect potential for renewables
C *Local human environment*	
7) Buildings	Availability and renewal of appropriate residential, social and commercial built space in convenient/accessible locations
8) Infrastructure	Provision and renewal of necessary/safe transport and service infrastructure
9) Open space	Provision/renewal and cleanliness of accessible and appropriate open space
10) Aesthetic quality	Enhance perceived environmental quality in terms of sight, sound, smell, touch and association
11) Cultural heritage	Safeguard archaeological remains, historic monuments, good architecture, attractive townscapes and landscapes

3) Human environmental quality: which encompasses the manmade stock of buildings, infrastructure and adapted landscape in terms both of appropriate space for human activity, and of its perceived aesthetic quality.

It should be noted that this categorization is based on the DoE's *Guide to*

Environmental Appraisal of Development Plans (DoE,1993) though it goes beyond the guide in suggesting the inclusion of human artifacts.

There are, inevitably, overlaps between categories. For example, reducing energy use in transport to moderate the level of CO_2 emissions also acts to conserve non-renewable fuels, and in addition is likely to have an impact on accessibility. Any list is bound to involve a degree of arbitrariness about where to draw boundaries. At the edges, environmental issues grade into social and economic issues. Some analysts might exclude the quality of life factors altogether on the grounds that they are 'social'. Others might exclude the provision of residential and commercial buildings as essentially 'economic'. But that is to miss the point. The environment is not being defined as something 'out there', separate from humanity. We are interested in it because it *is* the human habitat. Every element of environmental stock has profound implications for human well-being – physical, social, economic or spiritual.

GRADING AND TRANSFERABILITY OF STOCK

There are clearly degrees of sustainability. What this section does is first discuss some of the key distinctions that can be drawn between different grades of importance in the environment stock, and then to examine the question of substitution and transfer between elements of stock.

Strong and weak sustainability

Strong (or 'deep green') sustainability refers to factors critical to global ecology – for example CO_2 emissions and deforestation; while weak (or 'light green') sustainability refers to lower order or more localized concerns – for example architectural heritage or open space. In general terms therefore strong sustainability equates with sections A and B on Table 3.1, while weak sustainability equates with section C. More particularly it may be useful to analyse the global significance of local actions using four criteria:

1) Are emissions, especially CO_2, NO_x, SO_2, NH_4, O_3 affected?
2) Are non-renewable resources (especially but not exclusively energy resources) conserved, consumed, or substituted?
3) Is the resilience/absorptive capacity of the biosphere degraded or enhanced?
4) Are rare or vulnerable habitats damaged or threatened?

Caution: the use of terms such as 'strong' and 'weak' may be a good way to lose friends! Local public and political opinion often gives higher priority to weak factors (such as litter and dog-fouling) than to strong factors (such as global warming) which are perceived as distant and beyond effective influence.

Critical and constant stock

Critical environmental stock (or capital) are those elements which possess such scarcity value that they should be preserved at all costs, as 'critical' to sustainability of our natural/man-made heritage. The term is usually applied to specific sites or areas, such as Sites of Special Scientific Interest (SSSIs) or outstanding conservation areas. Used with discretion such highlighting of unique value in the audit has merit. Threats to any 'critical' element of stock would cause justifiable outcry.

Naturally environmental agencies are keen to see their own interests reflected in the identification of critical stock. Organizations such as English Nature, Royal Society for the Protection of Birds, English Heritage and the National Rivers Authority are lobbying to ensure what is perceived as this highest level of protection is afforded to key elements.

Their demands may not necessarily be right. The alternative defence of constant environmental stock (or transferable stock) may be more appropriate in some cases. It is an altogether more subtle concept. Rather than equating environmental value with specific site resources it equates value with a broader resource base which needs to be maintained in balance.

Examples where a 'constant stock' approach could be appropriate are in relation to anthropogenic (ie human-generated) greenhouse gases in the atmosphere, and energy resources. Both of these are discussed later in the chapter. Constant stock might also be best for habitat preservation where natural plant succession and/or human impact can lead to quite rapid change on any particular site, and the important thing is the general survival and enhancement of that habitat over a wider area.

Constant stock should therefore not be seen as a weaker level of protection than critical stock. It is appropriate in different circumstances. It is less locally fixed, more flexible, allowing – within defined limits – replacement, substitution and trade-offs to occur. The vital policy question is whether the local authority has in place the mechanisms to define, monitor and police stock levels.

Transferability and substitution

It is worth distinguishing between different kinds of transfer or substitution:

- **Replacement of like with like** in the context of maintaining overall stock levels. For example one area of woodland due for felling may be replaced by another maturing on a neighbouring site.
- **Substitution of one resource for another.** For example the use of non-renewable mineral reserve may be compensated by an equivalent increase in long-term capacity to recycle the material (but see later discussion).
- **Transfer or trade across boundaries.** In most instances local authority

boundaries do not represent autonomous geographical or economic units, so it will be necessary to see the locality as part of the wider region or country.

The SoE survey needs to recognize and pick up these distinctions in order to adequately relate resources to policy.

STANDARDS, TARGETS AND ENVIRONMENTAL CAPACITY

Monitoring the environment has little value unless objectives are set against which the performance of the environment, and the effectiveness of policy in improving environmental quality, can be judged. Such objectives come in a variety of forms:

1) **Desired direction of change:** eg reduced car reliance in terms of the share of trips made.
2) **Standard:** eg permitted levels of CO, or SO_2, in the air, as defined by the EU.
3) **Targets:** eg return CO_2 emissions to 1990 levels by 2000 AD.
4) **Environmental capacity:** eg the maximum number of people able to live in or visit an environmentally-sensitive area without sacrificing the value of the area.

These objectives provide *criteria* for evaluation: eg has the share of car trips increased or decreased? How often have permitted levels of SO_2 been exceeded? Have CO_2 emission levels moved towards the target at the right pace? Has the environmental capacity been exceeded? The SoE thus becomes a *normative* tool, seeking not merely to observe the environment, but to evaluate it in relation to politically-set goals. The sources of standards, targets and capacities may be diverse. Of the examples above some are exogenous to the local authority: SO_2 levels set by the EC; CO_2 targets by the UK Government. The others are home-grown, determined by local political process, presumably written into development plans, transport policies or wildlife strategies.

CAPACITY PLANNING

It cannot be emphasized too much that such criteria for environmental stock do not somehow emerge from natural laws: they are not 'objective'. They are policy-driven, dependent on the views and preferences of policy-makers. This distinction becomes important when dealing with the concept of environmental capacity. There is a temptation to search for some kind of absolute capacity, and use it to fend off development pressures. Wildlife groups are prone to this, and so are communities who argue 'not in my backyard, its full!'[1] But the capacity of an area (to accept human activity) depends heavily on the way the area is managed, or on the balance of environmental priorities with other social or economic goals. A fragile hill landscape, for example, may be threatened by too many visitors, but its capacity might be effectively increased by new visitor management policies, such as moving car parks away from the most vulnerable zones. In this case the defined capacity becomes a *threshold* which should trigger action by the local authority to deter, or cope better with, visitors.

It is important to 'unpack' the concept of environmental capacity. The first point to make is that 'capacity planning' is not entirely new. In some ways it is simply a refinement of the traditional process of planning by constraint. Sieve mapping and development potential analysis have been used to analyse constraints. GIS (Geographical Information Systems) bring the approach up to date.

The second point is that there are various different types of environmental capacity, encompassing both the built and the natural environment, and extending to include the human environment:

- **Built environment**   Capacity of building stock; capacity of infrastructure; capacity of the aesthetic and cultural heritage.
- **Natural environment**   Capacity of wildlife habitats/landscapes; capacity of the natural resource base:
  — absorptive capacity
  — resource capacity.
- **Human environment**   Capacity in relation to traffic impact; capacity in relation to social impact.

These capacities are not immutable. On the contrary, they are open to a great deal of manipulation. The discussion below examines the nature of the different types of capacity as a means of evaluating the concept.

Building stock capacity

This is particularly important in relation to housing. Falling populations in urban areas are not usually because of lack of demand but because the effective capacity of the dwellings is reducing as household size reduces. Population forecasts for urban areas are thus often best done by analysing *capacity*, not demographic trends. The capacity of a given area will gradually alter under market pressures and be reflected in applications for extensions, divisions, change of use, and renewal.

---

1 Known as the NIMBY syndrome.

Infrastructure capacity

This is probably the least mutable. The roads, sewers, water mains, have a certain capacity and are subject to centralized control. 'Threshold analyses' identify the degree of overload or spare capacity and the population levels at which extra investment would be needed to permit further growth. Even in this case, however, management techniques can alter the relationship between infrastructure and human activity. Traffic management can effectively increase road capacity. Water management can increase the amount of development and population relying on a given drainage system.

Both these types of capacity have a direct relationship to population, are relatively predictable, and ingrained in planning practice. 'Natural environment' capacities are altogether less tangible.

Wildlife habitats and fragile landscapes

Both of these are vulnerable to excessive human activity. The range of impacts is wide: walkers, tourists, quarrying, agriculture, traffic, any kind of development. In this situation of multiple impacts, each different, it can be awkward to find a common denominator in terms of capacity for what. Even when one kind of impact is clearly dominant then the capacity of a habitat or landscape to cope with human invasions can be altered by management, eg changing the location of car parks, providing 'honey-pots', creating a path. In some situations the natural ecology will itself regenerate, discovering a new equilibrium or invading new areas (eg derelict sites). When we are dealing with a living, fluid situation, it is difficult to define an absolute 'capacity'. It might be better to think in terms of 'thresholds' of impact which demand action.

Natural resource capacities

These are potentially the most fundamental and far-reaching and raise the issue of 'carrying capacity'. Two elements need to be distinguished: absorptive capacity and supply capacity. The capacity of local air, water and earth resources, to absorb the emissions and effluents of human activity without compromising their resilience or human health is central to sustainability. One main task of SoE monitoring is to assess progress against quality standards. Statutory bodies such as the National Rivers Authority and HM Pollution Inspectorate are critical to this. Such standards, however, do not of themselves allow definition of a 'carrying capacity' for an area. Rather pollution control and reduction is the principle – enshrined in the Environmental Protection Act. The theory is that development is fine, but must prove itself non-polluting.

The argument over the supply of resources is different. 'Carrying capacity' implies that development in any given region should occur only at the rate that can be supported by local supplies of, eg, stone, gravel, clay, maybe of energy as well. That has great attraction, a sense of elemental justice. But, the reality is that regions trade in minerals with each other increasingly across national boundaries. Some regions are and will remain net importers. Other are and will remain net exporters. Their wealth is built on it. So I see little social economic or political mileage in linking population and development directly to local resources for the foreseeable future.

Human environment capacity

A traditional form of this, promoted in *Traffic in Towns*,[1] relates to the capacity of residential or shopping environments to absorb traffic. A typical standard was, for a residential area, a maximum flow of 300 pcus per house, allowing relatively unimpeded crossing of local streets.

The new form might be termed *social capacity*: the capacity of a settlement, or a community, to accept growth without destroying the sense of place and the social milieu which are currently valued. That implies not an absolute limit to capacity, but a maximum *rate* of growth. As such the concept is very important. It is also of course very emotive and very political. Certain local authorities in the South East have gone so far as to argue that their areas have *reached* environmental capacity – ignoring the fact that they are not islands, but part of an expanding metropolitan region. In this case a possibly valid argument over the social capacity of a county has been confused with a probably invalid argument over natural carrying capacity.

This points to the dangers of the capacity concept: it is liable to be hijacked for political reasons, dressing up NIMBYism in ecological clothes.

Another example of the benefits and risks of capacity planning comes from Chester (Roebuck, 1994). In a very interesting exercise Cheshire County Council have defined the critical environmental stock of the city in terms of its aesthetic and cultural heritage. Capacity has then been calculated on the basis of the city's building stock, transport networks, open space and impact on that critical stock. Problems could arise, however, in so far as the process treats Chester as an island. If Chester is pronounced to be nearly up to 'capacity' space still has to be found for the people and businesses in a growing city region. The implications of limiting Chester's population for the smaller towns beyond the green belt, for commuting and transport energy use, and hence for globally damaging emissions, are set on one side.

2 Buchanan, C (ed) (1963) *Traffic in Towns*, the specially shortened edition of the Buchanan Report, Penguin and HMSO, London.

Conclusions

The idea of environmental capacity is capable of being used in relation to the built environment and the social sphere as well as the natural environment. Some of these uses – such as estimating housing capacity and residential traffic levels – are part of well-established planning practice. The extension of capacity arguments to questions of local ecology and the carrying capacity of natural resources is seductive. It gives the appearance of offering a kind of objective, scientific rationale to no growth or slow growth strategies – a handy weapon for nature conservation groups wishing to belabour ecologically-incorrect authorities.

But it is arguable that 'capacity' is not so easily pinned down, and has real dangers. It is not simply that environmental capacity arguments can become a cloak for NIMBYism (and thus lose credibility). It is that in some (but not all) situations the notion of capacity is not really valid. To summarize:

1) Capacity has validity when applied to factors such as the existing building stock, where the stock is relatively stable and exogenous variables predictable.
2) It has less validity when applied to elements such as natural habitats that have innate regeneration abilities, and where policy decisions can easily alter the context (for example, by changed management regimes) and thus capacity.
3) The population-carrying capacity of a particular region can only be usefully defined if that region is an island, sufficient unto itself. The island approach does not relate to normal, social and economic realities. Planners should resist politicians' desire to use it, except perhaps in the case of relatively isolated new settlements where ideals of resource autonomy could be a prerequisite.
4) Rather than capacities, which suggest absolute limits, it might be more constructive to work to *thresholds* – levels of activity or population that trigger action or review.
5) The definition of thresholds (or capacities) may be informed by technical analysis, but involve judgements which are essentially political – trade-offs of one need against another need. They should be recognised therefore as **policies** or **objectives**, rather than **facts**.

Finally, to relate thresholds and capacities back to environmental auditing:

1) **Monitoring environmental conditions (SoE):** Thresholds and capacities provide criteria against which to monitor progress. They provide reasons for choosing particular indicators and particular methods of data collection.
2) **Setting the right policy agenda**: Thresholds and capacities are policy

tools which may be appropriate to the needs of any authority. They are particularly useful as means of reeducation and motivation, forcing reappraisal of conventional practices.

3)   **Evaluation of current policy or of policy options (PIA):** Policies may be expressed in terms of their approach to environmental thresholds or capacities, eg to accept current limits or increase limits by management. Estimates of impacts on environmental stock could be in terms of whether critical thresholds are breached. Subsequent refinement of the plan would then have to specify how the situation was resolved.

We now turn from ways of assessing or measuring sustainability to look at two key issues that span across the specific topics of Part II of the book: climate change and non-renewable resources. The logic for tackling them now is that no one chapter in Part II encompasses them sufficiently. Yet they are central to the quest for the 'global grail' of sustainable development.

THE THREAT OF CLIMATE CHANGE

Global warming is the ecological threat which has forced governments to act on sustainability. This is not the place to discuss the science of global warming. But its significance for local authority policy, and therefore for environmental auditing, is great, and as yet little understood. So this section provides a brief introduction to the politics and the policy implications.

The key indicator in relation to greenhouse gases is the level of CO_2 emissions. The authoritative 'Intergovernmental Panel on Climatic Change' (IPCC) which reported to UN member governments in 1990, considers that a 'sustainable' level of CO_2 emission, where absorption rates could match emission rates, is about 40 per cent the current UK level. Since CO_2 is an inevitable consequence of burning fossil fuels, that implies a reduction in fossil fuel use in the UK by 60 per cent. That could be taken as a target by local authorities in environmental auditing of local activity and policies. Its achievement will require not only substitution of low-carbon fuels for high, but an absolute priority for energy efficiency in all spheres. Several chapters in Part II take up this challenge. A specific illustration of applying CO_2 targets is offered in the transport chapter.

Official policy

The UK government has committed itself to combat the threat of global warming. The 1990 White Paper *This Common Inheritance* (DoE, 1990) was honest about the problem and explicit about the direction policy should take. It has been followed up by an extensive research programme commissioned by the Department of the Environment. At the Earth Summit

---

Box 3.1   Global warming and climate change

1) The level of greenhouse gases in the atmosphere is rising due to increased human metabolic activity, particularly the burning of fossil fuels, the loss of forest, and the increasing intensity of agriculture.

2) This is leading, so most scientists believe, to the very rapid (geologically speaking) warming of the Earth – at the rate of between 0.3 and 0.7°C per decade. Feedback loops in the global ecosystem are not fully understood and *may* moderate the warming, but are more likely to exacerbate it.

3) Global warming, in turn, is affecting climate, and will do so at a greater rate next century. Climate change in many parts of the world is also being caused by land use changes, especially deforestation. The combined effect is to increase climate instability and, in the tropics particularly, the risk of drought or violent storm.

4) Warming also leads to ocean expansion, and *could* trigger polar ice-melting, causing sea level rise and flooding of low lying coasts.

(1992) the UK joined other nations in promising action to bring back CO_2 emissions to the 1990 level by the year 2000 – a target which the recession of the early 90s makes relatively unchallenging. The 1994 Strategy for Sustainable Development has a specific sub-report on climate change (DoE, 1994). In three spheres particularly Government is initiating change:

1) in relation to energy generation it is promoting the decline of coal and its substitution by gas, which has significantly lower emission levels;

2) in relation to land-use planning, it is requiring that development plans incorporate global environmental concerns;

3) in relation to pollution control, where the Environmental Protection Act now requires an integrated and consistent approach. There are also progressive changes in other spheres – such as building regulations.

Yet despite this it is clear that the government itself has no consistent strategy. It would appear that one section of government does not understand, or perhaps does not choose to understand, what another is attempting to do. Despite the existence of the Energy Efficiency Office (now in the DoE), the structure of energy supply industries ensures that different utilities (whether privatized or not) are competing to sell more energy rather than cooperating to conserve. This contrasts strongly with some other European countries: in Sweden the city and county authorities are charged with developing integrated energy-efficiency strategies incorporating conservation measures, energy from waste, transport and planning aspects, so that reliance on imported oil and unpopular nuclear electricity can be reduced. In Denmark urban authorities are moving towards combined heat and power schemes, using wind, straw, rubbish and gas fuels in order to achieve what the Danes perceive as higher standards and improved environmental quality.

Lack of consistency also appears in the transport field. Despite DoE commitments to emission control the Department of Transport persists with an investment strategy geared to private mobility. Both the trunk roads programme and the funding arrangements for transport authorities ensure the absence of a 'level playing field' for private and public transport. One recent study of the Bristol area, evaluating the potential for a sustainable transport strategy, points to the ineffectuality of local action to reduce car reliance in the face of the DTp determination to widen the M4 and M5 in the vicinity of the city. It is clear that when government perceives environmental priorities to be at variance with economic priorities (albeit the latter rather narrowly defined and reflecting sectoral interests) it tends to speak with a forked tongue.

In the face of government ambivalence, local authorities are not in a powerful position to achieve CO_2 targets. Limited influence, though, does not exonerate them from responsibility within their limited sphere. It also points to the desperate need for a consistent and collaborative approach to environmental auditing at regional and national levels as well as local.

Conclusion

Any targets for the reduction of greenhouse emissions relate to a *community* rather than *agency-specific* audit. They are in a sense 'pie in the sky', in the absence of more effective government action. But they can perhaps provide a rallying-cry and help galvanize political commitment.

Within the LA's own sphere of influence, the audit should assess at least whether policies and practices are shifting in the right direction – are positive trends being reinforced, and negative ones moderated?

NON-RENEWABLE RESOURCES

For most elements of environmental stock there are already examples of EU, national or local criteria which can be picked up by local authorities and adapted to their own needs. These criteria are explored in Part II of the book, under subject headings. But in the sphere of non-renewable minerals, including fossil fuels, it is still difficult to define sustainability criteria.

No adequate guidelines are in place from government that either promote the concept of mineral conservation or allow the interpretation of that to the local level. The locality has little relevance in a context where resources such as oil, stone or gravel are freely traded between different areas of the country. Sustainable exploitation of these minerals needs to be defined at national level but in the face of escalating commercial demand (sometimes called 'national need') this seems currently unlikely.

If a sustainable policy were developed it could be based around the principle of constant capital stock: in the case, say, of oil and natural gas the critical measure might be the extent of proven recoverable reserves. If this was falling because consumption was exceeding the rate of discovery, then the rate of consumption would need to be reduced, and the shortfall made up of increased energy efficiency or substitution by other (more renewable) forms of fuel. Put more pointedly: loss of non-renewable resources should be compensated by increased capacity to use those resources efficiently, so that the *rate* of loss will subsequently fall.

In other words the critical measure of sustainability is the longevity of reserves. *The level of proven recoverable resources divided by the rate of extraction per annum should be maintained or improve (grow) year on year* as extraction rates fall and new reserves are found.

This is a subtle measure. It recognizes the process of mineral discovery rather than an arbitrary fixed limit; it provides an incentive both to energy-efficiency measures and to substitution. It does not prevent economic growth but shifts its emphasis.

It may be a while before auditing is in a position to monitor such trends. It is a challenge for the future. Meanwhile the audit should at least try to identify:

- the level of reserves locally;
- the rate of exploitation of those reserves (rising or falling?);
- the number of planning permissions being granted (rising or falling?);
- the extent to which policy is moving to conserve scarce resources.

CONCLUSION

What this chapter has begun to do is link the concept of sustainable development to environmental auditing, particularly SoE and PIA reporting. The relation between internal auditing and external conditions is not necessarily direct. In Part II of the book the relationship will be investigated for each relevant topic.

General Recommendations

1) In the context of national and international moves towards sustainable development, the audit should adopt as far as possible a holistic and comprehensive approach to the environment.
2) The environmental (and economic success) should be judged by assessing the levels and quality of environmental stock itself.
3) The varying nature of the elements of environmental stock should be reflected in clear distinctions being drawn between global and local, critical and constant stock, with a recognition that in some spheres substitution and transfers of stock are appropriate.
4) Standards, targets, capacities and thresholds should be used in appropriate contexts to assess progress, and to pinpoint what progress *needs* to be made.

REFERENCES

Buchanan, C (ed) (1963) *Traffic in Towns* (the specially shortened edition of the Buchanan Report) Penguin and HMSO, London

Department of the Environment (1990) *This Common Inheritance: Britain's Environmental Strategy* HMSO, London

Department of the Environment (1993) *Environmental Appraisal of Development Plans: A good practice guide* HMSO, London

Department of the Environment (1994) *Sustainable Development: The UK Strategy* HMSO, London

Department of the Environment et al (1994) *Climate Change: The UK Programme* HMSO, London

Roebuck, S (1994) 'Calculating Capacity' *Planning Week*, **2**, no 24, 16 June 1994, pp14–15

Case Studies – Urban and Rural

Ruth Allen and Helmut Lusser

RURAL CASE STUDY: ENVIRONMENTAL AUDITING AND MENDIP DISTRICT COUNCIL – A CASE STUDY FOR PRACTICAL ACTION *(Ruth Allen)*

General background

Mendip is a small rural district in north Somerset, lying south of the cities of Bristol and Bath. It contains a rich variety of landscapes, ranging from the open views of the Mendip Hills to the more intimate farmlands and the wide marshland skylines of the Somerset Levels and Moors.

Over 98,000 people live in the district, with 40 per cent of the population located in five small towns – Frome, Wells, Glastonbury, Street and Shepton Mallet. The rest of the people live in villages and settlements scattered throughout the countryside. Over 70 per cent of the roads in the district are Class 4 or 3 and there are no motorways, the nearest being the M4 and M5, both over 30 miles away.

Although agriculture is the main land use (over 80 per cent is farmed, mainly dairying), the district also has a strong manufacturing base. This sector is now declining but in 1993 still accounted for 33 per cent of the workforce. The area is also rich in minerals and today is a major exporter of limestone aggregate from the Mendip Hills, mainly to the south-west and south-east.

Currently no political party has an outright majority in the District Council although the Liberal Democrats hold the largest number of seats.

ENVIRONMENTAL ISSUES AND MENDIP DISTRICT COUNCIL

In 1991 the Council agreed that environmental issues should be a core concern of its policies. It was decided to prepare a set of environmental aims and objectives and to establish an environmental reserve fund of £100,000. An environmental initiatives officer was appointed in 1992 to work corporately throughout the Council. One of the officer's first tasks was to undertake an environmental audit of the Council's policies and practices.

The underlying philosophy of the Council's approach to environmental issues is that they should be integrated in all the Council's work. The environmental initiatives office and the reserve fund are therefore used as pump priming agents, stimulating others to act.

This approach influenced how the environmental audit was undertaken – from the start it was intended that it should facilitate practical action and not just be an academic exercise.

HOW WAS THE ENVIRONMENTAL AUDIT PREPARED?

As it was essential to integrate environmental concerns in the Council's land use planning system, the audit initially concentrated on issues relevant to the district plan, particularly those affecting the countryside, an area of work which the Council wished to develop.

In contrast, the Council already had a well established energy management programme. As the audit could be used positively to coordinate existing programmes and to support further initiatives this topic was also chosen as one of the first areas for investigation.

Methods developed for undertaking the Mendip Environmental Audit were initially based on three main principles:

1) integration of the State of the Environment report and Policy Impact Analysis;
2) involvement of officers who would be implementing the audit recommendations in preparing the report;
3) preparation of an action plan as an integral part of the auditing process.

At the beginning of the project it was envisaged that State of the Environment reports would be prepared incrementally when each topic area was considered. This would ensure that up to date information was used when the environmental impact of the Council's policies was analysed. One of the main findings of the first audit report, however, was that the Council needed to gather more comprehensive, baseline environmental information about the district. This was essential if the Council was to enable practical action that would achieve tangible and relevant environmental goals.

Officer working groups were established for each topic area. They were multidisciplinary, involving staff from all relevant areas of work and included one director. They met 3–4 times during preparation of the report.

- **Meetings 1–2:** Discussion of main, relevant environmental issues and presentation of the initial findings of the state of the environment report.
- **Meeting 3:** Discussion of the environmental appraisal of the Council policies and actions and initial development of the action plan.
- **Meeting 4:** Final ratification of action plan to be considered by Council.

The initial meetings aimed to raise awareness of sustainability principles. Specialized, local knowledge of staff was used to help focus the audit report, ensuring that it was relevant to the district and the Council.

Working tables (Table 4.1) were developed to facilitate the environmental policy appraisal. Council policies and programmes were systematically documented (columns 2 and 3 of Table 4.1) within the context of issues identified by the working group.

The column which gave a detailed critique of the environmental effects of these policies was the focus of the most important and intense discussions of the working group. For these discussions to be constructive it was essential that they were preceded by the earlier meetings which raised awareness and understanding of the relevant issues.

The tables were presented to the group with draft recommendations (column 5) but with the action column blank. The working group then decided which actions could be undertaken by the Council and completed the column. It was then a relatively simple task to pull these together into a comprehensive action plan which could be presented to elected members.

Although using such an in-house approach was more time consuming than using an external agency it resulted in the action plan being implemented more effectively. The audit process itself also stimulated many actions, even before the final report was drafted. Although this was a very positive spin-off, it resulted in practical difficulty in finalizing the report. A 'cut-off' date eventually had to be imposed for completion of columns 1–5.

This structured method of documenting and appraising the Council's environmental performance resulted in the identification of:

- environmental issues which were not being addressed by the Council;
- Council actions which were helping to overcome environmental problems;
- Council actions which could potentially cause environmental damage;
- further environmental information to be held by the Council;
- policies which were not being implemented;
- programmes which were not related to agreed environmental policies.

Once the first practical improvements in the Council's performance were demonstrated, local outside agencies and groups were invited to establish a Mendip Environment Forum. This group now acts as an advisory body to

Table 4.1 Extract from energy section of audit report

Environmental aim: improve energy conservation in council buildings and encourage others to be aware of the need for increased conservation of energy

Issues	Existing Policies	Actions/programmes	Appraisal	Recommendations	Agreed Actions – 5.3.93
Reduction of energy consumption	Council housing stock: Housing service Aims to invest continually in the Council's housing stock to preserve and improve its condition	Affordable Warmth Programme: ■ More comfortable tenants ■ Lower fuel bills ■ Fewer condensation problems ■ Reduced CO_2 emissions ■ Saving energy and fossil fuels ■ Good value for money Includes some promotion of Affordable Warmth aims to private sector through exhibition meetings and competition	Structured documented programme with agreed policies is being implemented Monitoring the programme's performance could be improved No long term PR and awareness strategy prepared	Methods of more effective long term monitoring of the achievements of the Affordable Warmth programme should be investigated and implemented Long-term PR strategy promoting MDC's role in a national flagship scheme should be prepared	Investigating monitoring of individual tenants Sheltered housing communal areas energy consumption to be investigated with Senior Housing Officers and Tenancy Senior Officer Data from sheltered housing schemes to be included in current office monitoring system Long term PR strategy for Affordable Warmth Programme to be included in corporate PR strategy

the Environment Subcommittee. Future environmental audit reports will therefore involve the Forum in considering the topic reports and action plan.

STATE OF THE ENVIRONMENT AUDIT REPORT

The first significant action resulting from the audit was the Mendip State of the Environment project. This project was designed from the outset to ensure that environmental data which were collected would be available for people in the district as well as council officers.

The project involved gathering publicly available information and did not include primary data recording. Research officers were assigned to individual topics. Cross-disciplinary considerations were stimulated by project team meetings held to discuss the environmental issues relating to each topic.

Topics were divided into:

- **Natural resource:** land, water, air, wildlife
- **People:** population census data and health
- **Human influences:** industry, mineral extraction, agriculture, forestry, waste, noise, energy, transport.

This division was important for enabling the information to be used to devise the Agenda 21 strategy.

The information was contained in:

- a core report on Mendip's environment which was designed to lead people to further information sources;
- more detailed technical reports on each topic area;
- information held on Mendip District Council's Geographic Information System (with a linked database).

One of the main aims of the State of the Environment report was also to help people to care for their own local environments. Local people who are part of the Health of the Environment community project are able to easily access the environmental information relating to their neighbourhood by accessing the map-based information system. This will enable them to prepare community action projects within the strategic framework given by the State of the Environment project.

Lessons learnt

Local authority environmental audits can be very time consuming and negative exercises which often do not get implemented.

The example at Mendip District Council has shown, however, that they can be very positive agents for achieving practical action and change if they are used to help train staff and raise environmental awareness.

Involving people in the process may seem to lengthen the audit. It is, however, an essential element if the result is not just to be an empty public relations gimmick.

The main lesson to be learnt is therefore that environmental audits should be seen as an integral part of a local authority's work and not just a one off 'snapshot' of the Council's environmental performance.

URBAN CASE STUDY: ENVIRONMENTAL AUDITING – LONDON BOROUGH OF SUTTON *(Helmut Lusser)*

Auditing environmental performance has almost become a tradition in the London Borough of Sutton. The adoption of an environmental statement in 1986 was quickly followed by the introduction of a wide range of environmental initiatives. It soon resulted in the need to assess the environmental behaviour and impact of the authority.

A programme of specific topic audits was agreed in the third annual report on the Environmental Statement in 1989, with a number of audits carried out since then. These were principally **internal** (RIP) audits, that is looking at the authority's own behaviour. The exception was the recent audit on the performance of the Council's policy 'Environmental Awareness and Building', which in effect looked at one of the Council's service effects (PIA).

Audits 1989–1994

Three internal audits have been carried out so far: in-house transport, waste management and energy use.

The transport audit (1992)

For the first time the large amount of mileage that was driven on Council business was highlighted. Over one million miles per annum were recorded in a geographical area little larger than five by seven miles. This immediately threw up the need to look very critically indeed at mileage and this was amplified by the need to make substantial savings at the time. A whole range of other areas was also examined, such as the fuel control from the Council's own fuel pumps, which left much to be desired. A number of steps to rectify the situation and bring the use of cars and fuel under better control was agreed by the Council, but implementation of the recommendations has been slow.

The waste audit (1994)

This highlighted that up to 50 per cent of paper products from the Council's offices were still being thrown into the dustbin and hence sent to landfill. This was in spite of an existing high-grade office paper salvage system in place since the late 1980s. While the recovery of high-grade office waste was reasonably good in some offices (up to 70 per cent) there was little effort to use the Council's paper-banks or even the kerbside collection for the lower grade paper qualities. This process will now need a special impetus.

The energy audit (1994)

This focused on a number of Council buildings and sought to highlight options to conserve as much energy as possible. In spite of an existing energy team, the audit highlighted the scope for a range of cost-effective measures. Many of these would purely require a different attitude to the use of energy or the adoption of some very simple measures. It also highlighted the enormous importance of continuous education and information.

The exploration of the effectiveness of the Council's policy *Environmental Awareness in Building* revealed a widespread ignorance not only of the contents but also of the existence of the policy. The document had been an attempt to put forward non-statutory policies that, if widely employed, should have dramatically improved energy efficiency, layout from an eco-logical point of view, inclusion of sounder waste handling methods in new development and so on. Regrettably many of these points could not at the time be built into a statutory plan. Although government attitudes have now changed to a degree, there are still many ecological issues that can only be advisory rather than statutory at the moment. In the event, and in spite of considerable publicity and distribution of the document, little knowledge about its content or even existence was demonstrated. The policy obviously went the same way as so many other policy documents in the rapidly changing policy environment in local government where a constant flow of policy directives sometimes obscures yesterday's efforts. Clearly the document will need to be rejuvenated.

THE WAY AHEAD

On the whole the audit process has been useful so far. It has highlighted inadequacies and the need for constant vigilance if environmental objec-tives are to be implemented. Unfortunately the process so far has been too incremental and most importantly too slow. The reason for the long gestation periods of the individual reports has simply been the lack of staff and time available to carry out the work. Indeed the original approach was for members of the interdepartmental environmental steering group to carry out the audits themselves as a team effort. This was a laudable aspiration, regretfully always undermined by the need to carry through the main workloads.

One of the main conclusions that can be drawn from all four audits is that while seemingly sound policies have been put in place, the delivery mechanisms for those policies still need to be developed. Policies need an effective management system to ensure that they are implemented con-sistently over time.

In March 1994, after receiving the latest three audit reports, the Council decided to go for a different, arguably more assertive, approach. It was decided to gradually introduce Council-wide the **Eco-Management and Audit scheme** for local government, which was launched by government in October 1993. By October 1995 it is planned to have the first operational units ready for registration under the scheme. To achieve this ambitious target a number of steps had to be taken:

- **Eco-Management and Audit Coordination:** It has always been accepted that the process of audit should not require net additional resources, and should largely be self-funding. However at this stage it was necessary to concede a pump-priming resource, funded from within the participating department(s). A dedicated coordinator has been appointed with the role of guiding units which aim to register through the scheme, helping new units to understand fully the process. The coordinator will also act both as an advisor and a project manager for the introduction of Energy Management Assistance (EMA). Particularly careful advice will be needed in respect of the setting up of Environmental Management Systems, where the Council's ambitions are to pursue as simple as possible solutions. Clearly a coordinator cannot carry such a task through on his own back. Hence it has been decided to strengthen the Council-wide training programme and to ensure that there are at least some reasonably well informed and enthusiastic members of staff committed to Eco-Management and Audit in each of the units due for registration.
- **Training programme:** For about a year some thirty staff from across all departments have been introduced to auditing techniques. Two groups were formed to carry out the waste and energy audits referred to above, an exercise which combined training with carrying out a much needed project. The training has moved towards acquainting staff with EMA and its various concepts of significant issues, distinction between service and direct effects and the concept of best environmental practice. The members of the group are voluntary and will form the backbone of a Council-wide audit resource. It is proposed to work with these members of staff as unit by unit is taken through to registration. The possibility of mixing staff from the unit and staff from another unit when carrying out the audit part of EMA has considerable attractions as it starts to introduce an element of independence in the process. The training programme has one further important objective: it starts to deepen and spread the Council's important environmental messages across the board. It is unlikely that many of the staff trained so far will become technical audit specialists. They are the 'barefoot doctors' who will use common sense and enthusiasm to drive the environmental agenda forward.
- **Linkage to compulsory competitive tendering:** The timetable for

introduction of EMA in Sutton will allow the corporate framework required by the EMA regulations to be in place by October 1995. It is also planned to have the first four or five units ready for registration by then. This will give the Council a powerful argument for demanding that potential future contractors either already are registered with an Environmental Quality Management System (EMA, BS7750 or another compatible system) or that they are working towards such a system. The HMSO publication on the EMA scheme for local government is reasonably clear on the approach which local authorities can take to avoid being challenged for anti-competitive behaviour. As the first tranche of construction- and property-related white collar services needs to be let by October 1995 it can be seen how important it is for the Council to have the EMA framework in place by then.

- **A programme towards registration:** A broad programme for taking operational units towards registration has been agreed. The first units have been chosen due to their significant environmental impact. The first unit to be 'audited' will be the newly established strategic purchasing unit in Environmental Services Department. This is the unit that provides the strategic coordination of the department and masterminds the entire CCT process. This will be followed by the unit overseeing the bulk of the Council's environmental contracts (waste, highways etc), one of those units to be subjected to CCT and at least one of the regulatory environmental services (Environmental Health or Development Control). In addition it is intended to take the corporate policy and media unit located in the chief executive's department through the process. Following these initial units it will be necessary to take the remainder of the Council's departments through the same process. This is likely to take three to five years.

- **Environmental budget appraisal:** A key to environmental performance is how resources are being spent. EMA therefore requires an assessment of budgets as part of that process. A system of considering budgets in terms of concepts such as environmental value for money is being developed. The first steps have been taken by applying such a system to the annual Transport Policy and Programme in 1994.

- **Environmental information system:** This is key to the successful application of EMA and also needed to broaden the understanding of environmental issues both within the authority and also throughout the community. The development of such a system, making environmental information easily accessible to all, is therefore on the drawing-board. Resources for an air pollution monitoring system have already been agreed by the Council.

- **EMA and Local Agenda 21:** The two processes will run in parallel in Sutton. EMA equips and fine-tunes the organization to be able to behave and deliver services in an environmentally more sustainable fashion, constantly aiming for best environmental practice. The Local Agenda 21 process will build on the vast range of community involvement already in place and develop new partnerships and new directions broadening the environmental work by the social and economic dimensions. Clearly the two processes will inform each other: Local Agenda 21 will no doubt help to set the frame of mind of staff whose units are due for registration under EMA. Likewise the systematic management approach entailed in EMA is likely to have a role in ensuring that ideas and programmes under LA21 can truly be delivered.

CONCLUSIONS

Learning from several years of internal audit work, Sutton Council has recognized the value of such work in progressing vigorously its environmental agenda. By moving from an *ad hoc* system of internal audits, insufficiently resourced at best, to EMA, the process becomes more professional. In particular it has recognized that the Environmental Management Systems part of EMA is central to the Council, being able not just to propose policies but also to vigorously implement them. The process that the Council has now embarked on will be long and drawn out and one of constant evolution. The challenge of EMA to continuously ratchet up performance and the requirement to aim at best available practice will ensure that the process becomes a constant challenge. The complementary management tools of an environmental information system and environmental budgeting should help to firmly underpin the Council's management approach to environmental issues. Once the organization and its policies are able to stand up to scrutiny under the new systems it may be possible to extend the audit process to the Borough as a whole. This will no doubt make it an interesting tool to further Local Agenda 21.

Part II

AUDITING KEY POLICY AREAS

INTRODUCTION

Part II is concerned with the substance of the audit, the key environmental issues and the problems likely to be met in trying to address them.

It is organized on a topic basis, with the topics broadly related to areas of expertise and specific responsibilities within local authorities. In taking this approach it contrasts with most of the available guidance on auditing, which is structured around stages of the process – State of the Environment report, Review of Practices, Policy Impact Analysis, Management.

The merit of the topic-based approach is that it can make more explicit the links between the stages of the process. In particular it draws out the interdependence between the PIA and the SoE survey, showing how the kind of information collected should reflect the need to evaluate policy.

The demerit of the approach is that it segments the environment and could reinforce a blinkered departmentalism. We have tried to overcome that in two ways. First, because the topics, while usefully related to specific departmental remits, are not *confined* by them. Pollution control, for example, is the task of Environmental Health, but every department needs to take responsibility for reducing pollution levels. Second, we try to frustrate insularity by including express guidance on integration in Chapter 2 (page 42).

Taken together, the chapters of Part II provide a reasonably comprehensive guide to the substantive issues. They do not, though, cover everything. Each author has latitude to develop her or his own line of argument and offer a personal perspective on the issues. One specific gap is in relation to economic and financial policy. This is briefly addressed in Part III.

The chapters are ordered so as to move from broad aims of global sustainability towards more local concerns. The fit is not precise however, as all topics have some local and some global significance.

Chapter 5, Nature Conservation interprets the global goal of biodiversity into local priorities. While having many advocates, wildlife has no ascribed local authority department of its own, so Noel Bruder shows how different departments and agencies (including voluntary groups) need to be involved in both the SoE and PIA audits. He also examines the difficult issue of defining sustainable environmental capacities in relation to human impact on wildlife.

Chapter 6, Energy tackles the issues critical to the safeguarding of the global climate. The chapter deals with energy supply, the management and rehabilitation of buildings and the efficiency of new buildings. Richard St George stresses the importance not only of correct technology but of attitudes and awareness of users.

Chapter 7, Transport tackles the other main sphere where the local authority can influence fuel demand and global emissions. Hugh Barton suggests targets for sustainable transport and discusses the problems faced in making progress and monitoring progress towards them. He stresses that because transport behaviour is complex it is not necessarily appropriate to assess policy initiatives independently of each other. Their effect may be the opposite to that expected. Rather it is critical to evaluate the whole pattern of transport.

Chapter 8, Planning sees transport and transport emissions as a function of land use, and vice versa. In this field the auditor has been provided very recently with much greater ammunition in the form of revised Planning Policy Guidance Notes, and the guidance on the environmental appraisal of development plans. Hugh Barton links these together to provide the auditor with a coherent framework for evaluation. Issues of urban regeneration, commercial development, services provision, housing, open space and greenbelts are all drawn into the frame.

Chapter 9, Aesthetics and Conservation leads on naturally from land use planning. It focuses on people's direct experience of their own environment. Apart from concern for preserving our heritage (eg listed buildings and conservation areas) this is an aspect commonly and arbitrarily excluded from audits. But, as Richard Guise argues, a commitment to a sustainable future should embrace the concept of a satisfactory aesthetic environment for everyone. So this chapter deals not only with cultural heritage but also the quality of the visual, aural, olfactory and tactile environment in which people live.

Chapter 10, Pollution deals with issues of air, water and land quality which are central to sustainability and aesthetic perceptions. The monitoring of resource quality constitutes a key part of SoE reporting. David Dickerson addresses the questions: How adequate are current monitoring arrangements? How do we evaluate the significance of the results? How effective are current LA procedures for controlling the polluters?

Chapter 11, Waste and Recycling also deals with pervasive sustainability issues to do with reducing resource consumption and avoiding pollution. The focus here is on the specific duties of the local authority. Robert Keen takes the current reality of officer and councillor attitudes, often dominated by short-termism, NIMBY or cosmetic environmentalism, and demonstrates how the auditing process can begin to challenge them. He is at pains to encourage auditors to get deeper than the kneejerk response (eg to recycling initiatives) and examine the actual impact of policy.

Chapter 12, Purchasing moves the debate back to the internal practices of the authority. It is geared to the interests of purchasing managers and reflects the priorities that have already been explored in relation to pollution, wastes, wildlife and transport and energy. Dominic Stead stresses the importance of life cycle analysis and a systematic approach involving all relevant staff, and relating equally to external contracts as to internal arrangements.

Chapter 13, Community Awareness recognizes that the most significant influence of the local authority is through its role as catalyst and educator of the wider community. In the context of Local Agenda 21 that catalytic and coordinating role becomes more formalized. Jane Stephenson assesses how far the auditor can monitor the local authority's success in spreading environmental awareness to the business community, the voluntary groups and the schools.

The coverage of each chapter is summarized in Table PII.1, which sets out relevance to the three main aspects of the audit.

Table PII.1   Summary of chapter coverage relating to the audit

Audit **Topics**	*State of the Environment survey*	*Policy Impact Assessment*	*Review of internal practices*
Nature conservation	●	●	○
Energy	○	●	●
Transport	●	●	○
Planning	●	●	○
Aesthetics	●	●	○
Pollution	●	●	
Waste and recycling	○	●	○
Purchasing		○	●
Community awareness		●	○

Key		
	●	Prime areas covered
	○	Secondary areas touched on
		Marginal significance

NATURE CONSERVATION

Noel Bruder

INTRODUCTION

Nature conservation is one of the environmental issues which has long been institutionalized in the work of local government. The 1949 National Parks and Access to the Countryside Act placed a duty on local authorities to protect and promote the conservation of wildlife and habitats (see Box 5.1). In fulfilling this duty a number of related issues must also be addressed, such as landscape, land use, natural resources, access, education, etc... The relative importance of each of these issues will inevitably vary considerably between the tiers of local government and across regions. The difficulty with nature conservation is not in deciding what to include but in deciding what *not* to include within the concept.

This problem has been exacerbated by the growing realization of the inter-connectedness of all living systems in the world. Thus the conservation of a single local species or the protection of an important habitat has a role to play in maintaining global biological diversity. Set in a sustainable development context, the issue of nature conservation is inextricably linked with that of biological diversity.

Biodiversity simply means the variety of life in the world (usually expressed in terms of genes, species and ecosystems). Maintaining viable populations of species, preferably in their native habitat (as opposed to in farms, zoos, gene banks etc) is therefore a primary objective of sustainable development. Because of the huge difficulties in assessing diversity on a global scale the focus of attention is often on nations, regions and localities. This is recognized in the Convention on Biodiversity which the UK Government signed at the Rio Earth Summit. This may seem like a daunting challenge for a local authority but the task can be kept manageable by focusing on those nature conservation issues of local importance while keeping an eye on the broader context.

This chapter offers a framework for tackling this challenge and suggests

Box 5.1   Local authority powers and duties

The National Parks and Access to the Countryside Act, 1949.

Representation on National Park committees.
General responsibilities to protect wildlife and habitats and to pro-
mote nature conservation.
Powers to designate Local Nature Reserves (LNRs), National Nature
Reserves (NNRs) and Sites of Special Scientific Interest (SSSIs), in
consultation with English Nature.
Affords the opportunity for certain agencies (eg English Nature,
Countryside Commission, some NGOs) to make inputs to develop-
ment plans with regard to special sites and more general conserva-
tion objectives.

The Countryside Acts 1967, 1968.

General requirement for all government agencies to have regard to
nature conservation.

*Department of the Environment (DoE) Circulars 108/77, 27/87 and 1/92
on nature conservation and planning. Planning Policy Guidance note
(PPG) 9 on Nature Conservation.*

Specific advice defining the scope of nature conservation and the
duties of local authorities and other governmental bodies.

PPG9 implements the requirements of the EU Habitats Directive and
reinforces the importance of nature conservation in planning
matters.

The Protection of Birds Acts 1954, 1967.
The Conservation of Wild Creatures and Wild Plants Act, 1975.

Both these acts afford protection to wild flora and fauna.

The Forestry Act, 1967.
The Planning Act, 1971.

Protection for woodlands and control of felling.
Duty on a local authority to have regard to the preservation and
planting of trees when granting planning permission.
Powers to serve Tree Preservation Orders (TPOs) to protect individual trees and woodlands.

The Wildlife and Countryside Act, 1981 (amended 1985).

This act forms the cornerstone of current policy on nature conservation. It extends the provisions of previous acts. Some of its more important features include:

— Strengthening of the law protecting wild birds, animals and plants.
— Extension of local authority powers to appoint wardens to manage land and for officers to enter land in order to carry out the duties of the Act.
— Powers to enter into management agreements with owners and occupiers of land and to provide financial assistance to help implement the agreements.
— Revision of the powers relating to the designation and protection of SSSIs, NNRs and LNRs.

There are many other general powers and duties which are in the interest of nature conservation. These include:

The planning acts which confer powers to control development; require actions to be taken to protect amenity (which can be defined broadly); compulsorily purchase land which is of conservation interest; designate areas of open space and wildlife interest; enter into management agreements. The Acts are backed-up by a number of PPGs dealing with related issues.

how progress on the separate issues can be integrated within the overall audit strategy.

Establishing priorities

Nature conservation encompasses two interrelated and mutually supportive themes: wildlife and habitat. The wildlife or living components of an environment cannot be separated from the habitats in which they live. For example, there have been schemes to breed the barn owl in captivity and release adults into the wild, which in isolation is a shortsighted policy. Numbers of barn owls are diminishing, but simply increasing numbers achieves nothing – you need enough square acreage of suitable habitat for those owls to hunt, rear young, etc. The real issue is therefore habitat conservation. This is the essential purpose of a local authority's actions in this field and should form the cornerstone of auditing initiatives. Following from this it becomes obvious that the protection and enhancement of habitats and wildlife is very much part of the planning process. Later in this chapter, when examining the impacts of a local authority's policies and practices, the emphasis will be very much on the role of planning.

Once habitats have been successfully protected from damage a whole range of other local authority skills will come into play. Protected areas will require sympathetic management and careful enhancement; people will need to be informed and educated about the resources; there has to be coordination with other policy areas (eg to enhance access, ensure compatibility of goals); and monitoring to assess environmental change. All of these are issues of importance for EA.

As with most other topics examined in this book, the local authority role has evolved over time and in response to many needs. The basic rationale is that local actions are required to protect the local environment. To borrow a phrase from David Tyldesley (1986): 'nature conservation is about people and their environment, the very subject of local authorities!'

Levels of support

Never before has there been such wide-ranging support or such a pressing need for nature conservation. This support is evidenced at a political level by the apparent conversion of the major political parties to the environmental cause. The Government has recently reaffirmed its commitment to nature conservation in the 1994 national Biodiversity Plan (DoE, 1994a) and in a new planning policy guidance note (DoE, 1994b). At an individual level there has been a marked rise in environmental consciousness, a growth in 'green' consumerism and membership of conservation groups. The need for nature conservation is, unfortunately, equally apparent. In the UK, human occupation of the land is transforming the natural environment at an accelerating rate. Within the last fifty years, 50 per cent of ancient woodlands have been destroyed, 50 per cent of fens and coastal marshes have been drained, 95 per cent of flower-rich meadows have disappeared, 60 per cent of lowland heaths have been lost and over 100,000 miles of hedgerows have been grubbed out. Without immediate action this unprecedented destruction is set to continue as demands from transport, housing, industrial developments, farming, energy, forestry, extractive industries and services increasingly conflict with a diminishing natural environment. It is a resolution of this development versus conservation conflict that should be the primary aim of a local authority.

Role of the local authorities

Reflecting the political importance and popular support for nature conservation, a range of regulations and legislation has come into force with the aim of protecting and enhancing the natural environment. The powers and duties of a local authority are summarized in Box 5.1. In response to their responsibilities for nature conservation many local authorities have produced plans and strategies setting out their objectives and actions. An EA is not a replacement for these initiatives but instead should seek to expand and reinforce the authority's role, monitor progress on strategies and coordinate conservation with other policy areas. Where such a strategy does not exist, there should be a recommendation that one be undertaken.

The various approaches to EA, outlined in Part I, have been used by different authorities. This chapter will use the distinction between State of the Environment auditing (SoE) and internal auditing (IA). These two approaches are not of course mutually exclusive and a range of options exist to combine the two. The rationale of conducting a SoE survey prior to IA is so that the wildlife and habitat resources can be identified and then considered in terms of the authority's own policies and practices.

STATE OF THE ENVIRONMENT (SOE) AUDITING

The first consideration in conducting a SoE is, what will the local authority gain from doing it? It is essential to be clear about this from the start because the resources outlay may be considerable. As regards nature conservation, the main purpose is to get a picture, or more specifically a snapshot, of what exactly the nature resource is, how it has changed and is changing and thereby how to manage this change in a positive way. Much information exists on the status of species and habitats but in most regions this is fragmented and often non-comparable. For example, there may be hedgerow surveys done by a local Wildlife Trust and surveys of sites of known wildlife importance by English Nature. By drawing this information together, making the issues clear and comparable, the local authority not only aids analysis and decision-making, but also provides an information and educational resource for others. By updating this the authority can monitor trends over time.

Once the authority has established the need for a SoE the next stage in the auditing process is to define the scope of the natural environment in question and the level of data required. In general, the survey area will be equivalent to the administrative area of the local authority. This will certainly be the case when assessing the conservation value of particular land use types. However, when dealing with wildlife species the survey area may need to be considered more widely. For example a bird species, like a swallow or swift, may spend the summer within the local authority's area and then over-winter in southern Europe or Africa. The protection of this species is therefore not simply a local matter but requires consideration of the national and even international environment. Resource constraints will normally limit the area of direct interest but it is nevertheless important to be aware of the broader range of impacts at work.

Despite what is commonly thought, the data requirements for a SoE are usually from secondary sources and involve little or no primary surveying. In a field like nature conservation there may be information gaps which need filling, but this is more often a recommendation of an EA than a requirement for it. This is important from a cost point of view because a very adequate SoE can be drawn up with limited resources directed towards data collection and analysis.[1] There are innumerable sources of data open to the Council for nature conservation; the principle ones are listed in Box 5.2. This list is far from exhaustive and much will depend on the particular region and the level of analysis required.

Having identified the sources of data the next step is to collect and analyse it. Nature conservation is principally about protecting habitats. A convenient and practical approach is therefore to separate the natural environment into land use types and deal with each of these individually. The matrix illustrates the principal land use types, divided into three categories, and the sorts of issues which should be addressed in the SoE, under the headings of status, trends and actions. Expanding on each of these issues in the context of the local authority region would be the minimum requirement of a SoE.

The following section assesses briefly some of the main issues involved for three different land uses, each chosen as representative of the habitat categories in the matrix. The purpose is to show the range of information that should be sought and the scope for resultant actions. When an IA is done in conjunction with the SoE, recommendations for action will normally be considered as part of the overall assessment of policies and practices. They will therefore be addressed in the IA section.

AGRICULTURE

Status

Agricultural land will probably form the largest single land use in rural districts. Land is classified according to a Ministry of Agriculture, Fisheries and Food (MAFF) national grading system (Table 5.1). Topography, soil and climate are the principle determinants of quality. Information on the extent and distribution of each grade of land should be sought, as should a breakdown of the factors affecting quality (nutrient content, erosion, fertilizer and pesticide use, micro-climates etc). The main source of agricultural data are the annual statistics collected by MAFF and available at parish level. This provides information on the type of farming practised,

---

1 See, for example, the reports produced by Basildon District Council, 1991, and Kirklees Metropolitan Borough Council, 1989.

Box 5.2   Sources of data

Government Departments

Principally MAFF and the DOE (and Scottish and Welsh equivalents). Source of statistics policy guidance and funding.
In some regions the Ministry of Defence (MoD) may be a large land owner and source of data.

English Nature (formerly the Nature Conservancy Council (NCC)).

Responsible for national wildlife and habitat conservation. Statutory powers to protect habitats and to administer the SSSI schedule. Discretionary powers to finance nature conservation initiatives. A limited local role. Generally supports and advises local authorities. Provides information on nature conservation sites; advice and consultation on development control, the preparation of development plans, the management of council land, management agreements, environmental education and interpretation.

Countryside Commission (CC) (now in England only).

Remit covers landscape conservation and countryside recreation. Designates National Parks and Areas of Outstanding Natural Beauty (AONBs). Offers advice and grant-aid for a variety of nature conservation tasks, including the provision of countryside facilities, tree planting, country parks, wardening, community forests and land acquisition.

The Forestry Commission (FC)

Promotes conservation within its own forest estate, manages Forest Nature Reserves, and provides grant-aid and advice to the private sector.

Farming and Wildlife Advisory Group (FWAGs)

The principle advisor to farmers and increasingly promoting conservation initiatives. Source of information and useful link between MAFF, the farming community and the local authority.

Other Local Authorities.

Valuable information can be gained through consultation and collaboration with other authorities, both nationally and regionally. The local authority associations and the Local Government Management

Board (LGMB) collect, analyse and disseminate environmental information and offer advice and training.

The Natural Environment Research Council (NERC)

Carries out and commissions research on all aspects of nature conservation.
Source of impartial advice.

The Royal Society for Nature Conservation (RSNC) and the local Nature/ Wildlife Trusts.

Every country and almost every district (including metropolitan areas) has its own nature trust, often affiliated to the umbrella organization, the RSNC. They are often the leading local voluntary nature conservation body. They may have a variety of information and expertise on site management and ownership, surveys of local wildlife and interpretative material.

NGOs

Besides the RSNC and local nature trusts, a range of other national and local voluntary organizations may prove useful as sources of data and expertise. These include: The Royal Society for the Protection of Birds (RSPB), The British Trust for Conservation Volunteers (BTCV), Friends of the Earth (FoE), Greenpeace, Groundwork Trusts, The Worldwide Fund for Nature (WWF), Civic Trusts, The Ramblers Association, The British Trust for Ornithology (BTO), The Wildfowl Trust, The Woodland Trust, The Botanical Society of the British Isles (BSBI), The National Trust and the Council for the Protection of Rural England (CPRE).

Other agencies which may be of use include:

The National Rivers Authority (NRA); regional water companies; academic institutions; power companies; National Farmers Union (NFU); Country Landowners Association (CLA); angling and field sports societies; environmental consultancies; tourist boards; national park authorities....

Environmental Forum

Establishing a countryside or environmental forum, with representations from the relevant bodies listed above, is probably the best way to gather information while at the same time consulting and involving others in the EA.

Table 5.1 Matrix of SoE issues by land use type

	Status								Trends							Actions			
	Extent	Distribution	Quality	Species present	Conservation value	Economic factors	Social factors	Institutional arrangements	Changes in status	Patterns of changes	Local impacts	National impacts	International impacts	Effects on other natural systems	Monitoring	Information requirements	Local authority practices	Local authority policies	Management plan
Commercial land uses																			
Agriculture																			
Forestry																			
Fisheries																			
Natural/semi natural habitats																			
Scrubland																			
Heathland																			
Grassland																			
Moorland																			
Lowland																			
Peat moss																			
Woodlands																			
Wetlands																			
Open water																			
Rivers																			
Coastal areas																			
Urban habitats and wildlife corridors																			
Parks																			
Playing fields																			
Golf courses																			
Playgrounds																			
Recreation sites																			
Country parks																			
Nature reserves																			
Commons																			
Cemeteries																			
Allotments																			
Gardens																			
Green Belts																			
Roadside verges																			
Railway embankments																			
Rivers																			
Canals																			

size of farms, land use, livestock, ownership and employment. There may also be more locally collected information available (eg from the NFU).

Trends

Intensification since World War Two has led to higher yields, mechanization, falling employment and increased pressure on the environment (directly to wildlife and habitats and indirectly through pollution). If historical data are collected a comparison can be made with current circumstances. Agricultural trends may be assessed from both a structural and an environmental perspective. Structural factors include employment, land values, crop area, crop yield, livestock operations and institutional arrangements. Since the 1986 Agricultural Act a new balance is being sought between Agriculture and the Environment. Changes in the EU Common Agricultural Policy (CAP) have accelerated this trend. There is now more support for conservation initiatives, eg Set-aside schemes, Diversification Scheme, Farm and Conservation Grant Scheme, Farm Woodland Scheme and Environmentally Sensitive Areas (ESAs). The take-up and success rates of each of these schemes should be monitored. Because there is no planning control over agricultural land uses, the influence an authority can have is limited. However, councils are increasingly getting involved, in collaboration with bodies like MAFF and the NFU, with activities that promote environmental protection.

The environmental impacts of agriculture have been well documented (see, for example, Blunden and Curry, 1988; NCC, 1984). Important factors for assessing local trends are:

■ land use changes;
■ effects on water, air and soil systems;
■ effects on foodstuffs, amenity and life quality;
■ effects on other ecosystems.

WOODLANDS

Status

Commercial coniferous plantations and mainly deciduous woodlands represent quite different ecosystem types and as such should be treated differently in an SoE. Woodlands play a very important nature conservation role. They provide a habitat for numerous native species of flora and fauna, help prevent erosion and waterlogging, act as a windbreak for crops and settlements, help fix atmospheric carbon dioxide, are a useful amenity resource and are a source of income.

Ancient woodlands are those which have stood since at least 1600 and may be remnants of the original trees which once covered most of the UK. They are particularly valuable because of the stability and diversity of their plant and animal communities. Secondary woodlands originated after 1600. They are more widely distributed than ancient woodlands but are not as species rich.

Data on extent, distribution and condition of woodland habitats and on species present is available on a national level from bodies like English Nature and the Forestry Commission (see Box 5.2). More local information will probably be available both within the local authority and from conservation groups such as the local Nature Trust.

Trends

Despite the useful functions they serve, much woodland cover has been lost to over-exploitation, removal for other uses, disease, air pollution and poor management. Because many species rely on woodlands for their survival, their disappearance is resulting in a growing list of endangered plants and animals.

A range of designations exist for protecting woodland habitats. These include:

- Sites of Special Scientific Interest (SSSIs)
- National Nature Reserves (NNRs)
- Local Nature Reserves (LNRs)
- Country Parks
- Non-statutory Reserves (eg owned by Nature Trusts or the RSPB)
- Tree Preservation Orders (TPOs).

A Woodland Grant Scheme, administered by the Forestry Commission, provides funds for the management of existing broadleaf woods. In addition, DoE derelict land reclamation grants may be sought for tree planting and the Countryside Commission provides support for planting and management schemes.

As for agricultural land uses (see above), the factors impacting on the health of woodlands should be examined. Where information is scarce, the authority may need to consider commissioning additional research. Many Nature Trusts now offer these services along with a range of specialist environmental consultancies.

URBAN PARKS

Status

Particularly for city councils, but also for many county councils, habitats within urban areas and on the urban fringe are an extremely important wildlife reserve. Because of pressures in the wider countryside many animal species have found refuge in towns and cities, taking advantage of the supply of food from rubbish dumps, gardens and parks. Mammals such as foxes, squirrels, rabbits, mice and rats and birds like the sparrow, starling, pigeon and magpie have become especially adept at urban living.

As with other habitat types, the conservation value and potential of parklands should be surveyed and the wildlife quality assessed. The council's parks department and local conservation groups should be able to provide most of the relevant information.

Trends

Urban parklands are designated as public open space in development plans and as such are afforded almost complete protection. The primary issue is therefore the type of management practices which are undertaken to maintain the parks. Far too often parks are kept as 'formal' spaces with tidy flowerbeds, lollipop trees and expanses of neatly mown grass. Happily there is now a movement towards creating more informal areas within parks where wildlife is given equal weight alongside the more traditional considerations of recreation and aesthetics. These areas are easier to maintain and are also much cheaper to manage. Another important issue is that of access. Areas of relatively low wildlife significance may prove excellent from a recreational or educational perspective because of their location within population centres. In such cases their potential lies in raising awareness of nature conservation issues.

TURNING ISSUES INTO ACTIONS

Having assessed the land use resources as outlined above, the authority is then in a position to present an overall picture of nature conservation in the region. This overview is invaluable not only as a summary for the policy makers and public but also because of the interrelationships between elements of the environment (both living and non-living). The linkages in ecosystems are often poorly understood and should form a distinct area of analysis.

The overriding goal of the SoE is the improvement of the natural environment, therefore the result of the work must be a programme of implementable actions. These should be defined in terms of locally achievable sustainable environmental capacities. The issue of environmental capacities has been discussed in Chapter 2. With regard to nature conservation it will involve identifying a set of targets and a range of indicators for environmental quality. The targets may be set in the first place by strictly applying the guidelines outlined in the relevant policy and legislation. There could be a recommendation, for instance, to apply TPOs everywhere appropriate with an interim target of a specified number per year. Similarly, there could be an overall target to afford statutory protection to all sites considered to be of nature conservation importance. The indicators of whether this target was being met would be the amount of designated land area and the quality of the wildlife and habitat therein (measured in terms of species variety, abundance, rarity etc). All capacities are politically defined and it is a function of the audit to identify those which are appropriate and achievable. The important thing is to ensure that the highest standards are maintained and that targets are continually revised and where possible upgraded. An ongoing SoE will facilitate the monitoring of environmental indicators and thereby allow progress to be regularly checked.

The checklist at the end of this chapter notes some of the types of recommendations which should result, either in a plan of action or as issues to be followed up in another stage of the EA. There are no simple solutions to environmental problems. If there were, the problems would not exist in the first place! The SoE should point the way to some opportunities for improving the environment and directing change in a beneficial way. The next section will examine the IA phase of an EA, beginning by making the connection between SoE and IA.

INTERNAL AUDITING (IA)

The information collected for the SoE will now also be of use for the IA. If no SoE has been undertaken a certain amount of external data may still be needed though much will already exist in some form within the local authority. An environmental forum (see Box 5.2) would be the easiest way to access any additional information required.

As with SoE there may be many different reasons for undertaking an IA but of overriding concern will be the improvement of the natural environment through the activities and policies of the authority. The scope of the IA is therefore defined by the points of contact between the environmental topic areas covered in the previous section and the council's internal practices and policies. In tracing the role of an authority in nature conservation it is useful to look at the different functional areas that are involved. For convenience these have been divided into three:

1) forward planning;
2) development control; and
3) land management.

These areas will obviously vary at different levels of local government, so what is given here is a broad picture of activities and opportunities. As with the section on SoE, what is outlined are the basic requirements which would need elaboration and expansion in the context of each particular authority.

Forward planning

A local authority's development plans establish the overall strategy for ensuring a balanced approach between competing demands of development and conservation. Inclusion of nature conservation policies and proposals is mandatory. Although this has been continually re-emphasized, most recently in the Planning and Compensation Act, 1991, and PPG 9 on nature conservation, there is still little guidance as to their substance.

Structure plan policies set strategic objectives which should be further developed in local plans. Local authorities are required to invite conservation bodies to submit information for plans and to consult widely on draft proposals.

Development plan policies on nature conservation should be listed, their purpose and success examined and gaps in coverage highlighted. Statements of policy should be clear, unambiguous and comprehensive, thus indicating a firm commitment. London Borough Councils provide a good example of clear and consistent policy statements. There should be policies on all sites of conservation significance and the management of such sites should be examined. The minimum requirement is a general presumption against development, though where possible this should be strengthened to prohibit any development at all. Opportunities for new site creation and further designations should be assessed, with particular attention to new developments and derelict/reclaimed land.

There should be wide consultation and the public should be encouraged to participate in all development plan activities. It is imperative that all sites of nature conservation significance are covered by statutory plan policies; non-statutory plans do not carry the same legal status. Expert advice should be sought where necessary to augment in-house knowledge. All sites of wildlife significance should be mapped, if possible using a Geographic Information System (GIS).

Be pro-active! Direct policies and practices in a positive fashion rather than waiting for damage to occur.

Development control

Through the planning system, local authorities can exercise considerable control over developments which may affect nature conservation. Planning permission may be refused on conservation grounds, particularly where habitats are under greatest threat. Conditions of approval and management agreements may be used to forward conservation interests. All developments must be checked against the SSSI schedule and English Nature consulted on proposals. If a SoE has not been carried out then an up-to-date map of all important nature conservation sites should be produced.

There is a statutory duty to protect all designated areas. A local authority must consider requesting an Environmental Impact Assessment (EIA) for developments with significant environmental effects. Green Belts and open spaces, though not specifically designated for conservation purposes, are recognized as having a valuable role to play. Tree Preservation Orders (TPOs) may be used to protect individual trees and woodlands for 'amenity' purposes.

The development control system offers possibly the greatest opportunity for the local authority to effectively protect habitats and promote nature conservation. All planning applications should be monitored and their likely environmental impacts assessed. Where there are significant adverse impacts the development may be refused on conservation grounds. Where impacts are less severe, more information or, in specific circumstances, an EIA may be requested. Planning conditions and management agreements should be used to the full, not only to restrict damaging activities but also to encourage positive conservation initiatives such as site creation and tree planting. There should be clear guidelines on planning permission for all sites but particularly on or near sites of special importance. Duties with regard to SSSIs should be strictly adhered to. Incremental developments should be carefully monitored so as to avoid cumulative and indirect impacts.

There should be consultation with other local authorities, public agencies, industry, voluntary organizations and the public so as to provide clear advice and guidelines to encourage cooperation. General planning and design guidance for developers on protection, management and site creation would be particularly helpful in getting the local authority's message across. Public open spaces should be vigorously protected and where possible managed with conservation in mind.

With regard to TPOs, the authority may adopt a broad definition of amenity, encompassing conservation interests. There may be opportunities to expand the use of this mechanism.

Land management

Many councils are major landholders and as such have the potential to effect positive environmental impacts. It is on its own land that a local authority can use its policies and practices to set an example for the community by promoting nature conservation. There are many opportunities for the preservation and enhancement of existing sites and for new site creation.

The first task is for those in the local authority responsible for land management to assess the nature conservation potential that exists. Some sort of classification of sites may be useful, for instance, into sites of known conservation importance (SSSIs etc), sites considered to offer some value (eg parks, cemeteries) and sites where the potential exists to create new habitats of value to wildlife (eg quarries, derelict land). Habitat types should be established and mapped, and species surveys carried out where they do not already exist.

Management practices will vary between these different groups of sites. Of primary importance in all is the need for comprehensive management strategies. These should cover a range of levels, from an all-encompassing conservation strategy to site specific management plans. The former should constitute an overview of the council's policies towards conservation sites and the wider environment, providing overall aims and strategic guidance. The latter should focus on a particular habitat or group of habitats within a specific area, detailing management practices, objectives and the means by which these will be met.

The emphasis in all conservation strategies should be on enhancing the wildlife value of sites. The existence of formal policy guidance, developed with the participation of all departments and outside bodies, provides a benchmark against which progress can be monitored. It also facilitates the consideration of nature conservation in decision-making, plan development and council practices.

There are a number of issues to consider:

Pesticides and fertilizers

This issue is also covered in Chapter 12 on purchasing policy but, in general, artificial chemicals should be avoided wherever possible, especially on sites of known conservation importance. More organic methods should be used instead (eg composting leaves and grass cuttings, bark mulches).

Native species

Use of native species is preferable to exotic varieties. They support a more abundant and varied ecology and are generally more adaptable. The wildlife value of species should be considered in both new planting and the management of existing areas.

Peat

Peat extraction has proved to be extremely destructive of natural habitats. There are many alternatives available and its use should be discontinued.

Management regimes

The day-to-day maintenance of the site should be carefully considered. The emphasis should be on low input, non-intensive practices. It is possible to greatly improve wildlife value without undue expense or, in some cases, actually save money through reduced labour and material requirements.

Education

The key to effective nature conservation is public awareness. All parts of the Council should have a role to play, including those responsible for land management. Sites should be actively promoted and interpreted to the widest audience possible. On-site information panels, open days, guided walks etc can be used to explain the purpose of a wildlife area, what sort of species are present and why the site is valuable. Relating this information to the viewer's own environment (home, school, work etc) could both raise awareness and influence behaviour in a positive fashion. The support and participation of the public should be sought for all activities.

Site creation

Derelict land reclamation, restoration of refuse tips and mineral workings, improving unsightly land and new development areas all offer opportunities for a local authority to enrich wildlife quality by creating new habitats themselves or supporting others to do so.

Sites not under Council control

Sites of known importance may be secured through purchase or lease. Where possible such sites should be designated as LNRs, thus establishing a firm commitment to their conservation and enabling access to grant-aid from English Nature. A secondary form of safeguard is through securing an agreement about the use or management of land with the owner. Such agreements may range from informal, unwritten arrangements to more formal, enforceable management agreements with financial inducements. Most local authorities have been slow to designate land as LNRs and to enter into management agreements. Despite the obvious financial and administrative implications, both methods represent a wonderful opportunity for directly securing the conservation of important sites.

Having identified the three principle functional divisions within the local authority and the issues to consider within each, it is now appropriate to consider the resources which are available for nature conservation. These are considered in two parts:

1) resources within the authority;
2) resources within the wider community.

RESOURCES WITHIN THE AUTHORITY

Elected members

These are the greatest asset for nature conservation, if they have sufficient commitment and if they have a high level of involvement. Ultimately it is the politicians who direct policy and practice and make decisions on resource allocations. The principle gauge of member commitment is whether there is a committee or subcommittee with responsibility for environmental matters, and specifically nature conservation. Most local authorities now have such a committee. Their level of involvement can be traced by reference to committee papers and statements and by examining budgetary allocations to conservation initiatives.

Professional staff

Having sufficient expertise within the professional staff of the authority is a prerequisite for a successful approach to nature conservation. All councils should have at least one person with specific responsibility for nature conservation and larger councils should have a conservation unit comprising various skills. This is very important in order for there to be a coordinated approach across all departments and sections; to allow for effective direction of resources and implementation of strategies; to have an identifiable person for liaison with other bodies and members of the public. Ideally staff will be employed full-time, have the necessary qualifications and experience and will be located at a point within the authority where they can have the greatest interdepartmental contact. Many employees within an authority will have skills of use to nature conservation (for example, as members of local wildlife groups). There are also various government employment training schemes which offer skills and manpower for conservation work. All such opportunities should be used to the full.

Information

Information is an essential resource for forward planning, development control, land management and for formulating comprehensive conservation strategies. The purpose of the SoE is to collect all relevant information and to make it available in an accessible format. If a local authority does not have sufficient in-house expertise to assess the significance of a habitat or to formulate strategies, they should be able to call in expert advice.

RESOURCES WITHIN THE COMMUNITY

In addition to auditing their own policies and practices on nature conservation, local authorities can also encourage positive actions in the private and voluntary sectors. There exists a whole range of voluntary bodies engaged in conservation work (see Box 5.2).

The authority should make themselves aware of the activities of these bodies and provide financial assistance in the form of grants and material aid to support them and their activities. A local authority can often usefully provide a coordinating facility for these groups, especially where an environmental forum exists, motivating community action and promoting collaborative working.

The aim of the local authority should not be to preserve the countryside but to conserve and enhance it for its intrinsic value and for the enjoyment of all. This can only be achieved by engendering a more positive attitude to nature conservation within the whole community.

CONCLUSION

Completion of the IA should harness all resources towards improving policies and practices and thereby protecting and enhancing environmental quality. The SoE feeds into this, firstly by providing baseline data and then by monitoring progress in implementing actions and meeting targets.

Efforts should be made to become aware of all areas of nature conservation importance and policies pursued to afford an overall level of protection. This includes non-designated sites, which on a national level account for 90 per cent of the wildlife resource. Even sites of only local importance have a role to play in maintaining biodiversity. This is especially true for wildlife corridors, such as rivers, canals, railways and hedges, which are not only of value in their own right but are vital links between habitats. Protection policies need to be supported by a firm commitment at the highest level of the local authority. The source of this commitment may stem from the perceived value of nature for humans – aesthetically, for recreation, as a 'larder' of resources, etc. This is of course a valid basis for pursuing nature conservation but it should be backed up by a recognition of the intrinsic value of nature and the moral obligation to act as 'steward' of the environment.

CHECKLISTS

SOE

▶ Have all land use types been surveyed and their significance assessed?

▶ Have the issues of status, trends and actions, listed in the matrix, been addressed?

▶ Have environmental capacities been defined in terms of targets with supporting indicators?

▶ Are impacts and trends continually monitored for all wildlife resources?

▶ Are opportunities for habitat creation and enhancement addressed?

▶ Is there a list of all designated areas and sites of special importance?

▶ Have the ecological linkages within and between habitats been considered?

▶ Is there a central database of all environmental information?

▶ Is this database user friendly and open to the public?

▶ Are there plans for periodic SoE reviews?

▶ Are all possible sources of information utilized in the preparation of SoE reports?

IA

Forward planning

▶ Are there policies in all development plans for nature conservation?

▶ Are these policies clear, unambiguous and comprehensive?

▶ Are opportunities for new site creation, habitat enhancement and designation of sites of wildlife importance considered in all plans and policies?

▶ Is there extensive public consultation and participation in all planning with regard to nature conservation?

▶ Are all sites of conservation importance listed and mapped in development plans, their significance described and specific policy objectives outlined?

Development control

▶ Are all development proposals checked against the SSSI schedule?

▶ Are all development proposals checked against other lists of sites of nature conservation importance?

▶ Does the authority request an EIA for all developments with significant environmental impacts?

▶ Are TPOs used to protect all important trees and woodlands?

▶ Are planning conditions used to protect and promote conservation interests?

▶ Is there sufficient consultation and cooperation with all interested parties?

Land management

▶ Has the nature conservation potential of all council owned land been assessed?

▶ Does the authority have a formal wildlife/countryside/conservation strategy?

▶ Is there a management plan for each site of importance?

▶ Are all council sites managed with nature conservation in mind, ie low input, non-intensive practices?

▶ Are sites of known wildlife importance purchased or leased?

▶ Are formal and informal management agreements entered into with private land owners to encourage environment-friendly practices?

Resources

▶ Is there a committee with specific responsibility for nature conservation?

▶ Is there a full-time professional conservation/wildlife officer?

▶ Is there a separate budget for nature conservation initiatives?

▶ Is there a register of all useful skills within the authority?

▶ Are external conservation experts used, where required, to augment in-house expertise?

▶ Are all powers being used to reduce air, land and water pollution?

▶ Is grant-aid from government and governmental agencies utilized?

▶ Does an environmental forum exist?

▶ Is there coordination between policies on nature conservation, recreation and education?

▶ Are local conservation groups grant-aided?

▶ Is other assistance provided to local conservation groups – both financial and in kind?

▶ Are all opportunities taken to motivate community action and promote collaborative working?

REFERENCES

Basildon District Council (1991) *State of the Environment Report,* BDC, Basildon, Essex

Blunden, J and Curry, N (1988) *A Future for Our Countryside* Basil Blackwell, Oxford, in association with Countryside Commission

Department of the Environment (1987) *Circular 27/87: Nature Conservation* HMSO, London

Department of the Environment (1994a) *Biodiversity – The UK Action Plan* HMSO, London

Department of the Environment (1994b) *Planning Policy Guidance Note 9: Nature Conservation* HMSO, London

Kirklees Metropolitan Borough Council (1989) *Kirklees State of the Environment Report* KMBC, Huddersfield

Nature Conservancy Council (1984) *Nature Conservation in Great Britain* NCC, London

Planning and Compensation Act (1991) HMSO, London

Tyldesley, D (1986) *An Analysis of the Role and Performance of Local Authorities in Nature Conservation* British Association of Nature Conservation, Pisces, London

6

ENERGY

Richard St George

INTRODUCTION

About half of UK emissions of CO_2 are attributable to the use of energy in buildings and about 60 per cent of this is attributable to dwellings (Shorrock and Henderson, 1990). This immediately illustrates the difficulty of separating energy out from other environmental issues. Nor can one divorce patterns of national energy use from social issues either. A report by the Joseph Rowntree Trust identifies four definite links between poverty and power supplies:

1)   a rise in mortality in winter;
2)   respiratory disorders in children;
3)   depression amongst women at home; and
4)   debt in low income households

(Boardman and Houghton, 1992)

While a profligate waste of energy exacerbates social problems, a conservation approach to energy can actually reduce such problems. This is best illustrated by Davis, a small town in the Sacramento Valley in California. In the early 70s Davis was expanding fast as home to the Agricultural Department of the University of California. A number of students were elected to the town council and initiated the passing of a series of local environmental by-laws (Box 6.1).

The result is that now Davis, per head of population, has a third less energy consumption than other local townships. Travel is also reduced because the inhabitants tend to stay in Davis with its high level of local provision rather than visit other communities.

General and specific health problems are also directly related to the use of energy in buildings. Buildings suffering Sick Building Syndrome tend to be energy inefficient buildings also. One survey came to the conclusion that 60 per cent of the UK workforce showed some degree of seasonal depres-

---

Box 6.1 Davis environmental by-laws

Bicycles have priority over cars
Superinsulation building regulations
Domestic dwellings must be fitted with solar collectors.
A tree must be planted outside every dwelling (to provide shade)
A tree must be planted next to every parking lot (again for shade).

---

sion (Seasonal Affective Disorder or SAD) due to a deficiency of daylight. Asthma and arthritis in children is often linked to condensation problems in the home.

Finally the greater the reduction in demand for grid-based electricity, the greater the potential significance of non-polluting renewable energy technology as a provider of primary fuel and therefore its greater likelihood of being developed. It is no coincidence that the two states with the greatest concern for energy conservation are also leading in the grid-based use of renewable energy. Thirty per cent of Denmark's energy demand is now provided by windpower as is 30 per cent of the electricity used by the city of San Francisco.

This chapter deals first with broad energy issues, before focusing more specifically on the energy audit of the authorities' own buildings and housing stock (Review of Internal Practices – RIP). It then turns to reviewing policy for rehabilitation and new build (Policy Impact Assessment – PIA). It does not, however, address the issue of renewable energy sources for electricity in any detail.

ENERGY PLANNING

A large scale reduction in the use of fossil energy can be achieved if a rational systematic approach is taken through the establishment of a strategic plan. The auditing process should assess how far the authority has progressed down the following path:

1) **Has it approved an Energy and Environment Policy?** The first step is a collective commitment to energy conservation. This should be achieved through the local authority adopting a wide range 'Energy and Environment Policy'. This provides the direction and commitment to action on behalf of the community's public officers.

2) **Has it prepared an Energy and Environment Plan?** It should encompass analysis of the current situation in generation and use, and plan for energy supply (including renewables and Combined Heat and Power (CHP)), plus a programme for improving energy efficiency,

related to each major sector of use. This will set out a strategic plan of action and again energy conservation will be a major plank in this plan.

3) **Has it established current energy consumption?** This is an important exercise. It is important to establish a baseline from which future changes in the pattern of energy consumption can be measured. There may also be assumptions about energy use which are not actually true and it is important to find this out early on.

Macro energy consumption can be gauged by the power supplied by the fuel utilities – gas, electricity, heating oil, transport fuels, coal etc – supplied to the area. Remember to take into account power generated privately in some process and manufacturing industries. This will also give a figure for the area's gross production of CO_2, NO_x, SO_2 etc, which itself might be a spur to action. Next, this gross consumption has to be attributed to the different sectors, eg public housing, private housing, public buildings, commercial buildings, industry, transport, street lighting, etc. An estimate is then made of approximate conversion efficiencies in each sector. Once completed this will reveal a set of priorities for proactive action below.

4) **Has it established a monitoring system?** One of the best methods of monitoring is to set up a database of the building stock into which all the relevant agencies can input data. There are some legal implications to be overcome here but there is much to be gained from such information, especially in the setting of priorities.

Base information on the building stock and energy use should be related to some form of energy labelling. The most general form of labelling in common use is 'BREEAM'. This is a tool for gauging the total environmental impact of a building on the environment. It is useful for identifying potential 'sick buildings', for example, as well as levels of energy efficiency.

An extremely useful subset of this exercise might be the energy labelling of the existing housing stock for which the local authority is responsible. This is examined on page 104, where more specific home energy rating systems are also described.

5) **Has it adopted a set of specific measures? – for instance:**
   – the planned upgrading of all public housing on the lowest NHER rating by, for example, two points;
   – the release of land for newbuild private housing dependent on a minimum NHER rating of the houses of say 9 (two points above the minimum);
   – all future planning applications for commercial buildings to include an environmental assessment;
   – all local government buildings to undergo an environmental assessment;

    –   controls and/or incentives to encourage combined heat and power (CHP) schemes;

    –   support and/or encouragement for the setting up of a local energy centre as a source of expertise to promote local energy conservation measures;

    –   the training of public housing managers in energy awareness and planning controls in support of solar energy in buildings.

This whole process may sound rather theoretical but it is actually being done, for instance by the City of Bristol (see Box 6.2).

Box 6.2   City of Bristol – energy planning measures

1990 – Launch of Avon Environment Plan
1990 – Support for Bristol Energy Centre
1990 – Appointment of green surveyor in Housing Department
1991 – Appointment of energy manager in Engineers Department
1991 – Energy Awareness Training of housing managers
1992 – Launch of Bristol Energy and Environment Plan
1992 – Energy labelling of selective public housing begun

ENERGY MANAGEMENT OF THE AUTHORITIES' OWN BUILDINGS

The first step in tackling energy issues in any organization is to give it a high priority. One way to initiate this is to write a mission statement which states the organization's commitment to energy conservation. The standard statement issued by the Energy Efficiency Office to participating signatories is set out in Box 6.3.

Appointing a controller

The next step is to assign someone the responsibility for carrying out this commitment on behalf of the organization. Generally this is to appoint a member of the board, staff, etc to the post of site energy officer. The job specification for the energy officer could include a target for what is to be achieved within a certain time frame, ie a 20 per cent reduction in energy use in twelve months. Having established the current energy situation the officer can check that the organization is on the most advantageous tariff structure with the fuel utilities. Often in a commercial situation one finds a serious mismatch which is extremely costly. The author has done one audit for a charity where over two and a half years only 45 per cent of the total

> **Box 6.3**   Energy management declaration of commitment
>
> **This company is committed to responsible
> energy management and will promote
> energy efficiency throughout its operations
> by the following actions:**
>
> ■ Publish a corporate policy
> ■ Establish an energy management responsibility structure
> ■ Increase awareness of energy efficiency among employees
> ■ Hold regular reviews
> ■ Set performance improvement targets
> ■ Monitor and evaluate performance levels
> ■ Report performance changes and improvements to employees and
> shareholders

electricity bill of thousands of pounds was for units actually consumed. The other 55 per cent of the bill was for unused maximum demand and capacity charges. Renegotiation of the tariff may immediately save money, giving all concerned extra encouragement to continue the process. The next step is to identify all the plant and equipment that use energy and how much. Often the figures do not add up and this will enable equipment that has been forgotten about to be traced. At Bristol Energy Centre a continuous 0.2kW drain on electricity was eventually traced to the relays on the Centre's telephone switchboard.

Once it is established where the energy is going then rational decisions can be made about minimizing the wastage. This will involve drawing up a list of priorities from 'Do Now' actions (often linked to passive energy conservation such as insulation and draught-proofing), through 'do this financial year' projects such as replacement of lighting and heating controls to long-term plans for replacement of inefficient plant such as boilers or switch to a different fuel. All this can be written into a strategic plan for board approval and a budget allocation, with the energy officer being charged with carrying it out.

If there is air conditioning present then the heat from inefficient lighting will add to its load. In New York lighting accounts for about 20 per cent of the electricity consumed directly but the waste heat from it also adds a further 5 per cent to the load attributable to air conditioning.

Raising staff awareness

However, this is far from the whole story of energy management. Tinkering with the technology is generally only ever half the battle. Any organization is made up of people and at least half the effort should be directed at them. Changing behaviour patterns relating to the use of energy can be just as effective at reducing the waste of energy as changing the technology. In 1991 Bristol Energy Centre undertook three months of energy awareness training of staff on a large site in a high technology industry with a very skilled workforce. This training was monitored by a firm of independent management consultants who came to the conclusion that the exercise paid for itself in saved energy bills in just three weeks! A programme of staff awareness raising should be an inherent and early component in any energy management strategy.

The mission statement on energy can be part of a wider document on the organization's intentions regarding energy and other environmental issues which is distributed to all staff or otherwise well publicized, asking for the cooperation of all concerned. Usually the staff will be glad something is being done by their organization and will give it a positive response.

CARRYING OUT AN AUDIT OF HOUSING STOCK

An audit of council housing stock enables a local authority to establish a 'baseline' position of the energy performance and condition of its properties. It provides information on the distribution of certain property characteristics, and is the first step in assessing the efficiency benefits of annual maintenance improvements to the stock, and planned improvement programmes. It can be used to produce average 'energy ratings' for the stock and CO_2 emissions, and pictorial representations of these. A baseline study also forms an essential prerequisite to any housing energy or environmental policy.

There are a number of key steps in completing a successful audit:

- Appoint a member of staff to coordinate the audit on the stock and to publish the results.
- Gather information on tenants' circumstances and assess their needs. This may be initiated by collating information which is already gathered as a matter of course, for example when complaints are made. Information and views can also be gathered from tenants' representatives and tenants' group meetings.
- Identify existing sources of information for the age of dwellings, built form, heating, and insulation in the stock. These are likely to come from existing stock databases, property registers, stock condition surveys, building control records, servicing contracts, installation records, and historical OS maps.
- Decide how the energy efficiency of the stock will be measured. Several computerized systems now exist which give a 'stock profile', average

energy rating and CO_2 emissions. An assessment of the various options needs to be made before selecting a system.

- Decide what is required of the energy rating system selected. What level of rating is required for the stock as a whole? How precise does the rating of each property need to be and how will the information be processed? Will additional software be required for this? Will the information form part of an energy policy?
- Decide what the key indicators for the stock are going to be and then produce stock profiles of these, eg the average 'energy rating', CO_2 emissions.
- Find out how much is being invested currently in energy related work, and how it is being spent.
- Decide how the profile of the stock will be updated, and how often. What sources of information will be used to do this and which staff will be involved?
- Disseminate the information to all relevant staff.

Assessing the energy performance of the housing stock

A number of tools now exist which, given the right information, will produce an assessment of the energy performance of the stock, an 'energy rating'. Some base the rating on the Standard Assessment Procedure (SAP), some use a greater number of parameters but incorporate the Standard Assessment Procedure as part of the rating.

At its most detailed an energy rating is produced by carrying out a full audit of each individual dwelling. However, in most cases this is likely to be prohibitively time-consuming and expensive. A simplification of this method is to carry out a full audit on examples of each dwelling type, and then extrapolate the results for all dwellings of the particular type. An alternative is to carry out a lower 'level' of audit on all the properties to produce a rating for the stock as a whole.

Different 'levels' of rating can be produced by varying the number of parameters required about each dwelling. A low level rating based on half the questions of a high level rating will produce only an approximate energy rating for an individual dwelling, but for the stock as a whole the overall rating becomes highly accurate.

Standard Assessment Procedure (SAP)

SAP was published by the Government in July 1993 as the standard system for home energy rating. SAP is defined on a 100 point scale and is based upon the space and water heating running costs per square metre at a fixed location in the British Isles. Cooking, lights and appliances are excluded as is the dwelling location. Its introduction was in part to provide a means of direct comparison between rival assessment systems.

To take two of these systems as examples, the MVM-Starpoint system uses the SAP as its basis, but expresses the energy efficiency of the dwelling in a star format by converting the SAP rating to a star grading. One star (*) indicates a dwelling with a poor energy performance, and five stars (*****) excellent energy performance.

National Home Energy Rating (NHER)

This assessment procedure, run by the National Energy Foundation, is a BREDEM computer programme based on a two zone, variable base, degree day calculation of space heating demand. Over the last decade this has been supplemented by algorithms for estimating ventilation rates in dwellings, water heating use, the fuel use from cooking, lights, and appliances, the effects of controls on heating system performance and internal temperatures, and the effects of conservatories or sun-spaces.

The NHER scale runs from 0 to 10 where a rating of 0 is very poor, a rating of 10 is excellent. Both the Starpoint and NHER schemes operate through trained assessors, and operate a quality control system.

The difference between systems based on SAP and those such as the NHER which incorporate it, is that the latter sort includes location and so reflects the local running costs. It can also take into account occupancy and can therefore give a detailed analysis of affordability.

Information sources and updating

To be useful at a later date, sources should be listed for all the information which goes to make up the audit of the housing stock. If stored on a database, consideration must be given to the interface with other storage systems, and planned development of these.

To be of real benefit the stock profile needs to be updated annually. This allows progress towards energy efficiency objectives and targets to be tracked. In later years the accuracy of the rating can be improved by feeding in additional sources of information, including option appraisals, maintenance visits and tenants' comments. However, if it is planned to improve the accuracy of the rating in this way this should be borne in mind when deciding which system to adopt.

REHABILITATION

The internal energy audit can extend beyond assessing management and monitoring procedures. Rehabilitating an old building rather than demolition and replacement can in itself be an energy conservation measure. A sizable proportion of the energy budget of a building can be in the energy content of the materials in its fabric.

Even with old buildings much can be done to upgrade their energy efficiency. Often the building can be reorientated to the south with additional glazing, eg oriel windows, to the southerly aspect and reduced glazing to the northerly walls. There is often potential for the addition of sunspaces, especially between neighbouring buildings, and the provision of light wells to increase daylighting in dark central areas.

If all the gaps around windows and doors are added together the average UK dwelling has the equivalent of a foot square hole in it! Here too, much can be done to improve the situation by the addition of draught stripping and excluders. Any replacement windows and doors should have integral draught exclusion.

The building can be thermally upgraded by the addition of insulation to the loft (up to 200mm), cavities, walls and floor. Some insulation measures will probably be only economically viable if the external or internal surfaces need replacing, eg external wall insulation or insulated dry lining. However the converse is also true in that the extra cost of adding the insulation is minimal if the surface treatments have to be done anyway. If ground floors have to be relaid, then they should be insulated, either by a rigid slab in the screed, a quilt between the joists or an insulated flooring board. Also look for any signs of cold bridging which should be thermally broken with cladding or other appropriate insulation. This is particularly important in ferro-cement buildings.

Any replacement windows should be doubled glazed, preferably with a 16mm air gap and argon filled, and those retained windows should be secondary glazed.

If renewing the heating system this is the time to consider a change of fuel, eg from off-peak electricity to natural gas. Consider installing a condensing boiler. If retaining the existing heating system then upgrade with a 7-day controller incorporating optimization such as pump overrun and weather compensation. Fit thermostatic radiator valves.

If replacing lighting then provide fittings which take compact electronic fluorescent lamps, especially for corridors, stairwells, external and security lighting. If replacing strip lighting use high frequency ballasts.

If the building is subject to overheating in summer then consider fitting solar control film to the windows. This will reduce the load on the ventilation or air conditioning system (as will fitting low energy lighting) and also provide some insulation in winter.

If there is a heavy use of hot water in the building (such as dormitory accommodation or a canteen) then consider fitting solar collectors. In commercial or public buildings fit occupancy controls to appropriate areas, eg lavatory blocks.

NEW BUILD

One of the areas of greatest potential for energy conservation in the design of new buildings is to maximize for the passive use of solar energy, both in heating the building directly and also in creating passive stack or vortex ventilation without the need for any mechanical assistance. The audit should assess the degree to which new buildings built or sanctioned by the authority are recognizing such techniques.

Unless the building has exceptional demands (such as a lecture hall or financial dealing room with a very high cooling load from all the electronic equipment) there should no need for air conditioning in the UK. If a new building designed for a UK site incorporates air conditioning then one has got the wrong building (or the wrong architect!).

Installing a wet underfloor radiator system can be a move towards a low energy building and increasing health and comfort levels. Wet underfloor systems are particularly well matched to condensing boilers because the heating circuit is run at only about 35°C. Using a wet underfloor system can save about 20 per cent of fuel over a conventional radiator system. Such systems are installed in 55 per cent of domestic housing in Switzerland and Germany and 50 per cent of dwellings in Scandinavia but there appears to be a taboo against the use of such systems in the building industry in the UK.

Private passive solar houses built in southern England have been monitored over the last five years by the Energy Technology Support Unit at Harwell. These have regularly turned in space heating bills of £10–15 a year and the technology has already moved on since these houses were built. In 1991 there were 40 houses built in Europe requiring a zero heat load!

While the perception of the house building trade has often been that unconventional solar houses will not sell, experience has tended to prove the reverse. Indeed, solar houses in Milton Keynes have sold readily, and some have attracted a premium on the price.

THE FUTURE

Provided the house is of a passive solar design, it is now technically possible to build domestic housing in the UK that does not require connection to mains energy. Electricity for lighting and appliances can be provided by small scale photovoltaic (solar cell) systems either alone or in conjunction with small wind or water turbines. Water heating can be provided predominantly by solar collectors with back-up from the independent electric system as a dump load. Because of the increasingly high cost of connection to mains services, if one is building new on a green field site in a rural area in the UK, this will be the most economically favourable option by the year 2000. The attitude of local planners is likely to be the biggest hurdle.

Other options are likely to present themselves over the next few years, which go beyond the conventional. Local authorities should be open to change in building practices. The high cost of new housing and the issue of homelessness may well lead to the introduction of cheap self-build timber frame kit housing. Similarly while the average size of households, especially in the cities, is getting ever smaller, there is likely to be another movement towards people living in small intentional communities. There will be very good energy arguments for this (car sharing, district heating, CHP, etc) and in Denmark such fledgling communities already receive government subsidies.

The movement of middle class families from London to rural Devon has prompted Devon County Council to set up a special unit to study their new needs. The incomers to rural areas are unlikely to want to import suburbia with them and the local population certainly will not. One response to demand for new rural dwellings is likely in the next twenty years to be a new architectural movement for 'hidden housing'. This movement will be characterized by designing buildings that blend into their backgrounds so that they can only be identified when one is close up to them. In this case such elements as earth sheltering, turf roofs, rammed earth and green timber building, and reflective glazing will all be in demand.

What will be the attitude of the next generation of planners to such new ideas? Generally politicians and officials tend to reflect what they perceive to be public opinion (which in reality has already moved on ahead of them).

CONCLUSION

Reviewing this chapter now should give the reader a sense of how much could be achieved by a national commitment to energy conservation. The Building Research Establishment believes that simply by utilizing only those technologies and techniques that are currently cost effective, the energy consumption of UK buildings could be reduced by 25 per cent. If the *best* currently available technology were used then this figure would rise to 50 per cent. This is a considerable challenge but it should not be viewed as one with only costs attached. There are many positive benefits to be gained by meeting the challenge. With hindsight it could be argued that western industrial society tends to solve problems by creating two more. One of the indicators of an environmental approach to problem solving is that tackling one problem also helps the solution of two or more others.

Thus a concerted effort by national and local government, by developers and the building industry, by managers and homeowners would have many secondary benefits beyond saving energy (see Box 6.4). The energy audit can be used to trigger this effort on the part of local authorities.

Box 6.4   The national benefits of saving energy

- Reduction of CO_2 emissions which contribute to the greenhouse effect
- Reduction of NO_x and SO_2 emissions which contribute to acid rain
- Reduction of dependence on ozone depleting refrigerants
- Reduction of environmental pollution from fossil fuel exploration
- Increasing of people's real income and company profits and a reduction in tax burden
- Reduction of social problems associated with fuel poverty
- Revitalization of a depressed UK construction industry
- Encouragement of UK renewable energy industry and reduced dependence on fossil fuel and nuclear power
- Buffering of UK economy from worldwide fluctuations in primary fuel prices

CHECKLISTS

Energy management
▶ Is there a mission statement on energy?
▶ Has an energy officer been appointed?
▶ Has a monitoring programme been instigated?
▶ Have realistic conservation targets been set?
▶ Are fuel tariff structures appropriate?
▶ Has an audit of current energy use been undertaken?
▶ Has a plan been made to reach targets?
▶ Has a programme of awareness raising been instigated?
▶ Is the performance of the energy officer monitored?

Council housing audits
▶ Has sufficient information on tenants' heating circumstances and needs been collected?
▶ What is the current budget for energy related housing improvement, and in what areas is it currently being spent?
▶ Has information on the condition, design and insulation of the dwellings been collated?
▶ Consider the most appropriate method for rating the energy efficiency of housing stock: what information needs to be included in the audit?

▶ Which key indicators will be used in the audit? (eg average energy rating, CO_2 emissions etc).

▶ Consider how frequently the profile of the stock will need to be updated. What sources of information and staff input will be required to do this?

▶ Are the recommendations resulting from the audit reaching the relevant staff?

Rehabilitation of old buildings

▶ Has reorientation of the building to the south been considered?

▶ Can sunspaces and/or lightwells be added on?

▶ Have cold bridging points been cladded or insulated?

▶ Has extra insulation to external envelope been considered?

▶ Have windows and doors been draughtproofed?

▶ Has double or secondary glazing been evaluated?

▶ Would a change of fuel be beneficial?

▶ Consider upgrading heating controls.

▶ Have low energy lights been installed?

▶ Have occupancy controls been considered?

Design of new buildings

▶ Has design for passive solar heating been maximized?

▶ Have designs for passive stack ventilation been considered?

▶ Have whole house ventilation systems with heat recovery been considered?

▶ Does the design maximize daylighting?

▶ Is the fabric super-insulated (U value: 0.2W/m2/degC or less)?

▶ Is double glazing with low emissivity glass used?

▶ Does the heating system maximize radiant heat?

▶ Has a wet underfloor radiator system been considered?

▶ Have condensing boilers been fitted?

Commercial buildings:

▶ Have heating and lighting circuits been zoned?

▶ Has the use of heat pumps been considered?

▶ Has a micro combined heat and power unit been evaluated?

Long-term potential for the local authorities to consider

▶ Timber frame, self build, kit housing.

▶ Earth sheltering, turf roofs, rammed earth, green timber.

▶ Glass houses.

▶ Solar power, wind power, water power, mini CHP.

▶ Heat stores.

▶ Water recycling.

▶ On site biological sewerage treatment.

REFERENCES

Boardman, B and Houghton, T (1992) *Poverty and Power* Joseph Rowntree
  Foundation, York
Shorrock, L D and Henderson, G (1990) *Energy Use in Buildings and Carbon Dioxide
  Emissions* Building Research Establishment Report, Garston, Watford

TRANSPORT

Hugh Barton

INTRODUCTION

Transport is about getting to places. It is not valued primarily for itself but for the level of accessibility it affords. An environmental audit of transport policy is not directly concerned with measuring accessibility but cannot avoid having implications for it. Accessibility relates to basic questions of individual choice, equity and economic growth, so in raising the profile of environmental issues the audit may challenge fundamental political goals. It may also work to reinforce or redefine them. Either way, a transport EA is liable to be contentious.

The challenge of creating an environmentally sustainable transport strategy is to move away from high dependence on road transport and the satisfaction of the demand for car use towards a balanced 'demand management' approach offering real choice to travellers while maintaining levels of accessibility. Government is, at least in principle, backing this change of approach.[1]

The Departments of Transport (DTp), and of Trade and Industry (DTI) are at best ambivalent about the shifting emphasis. Local transport authorities – shire counties, metropolitan districts and London boroughs – are not free agents. Their freedom of action is largely constrained by DTp funding criteria which are still geared to road provision rather than public transport. At the same time other agencies such as Railtrack, private rail and bus operators, freight firms and development companies are making decisions within their respective remits. Transport authorities therefore have limited room for manoeuvre.

The environmental auditor is thus faced with an unenviable task. The decision may need to be made early in the audit process whether to be

---

1 Key official documents are *Sustainable Development: The UK Strategy* (DoE, 1994) and the Planning Policy Guidance Note on Transport (DoE, 1994: PPG13).

cautious or bold. The more cautious approach would recognize the limits to LA power and tailor auditing to those factors directly amenable to influence. The bolder approach is to do a 'community transport audit' looking at overall impacts and evaluating the combined impact of all the relevant agencies. This guide recommends the latter as being appropriate in the context of Local Agenda 21. However, the testing of specific LA policies and practices remains a crucial part of the audit.

The chapter is organized in six main sections:

- an overview of transport trends and environmental issues;
- how to tackle the transport SoE;
- choice of indicators and targets;
- evaluating transport policies;
- the problems of achieving policy consistency; and
- the review of internal practices.

TRANSPORT TRENDS AND ENVIRONMENTAL IMPACTS

The significance of transport in the pattern of British energy demand is growing (see Figure 7.1). While most other sectors of energy use have experienced only marginal increases or even decreases, the transport sector's share of the total has risen from 19 per cent in 1970 to 33 per cent in 1993. Land passenger movement accounts for a major part of the growth, and in 1989 amounted to 20 per cent of *total* energy use. Within the land passenger total the motor car dominates – with roughly 95 per cent of fuel used.

The increase in passenger transport energy use reflects long-running social and economic trends. It is not only that more people now own and use a car, but also they make more trips, and each trip is on average longer. In the last few years in particular low petroleum costs have been fuelling profligate energy use. By comparison with major competitors, some with higher car ownership, the UK has become significantly more dependent on car use.

The Department of Transport expects these trends to continue. It expects a doubling of the motor vehicle population from the current 23 million vehicles by AD 2025, with an increase in vehicle kilometres of between 86 per cent and 142 per cent over the period (DTp, 1989). It has been calculated that the extra parking space required in 2025 to cope with this demand would be equivalent in area to a 257-lane motorway between London and Edinburgh (Adams, 1990); further, that even if present road building programmes were implemented in full, the expanded network could not keep pace with predicted traffic growth.

Our evident infatuation with the car comes at an environmental cost.

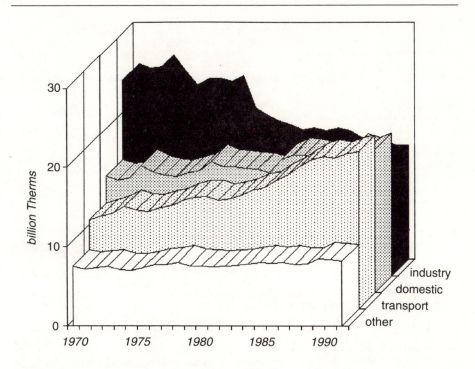

Figure 7.1 Contribution of the transport sector to total energy demand in Britain 1970–1993

Source: Barton, H and Stead, D (1993) *Sustainable Transport for Bristol* University of the West of England Working Paper 33, Faculty of the Built Environment, UWE, Bristol

Pollution is treated by the transport system as a largely uncosted externality. Transport is heavily implicated in a range of pollution problems, including smog, acid rain and global warming (see Table 7.1).

The critical importance of the greenhouse effect has been highlighted by the Climate Change Convention at the Rio Earth Summit, signed by John Major on the UK's behalf. Transport accounts for over 20 per cent of CO_2 that is causing global warming, and CO_2 accounts for half the total effect. Transport energy use also adds to emissions of other key 'greenhouse' gases – nitrous oxides and low-level ozone. In the 1990 White Paper *This Common Inheritance* (DoE, 1990), scientists, international agencies and national government recognize the need for urgent action to stabilize global ecology. The most authoritative statement so far by the scientific community was the final report of the Intergovernmental Panel on Climate Change (Houghton et al, 1990). It recommends a cut in CO_2 emissions of 60 per cent if we wish to halt global warming by the end of next century.

Table 7.1 Environmental impacts of transport

Global pollution	Local pollution	Resource use	Aesthetic impact	Physical impact
Emission of greenhouse gases CO_2, NO_2 and (indirectly) O_3	Health and fertility effects of carbon monoxide	Increasing use of the limited resources of oil	Visual impact of roads etc on town and country	Imtimidation of pedestrians and cyclists
Contribution to acid rain SO_2, NO_x	Child mental development effects of lead	Use of metal and other non-renewables in manufacturing	Visual impact of parked and moving vehicles	Accidents Creation of barriers to free pedestrian movement
	Health effects of SO_2, black smoke, volatile organic compounds (VOCs) and low level ozone	Use of scarce land resources for roads and parking	Noise, vibration and fumes	

Targets for global sustainability

In this context government – and local authority – plans for continued traffic growth take on a somewhat apocalyptic look. The environmental audit needs to identify clear and sustainable targets against which to measure progress in the local area and assess policies. The level of CO_2 emissions can be taken as one key indicator. The UK Government has so far only committed itself to stabilizing emissions at 1990 levels (DoE, 1990). In the transport sector even stabilization will be profoundly difficult to achieve, requiring the reversal of long-term trends. Part of the problem is that we have quite literally built energy profligacy into the urban and rural environment (see Chapter 9). Reviewing all the arguments, one recent study of Bristol recommends moving beyond stabilization to progressive reduction. The AD 2025 target – modest as it is in relation to the threat – implies a 50 per cent cut of emissions below trend (see Figure 7.2). That gives a measure of the task for local communities.

Such targets require concerted action on all fronts by the relevant agencies:

■ effective and consistent transport strategies
■ land use planning aimed at reducing the need to travel
■ the substitution of telecommunications for travel
■ technological innovation in engine and vehicle design
■ increased costs for motoring, eg through fuel tax and road pricing.

Local authorities can have a significant impact on only the first two of them. But they can also try to influence other agencies and the public in general by example, in their role as consumers, employers and operators.

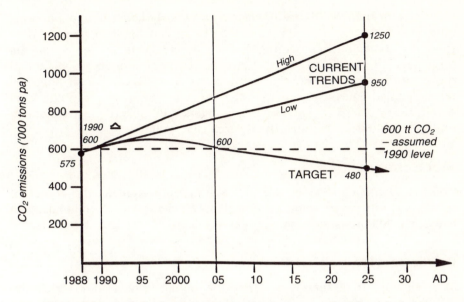

Figure 7.2 Forecasts and targets for Avon transport's CO_2 emissions

Source: Bristol Energy and Environment Plan 1992

THE REVIEW OF INTERNAL PRACTICES

The problem of unsustainable transport practices may be as much one of culture as it is engineering or finance. Habits of car reliance die hard. So as with other aspects of corporate behaviour, a prime purpose of any innovation is to change the attitudes of employees generally and key decision-makers in particular.

The main elements of in-house transport practice, all of which should be monitored and assessed on a regular basis, are:

- the choice of vehicles purchased;
- the quality of vehicle maintenance;
- the use of vehicles in providing public services;
- travel by staff for work purposes; and
- the staff journeys to work.

These five aspects are examined in turn below, and the key issues summarized in the checklist at the end of the chapter.

Choice of vehicles

The choice of vehicles for purchase by the authority can make an impact on the environment for a number of years. Two key decisions are the *size of* vehicles and their *fuel*. These decisions obviously affect budgets as well. Economy and environmental-friendliness can run hand in hand. Where there is a choice between petrol, diesel or electric vehicles the arguments on impact are equivocal. In most situations the greater fuel efficiency of diesel motors should sway the decision, but in areas of high air pollution more detailed analysis of comparative impact is appropriate. Some local authorities are actively encouraging innovation in fuels (eg the use of natural gas or biofuels) through their purchasing policy.

Maintenance

Good maintenance regimes are probably as important as the choice of vehicle. Priorities are the maximizing of fuel efficiency and the minimizing of emissions. Maintenance contracts can specify performance standards.

Public service vehicles

More difficult to assess is whether the public services for which the vehicles are used are provided with the minimum necessary number and length of motorized trips. Such assessment has to rely on the judgement of those managing the service. The role of the auditor, therefore, is to see whether the various service departments have given energy use sufficient weight in their decision processes, and to stimulate greater awareness where necessary.

A vital part of raising awareness is knowledge. If decision makers have access to regular information on (for example):

- number of trips made, by purpose and mode
- level of emissions implied by the mileage
- amount of fuel purchased: diesel and petrol
- expenditure of fuel and car allowances

– then they are much more likely to make sensible decisions.

All service departments should be involved, not only those which make regular site inspection and client visits. Two of the largest energy users are the refuse collection service and the parks and open space maintenance services.

Staff travel allowances

A further set of possible action points revolves around the need to use a vehicle for a particular trip. Individual car allowances may encourage profligacy. Allowances might instead be oriented to promote bike and public transport use and car sharing. Equally valuable can be the encouragement of multi-purpose trips – one trip serving several different purposes rather than several trips serving one. Increasingly, also, phone, fax and computer link-ups can substitute for travel.

Travel to work

Finally there is the journey to work. The *location* of offices and other workplaces is critical to both journey length and the mode of transport chosen, constraining the use of public transport, foot or pedal by employees. This issue of site choice is dealt with in the next chapter. Within the constraints of any given site the authority can make things easy for their environmentally conscious (and cost-conscious) workers:

- easy, direct access routes for pedestrians and cyclists;
- secure bike parking, and cyclist showering provision;
- bus passes/bike loans instead of casual car user allowances;
- limits on car parking provision, with regulations benefiting car sharers;
- car allowances at a standard rate unrelated to engine size;
- car pools at work instead of car allowances, allowing employees the option not to own (or use) their own vehicle.

STATE OF THE ENVIRONMENT MONITORING

More broadly, local authorities can trigger and focus public debate by coordinating and publicising SoE surveys.

There is clearly a difficulty in converting broad emission targets into practical criteria for evaluating current trends and policies. Detailed local figures on energy use and emissions are not as yet available. It is inevitable the SoE will rely on standard measures of transport activity and environmental impact. Typically information is available from transport authorities (often collated in the annual TPP – Transport Policies and Programme) on trends in car ownership and use, public transport ridership, levels of congestion or delay, accidents, and aspects of noise and pollution.

From the sustainability perspective the key indicator is the total amount of traffic. Total traffic levels are strongly correlated with energy use and emissions. It may well be that current traffic monitoring is more concerned with specific locales (such as central areas) than the overall. Reliance on such limited measures can be misleading, however, since it is quite possible for inner urban traffic to be effectively restrained or 'calmed' while at the same time the growth rate of traffic in the outer suburbs and rural hinterland is actually increased. So the critical indicator is the *overall* level of traffic in a functional region. This may, in highly urbanized areas, necessitate collaboration with neighbouring authorities to avoid the syndrome of one community simply exporting its problems (traffic in this case) to another.

The SoE checklist at the end of the chapter suggests some more specific measures of progress. They have been devised either as *primary* indicators (see Figure 2.1) to measure the use of resources by transport and the quality of the environment (for example the level of CO in congested streets) or as *secondary* indicators which assess effective policy implementation (for example, whether bike trip times are improving).

Both these kinds of indicators attempt to provide objective measures of success. But sometimes collection of such data can be beyond the scope of the study and constitute rather a recommendation for subsequent monitoring. It could be argued that it is at least as important to include subjective assessment – finding out what people *feel* is the quality of their environment.

Subjective assessment may be by social survey, interest group consultation and councillor involvement. This approach could be particularly relevant to perceptions of danger and intimidation, visual impact, noise and fume levels, and tie the audit in directly with public concerns. One criterion of environmental impact, in other words, is the level of public acceptability. As usual with this approach it is necessary to balance cases of special pleading with more comprehensive techniques – ensuring equitable treatment of, for example, articulate upper middle-class enclaves with less vociferous, often poorer, communities.

ASSESSING TRANSPORT POLICIES

In principle the environmental impact of policy is assessed by reference to SoE information. If the environment is safer, for example, with fewer traffic accidents, then policy would appear to be moving in the right direction. But in practice it is often not so easy. The SoE may provide only incomplete data. The relationship between LA policy and environmental impact may be distant, as for example in the sphere of public transport where the local authority has very limited influence. Or it may be difficult to disentangle the discrete influence of specific policies from that of others. An SoE is a *necessary* but not *sufficient* means of policy appraisal.

In this situation there are two other mechanisms that are needed: the test against 'good practice', and the test of policy consistency.

Good practice

The test against good practice can be relatively quick. In the transport field there are some useful reviews of the state of the art, and helpful (also challenging) lists of environmentally conscious policies from groups like Friends of the Earth and Transport 2000. The checklist at the end of this chapter provides one version of such lists. It examines good practice by 'mode' or aspect of transport policy, working from broad transport investment policy to more specific policies for walking, cycling, public transport, traffic capacity, car restraint, transport interchanges and freight movement.

The checklist has been devised so as to highlight the possible progression of policy in each decision area. For example in relation to traffic capacity: the first policy which restricts capacity and calms traffic in inner urban areas is seen as a halfway house to the second, which envisages a *general* reduction in capacities and speeds.

It is often difficult to define what policy actually is, and therefore difficult to assess whether it is having a beneficial effect. A typical case would be a cycling promotion policy, firmly stated in structure and local plans, but where there is no evidence of implementation either through investment programmes or through development control. Where there is a gap between rhetoric and action, the audit should attempt to pick it up.

Another contentious area is where different environmental criteria pull in different directions: for instance in relation to parking provision. Normal planning policy is to insist that new developments such as retail units or office parks provide for the expected level of car use, to avoid blighting nearby streets with extra parked vehicles. However, the fact of parking provision itself encourages car use, exacerbates congestion and emission levels, and hastens the spiral of public transport decline. Good practice in these situations can be very different according to which environmental impact is considered most important.

So the good practice test, while useful, needs to be treated with caution. The factor it very evidently ignores is conflict between policies or between objectives.

Testing for consistency

Car sharing

An example of policy conflict relates to car sharing and public transport. Both appear desirable, worthy of promotion as alternatives to low occupancy car use. Yet in practice one tends to undermine the other. An *effective* car sharing policy is likely to take passengers away from public transport and thus reduce the viable level of service.

Park and ride

Again, a much touted environmentally benign policy is 'park and ride' (P & R). Park and Ride stations at the edge of a city can play a vital role reducing in-city car use and enhancing the city centre environment. But at the same time it is encouraging car use in the outlying areas, deterring people from walking direct to nearby bus services, thus undermining the viability of local services and contributing to increased energy use. It also tends to increase the distance commuters are willing to travel, and so encourage further population dispersal to locations which are entirely car-dependent.[2]

These examples must be sufficient to indicate that policy assessment is a complex process. It is vital to avoid the crude assumptions – 'knee-jerk' environmentalist responses – that particular policies are automatically good. Rather it is the whole context of policy, the shape of the overall strategy, which will determine whether a particular initiative is worthwhile or not.

The compatibility matrix (Figure 7.3) illustrates how the consistency of overall strategy may be assessed. It lists the policies and/or objectives down the left hand side, then reading diagonally allows the compatibility of pairs of policies to be recorded. Compatibility is judged in relation to overarching policy goals: in this case 'reducing transport energy use' and 'maintaining a good level of accessibility' ... does a particular combination of policies work towards these goals, or does one policy perhaps undermine another?

The context for the illustration is a large city of over half a million people. The matrix would look different in this context to, say, a rural area or a metropolis such as London.

A matrix of this kind could be particularly useful where a number of agencies have a say in transport policy. The policies down the side can reflect precisely what the different agencies are doing, for example the road proposals of the DTp, the bus priority measures of the County, and the central parking policy of the urban district. The inconsistencies of approach can thus be highlighted in a graphic way. (For discussion of the basic principles of consistency analysis see page 42).

CONCLUSION

What is suggested in this chapter is one step ahead of current practice in auditing. Few audits at present go beyond the RIP and of those which do even fewer aspire beyond relatively simple checklists and basic monitoring. However, some transport authorities have undertaken sophisticated transport studies incorporating extensive survey work and with environmental variables given due weight. Bristol Integrated Transport and Environment Study (BRITES, MVA Consultants, 1991) is a case in point. Also transport authorities have the mechanism, through the annual Transport Policies and Programme (TPP), for publishing regular monitoring reports. These studies and mechanisms are likely to be very useful as Government

2 See further discussion of this point in Barton and Stead (1993).

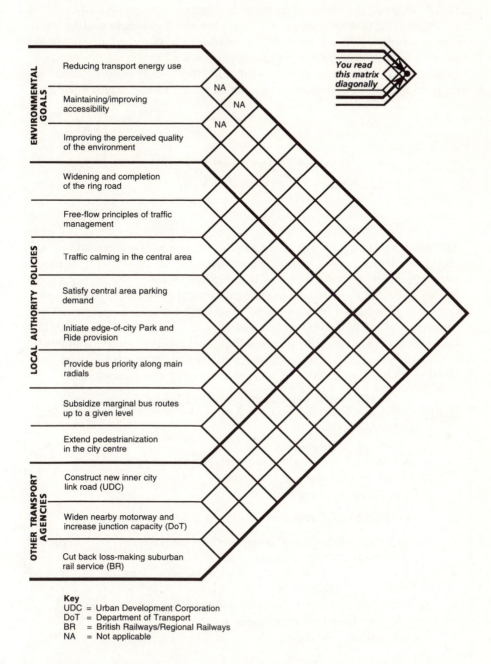

Key
UDC = Urban Development Corporation
DoT = Department of Transport
BR   = British Railways/Regional Railways
NA   = Not applicable

Figure 7.3 Illustrative transport compatibility matrix for a city authority

Note: Explanation of the use of this technique is given in Chapter 2, page 43

and EC legislation move haltingly towards Strategic Environmental Assessment (SEA). Already the DoE's guide to the 'Environmental Appraisal of Development Plans' (DoE, 1993) is required reading for land use policy planners. It should be so for transport planners as well.

Long-run sustainability depends on effective integration of land use, energy and transport planning. It is that to which the next chapter turns.

CHECKLISTS

The transport checklists attempt to give a guide to the range of issues an environmental audit might cover. Any particular exercise can then define its scope by reference to the checklist. Of the three sections the RIP and SOE lists are relatively straightforward. The Policy list is more complex. It is based around recognized best European practice. The problem is that the effect of individual policies can be very different depending on which other policies they are combined with. It is vital, therefore, that these checklists are read in the context of earlier discussion on consistent strategy and are not used mechanistically.

Reviewing in-house transport practices

▶ Have all main elements been considered:
  - choice of vehicles
  - quality of maintenance
  - use of vehicles for service provision
  - travel by staff for work purposes
  - staff journey to work?

▶ Is transport energy use etc monitored effectively?

▶ Are vehicles selected for purchase or hire as quiet, fuel-efficient and pollution-limited as possible?

▶ Are maintenance regimes and contracts geared to fuel efficiency and emission reduction?

▶ Does the provision of services occur with the minimum necessary number and length of motorized trips?

▶ Are work practices encouraged which reduce the need for motorized travel?

▶ Are there incentives to use low energy modes for the journey to work?

State of the Environment indicators

Information on energy use in transport is not amenable to collection in the UK. The first (and most important) indicator is a proxy both for energy use and carbon emissions, and is quite a challenge.

▶ Is *(a)* car use, *(b)* the overall level of traffic, falling:
  – in town centres
  – in urban areas
  – in rural areas
  – in the whole geographic region as defined by commuting patterns, *not* local authority boundaries?
▶ Are modal choices for personal travel moving away from energy-intensive transport towards walking, cycling and public transport:
  – for peak central area trips
  – for intra urban trips
  – for inter urban trips
  – for all trips?
▶ Are emission levels (C, NO_x, HCs, O_3, Pb etc) satisfactory in relation to WHO and EU standards:
  – in residential and shopping streets
  – adjacent to main roads?
▶ Is the number of road accidents falling:
  – in absolute terms
  – in relation to total vehicle miles?
  (Distinguish levels of severity, different user groups and areas)
▶ Are levels of traffic noise falling?
▶ Are levels of congestion/traffic delay falling?
▶ Are bus trip times and reliability improving?
▶ Are cycling trip times improving?
▶ Is pedestrian delay in crossing main roads reducing?
▶ Is infringement of 'environmental capacity' in residential areas and shopping streets being avoided?
▶ What is the *perceived* trend in environmental quality in relation to traffic? Has a social survey been undertaken to supplement councillor and pressure group views?

Transport policy assessment

As noted in the text, it is important to assess actual or programmed implementation of policy rather than policy objectives which may be little more than aspirations. The following questions can be applied to specific authorities or the combination of all transport agencies in an area. The two questions given under each heading are sequential, the first being a staging post on the way to the second.

▶ Capital transport investment
  - Are capital programmes progressively shifting the balance of investment away from pure road building?
  - Are capital programmes at least 50 per cent for pt investment linked to complementary land use policies?
▶ Walking
  - Are there extensive pedestrianization schemes in central areas?
  - Is a comprehensive pedestrian network being implemented, designed for convenience, safety and beauty, linked to land use policy?
▶ Cycling
  - Are there existing or planned commuting and recreational cycle routes, with some trip-end provision?
  - Is there a comprehensive hierarchical route network planned and being implemented for maximum convenience and safety?
▶ Public transport priority
  - Is there extensive priority on key radials and in the city centre being implemented?
  - Is there effective priority on the whole basic network, with all new development designed around pt?
▶ Transport interchange
  - Is there extensive Park and Ride or Bike and Ride provision in or close to commuter settlements?
  - Are comprehensive bike/bus/rail transfer facilities provided, with local dial-a-ride (etc) feeder services in low density areas?
▶ Car restraint
  - Is there restricted central area parking (long- and short-stay) and/or road pricing?
  - Are there general trip-end restrictions on car use – in suburban and exurban developments as well as central areas?
▶ Traffic capacity
  - Are there effective policies aimed at restricting traffic capacity and traffic calming in inner urban areas and environmentally sensitive areas?
  - Is there a general programme of reducing traffic capacity while at the same time giving priority to walking, cycling and public transport and increasing levels of safety and perceived environmental quality?
▶ Para-transit
  - Are there effective measures designed to promote alternatives to the car in low density/dispersed settlements and rural areas where public transport is not viable – eg car sharing, community minibuses, shared taxis?

> ► Freight transport
> – Are there implementable policies for freight consolidation and transfer points, linked to rail terminals as well as road transport?
> – Are policies designed to ensure that new freight-intensive activities locate on sites where direct access can be gained to motorway/lorry route network and existing/potential railways?

REFERENCES

Barton, H and Stead, D (1993) *Sustainable Transport for Bristol* University of the West of England Working Paper 33, Faculty of the Built Environment, UWE, Bristol

Department of the Environment (1990) *This Common Inheritance: Britain's Environmental Strategy* HMSO, London

Department of the Environment (1993) *The Environmental Appraisal of Development Plans: A Good Practice Guide* HMSO, London

Department of the Environment (1994) *Planning Policy Guidance Note 13: Transport* HMSO, London

Department of the Environment et al (1994) *Sustainable Development: The UK Strategy* HMSO, London

Houghton, J T; Jenkins, G J and Ephraums, J J (1990) *Climate Change: the Intergovernmental Panel on Climate Change Scientific Assessment* Cambridge University Press, Cambridge

MVA Consultants (1991) *Bristol Integrated Transport and Environment Study (BRITES)* Final Report, Avon County Council, Bristol

8

LAND USE PLANNING

Hugh Barton

INTRODUCTION AND ORIENTATION

This chapter deals with the auditing of land use planning policy, which is possibly the least well developed aspect of EA as currently practised. Conventionally the planning audit, if it occurs at all, focuses on reasonably discrete and identifiable issues that are amenable to some kind of measurement: for example, dereliction, the protection of the green belt, and the protection of urban green spaces from development. Any or all of these criteria may be important in particular circumstances. But the agenda has now broadened to embrace the whole gamut of planning policy. The chapter first describes this broader perspective and the reasons for adopting it, then explores some of the very real difficulties which the auditor is likely to have to confront. Subsequently the chapter deals with the land use SoE, PIA and RIP, including an urban and rural case study to help give form to the ideas.

The new agenda: sustainable development

The significance of sustainable development for planning policy has barely been grasped by many British local authorities. The relationship between the spatial arrangement of human activities and global environmental quality is fraught with conceptual difficulties and preconceptions. The uncertainties in this whole area mean that so far most audits have tacitly ignored it.

That attitude does not evade responsibility, however. The interdependence of global ecology, energy use and the form of settlements has long been understood. At least 70 per cent of energy use is affected at some time, to some degree, by land use planning decisions (Barton, 1990). Factors such as built form and layout, density and zoning, the concentration and dispersal of activities can lead to very substantial variations in energy used in buildings and in transport (Owens, 1986). High energy dependence in turn threatens the global environment.

Recognizing this, the European Commission is now actively promoting the vision of compact towns and cities, more urban and less suburban in character, with higher levels of accessibility but lower levels of energy use (DoE, 1992). Certain EU countries (eg the Netherlands) are energetically implementing the concept. The British Government, too, is altering its stance, albeit haltingly, to incorporate 'sustainability' objectives in planning policy guidance. The key document is PPG12, which came out in Spring 1992 (DoE, 1992). PPG12 defines the environment very broadly, and requires planning authorities to incorporate environmental issues systematically into land use policy decisions. Subsequently a series of PPG revisions have reflected the new priority. PPG13, on transport, is particularly significant in stressing the interdependence of transport, land use and energy use, and shifting the balance of locational policy away from personal car-based mobility towards public transport, walking and cycling (DoE, 1994).

There are hopeful signs that all this is not mere window-dressing, but that government will back the sustainability argument through the appeal system as and when the development plans (in a plan-led development process) incorporate appropriate policies.[1] This reinforces the potential significance of the planning policy audit. It is concerned to test two things:

1) Are plans promoting sustainable development?
2) Are ongoing development decisions reflecting the environmental priorities in plans?

THE ENVIRONMENTAL APPRAISAL OF DEVELOPMENT PLANS

The first of these two questions is effectively tackled by the 'environmental appraisal of development plans' (EAP). The term 'environmental appraisal' is enshrined in PPG12, and appraisal is now an obligatory part of plan making. The recommended process of EAP is set out in recent government guidance (DoE, 1993). It involves three key stages which make the connection with environmental auditing very clear:

1) Monitoring the state of the environment to assess the real impact of policy, and progress towards environmental goals.
2) Scoping of the policies in the plan to ensure that they reflect the full environmental/sustainability agenda and current best practice.
3) Evaluation of the policies contained in the plan to assess likely environmental impacts and mutual consistency, leading where appro-

---

1 eg *Planning Week*, 26 May 1994, p 2, 'DoE puts muscle on framework of PPG6'.

priate to policy modification and/or measures in mitigation of those impacts.

Thus EAP *requires* the planning authorities to be active in SoE surveys, and in policy impact assessment (PIA). It is in effect the main contribution of the planning department or section to environmental auditing. It is seen as an essential part of the normal process of plan preparation, monitoring and review, and in no sense some extraneous bolt-on extra.

The only elements of a complete planning audit *not* encompassed in EAP are the review of development control and the review of the authorities' own development decisions (the RIP).

DIFFICULTIES IN PURSUING THE AUDIT

Before turning to a more detailed examination of audit elements it is important to deal with some of the problems that have inhibited progress on incorporating planning in environmental audits.

In the first place there has been a *lack of knowledge*. Many planners have felt that while they have a very good understanding of certain issues (eg building and landscape conservation), they are ignorant of what policies are environmentally sustainable. This justification for inertia no longer applies. Research institutions, environmental agencies and now the DoE itself, through the Planning Policy Guidance Notes, are progressively refining broad principles into practical policies.

Secondly, there are severe *limits to LA power*: an important question arises as to extent to which planning authorities, by their action and policies, can really effect key environmental variables such as the level of greenhouse emissions. Decisions on travel and heating, for example, are made by a host of individual households and enterprises, not subject to LA dictate. Locating housing next to employment opportunities does not mean people will choose to work locally or employers will give preference to locals. Changes in employment of shopping patterns are more to do with economic and social trends than LA policy. The decisions of investment companies, multinational firms, government departments and privatized public utilities are often central. Local authorities, therefore, are only one of the players in the game, and by no means the most powerful.

There are two answers to these concerns. On the one hand, while the planners do not make development decisions, let alone control individual behaviour, they do help *shape the framework* within which those decisions are taken. If patterns of land use zoning provide few opportunities for working locally, then it is *obliging* people to use more energy to get to work, and at the same time hampering social welfare and, possibly, economic growth. Planning policy therefore needs to be geared not to restriction of choice, but increasing choices open to people, allowing them to choose whether to work near home or further afield; whether to walk or use bus or car. It is working on a probabilistic not deterministic premise.

On the other hand, the answer to the plurality of decision-makers lies in the nature of the auditing process itself. Ownership of the audit need not be restricted to the LA. A community audit, linked to an Environmental Forum or Local Agenda 21 committee, could draw in some of the other powerful agencies and win their backing.

Thirdly, there is the problem of making *very long-term commitments*.

One argument against incorporating sustainability into planning policy is the sheer time scale involved in moving from the *status quo* to a resource-efficient settlement pattern. Most of the buildings that will be standing in forty years have already been built. At the same time the formal plans have a time horizon of at most 15–20 years. So what real chance is there of changing direction? This line of reasoning is especially powerful in more rural areas (eg Cornwall) where the ability to reverse long standing energy-intensive trends appears remote.

Part of the answer is at the level of principle. Even if it is difficult, now, to plan an ideal long-term settlement pattern that would be energy efficient, that does not invalidate considering each new development project on its merits. Locational options (say in-town or out-of-town) for a new housing estate can lead to 100 per cent variation in lifetime energy use and emissions. Each new development, therefore, should be planned to save energy. Even if its immediate impact on the total energy use in the region is small, each increment will add a little more. This leads to a quite practical auditing approach. The audit is not concerned with blueprints of a future sustainable utopia, but with incremental change. It is concerned with the *direction* of policy, now.

THE REVIEW OF THE COUNCIL'S OWN LOCATIONAL DECISIONS

The land use planning RIP is often ignored in environmental auditing. Yet the locations chosen by the local authority for its own offices and public services are among the most significant decisions it will make, affecting journey lengths and modal choice of employees and the public. In the past critical decisions on, for example, schools and colleges, have been based on land ownership and other factors, largely ignoring the social and ecological significance of accessibility. The result can be to build in high costs both for people and for the environment, and indirectly for the economy.

The audit process should establish the importance of accessibility for all relevant groups in the population, setting the context for subsequent decisions. The responsibility for sound locational decisions rests with a range of departments, including housing and education. Coordination of these decisions should sensibly rest with the planners.

STATE OF THE ENVIRONMENT MONITORING

The purpose of the planning SoE is to evaluate the actual impact of policy. The primary indicators of environmental quality – such as pollution levels, resource use, habitats, aesthetic quality – shed vital light on this but are for the most part at one remove from policy where the LPA is only one influence among many. Those primary variables are in any case dealt with elsewhere. What there needs to be to make the planning SoE well targeted is study of secondary indicators that measure policy impact more directly. Such indicators also should have a clear relationship to primary environmental quality.

At present the monitoring of planning policy is driven largely by political necessities, limited to variables such as residential land available, derelict land and development control efficiency. These do not generally measure up to the SoE requirements. Extra resources may therefore be implied, but authorities investing in GIS systems should be able to reorientate information to satisfy some of the requirements.

Self-sufficiency

The key indicators describe the broad spatial trends of settlement patterns and behaviour. A central concept is that of self-sufficiency. How self-sufficient, or autonomous, are different settlements or residential neighbourhoods? Are the trends towards greater or lesser autonomy? One measure of this could be the job ratio: the number of jobs in an area divided by the number of people available for work. Research indicates a direct relationship between the job ratio, average travel to work distance, and the proportion of walking/cycling trips. The idea could be applied to other sectors, eg the shops ratio, the schools ratio – though there are problems of data availability.

Clustering

Another important factor in energy-efficient urban form, highlighted by the DoE in PPG13, is clustering. To what extent are job and service facilities clustered together, permitting multipurpose trips and encouraging public transport, or to what extent are they dispersed, increasing car dependence and the number of trips?

Density

Density is a further variable strongly correlated with energy use and emissions. The planning SoE could seek to establish how residential and commercial densities are changing, through both new development and the process of urban renewal.

Green space

To complement study of density there can also be study of green spaces. Green space is being promoted for sustainability reasons such as pollution absorption, wildlife diversity, water conservation and local recreational provision. The mapping of gains and losses of green spaces/corridors would throw light on the effectiveness of policy.

These secondary indicators are all land use-based, involving monitoring change to land use and use intensity, in other words of the *framework* for human behaviour. More fundamental is *actual* behaviour. Census information and the National Travel Surveys ideally need to be supplemented by local surveys of trip length, frequency, mode and purpose. The political process, too, may throw light on questions of accessibility. The expressed concerns of residents about access to local schools and other facilities, for example, can provide both useful information and the publicity necessary to get effective action.

There are, in other words, different levels and different approaches to monitoring the environment. The important factor is remembering the purposes: to assess actual environmental quality and social well-being; and to assess the effectiveness of policy.

POLICY IMPACT ASSESSMENT

As discussed earlier, the DoE guidance on Environmental Appraisal provides the main framework for assessing the impacts of planning policy. Policy is assessed by:

1) comparison with good practice and official guidance (PPGs);
2) establishing consistency of the strategy and the objectives;
3) checking policies against a checklist of possible impacts;
4) monitoring the real impact via SoE surveys.

Additionally, there is the need to assess development control decisions:

5) assessing conformity of DC decisions with the environmental priorities in plans.

Rather than repeat the DoE guide, the subsequent sections discuss the distinction between local and strategic policy scales, the problems of policy consistency, and then presents two case studies, one from an urban, the other a rural context. The checklist at the end of this chapter provides some clues as to best practice.

The local or urban design level focuses on the three-dimensional form and character of a neighbourhood, estate or project, and on the general policies/guides/briefs that shape such areas. The strategic or policy level encompasses the spatial distribution of activities within and between settlements, and the policies in Unitary Plans, Local Plans, Structure Plans and Regional Guidance that influence these patterns.

Strategic policy

At the strategic level the cut-off point may be difficult to define. What are relevant strategic land use/transport issues? Consider the situation of a metropolitan borough council, or a rural district council that looks towards a dominant city outside its area, or a County Council in the home counties. None of these are remotely autonomous in land use terms. The level and distribution of growth in such authorities will be a function of a wider subregional or regional pattern. The auditors can then adopt one of two approaches:

1)   They will restrict consideration to those matters that are strictly within the power of the local authority, on the grounds that anything more would be spurious and time-wasting;
2)   They will deliberately include broader strategic factors on the grounds that not to do so distorts the analysis.

The latter is ideal, but implies close collaboration with neighbouring/ superior authorities – which may not be forthcoming.

Another major difficulty at the strategic level is the need to establish consistency between policy areas (eg housing, employment, tourism, transport) that are often treated as discrete and separate. The next section tackles this issue.

Local policy

At the more detailed level the criteria for sustainability in the design and layout of development are reasonably direct and easily assessed (see the checklist). The audit can be handled mainly through simple observation and questions about existing policy content. The surprising thing is that the elements of sustainable design, some of them quite well known from individual projects, have not caught on in the planning system generally. Principles of good microclimatic design, the use of planting, orientation and aspect, attractive local provision for pedestrians and cyclists, good access to planned bus routes, good accessibility to services generally, all these are well understood and could be incorporated into normal practice with little inhibition. Other principles – to do with local recycling, local sewage and energy systems, wildlife enhancement, local organic food production – are being discussed, though the layout implications are not always clear as yet.

Local planning authorities, stimulated by the audit, could make rapid improvements in their urban design policies and development briefs, cultivating new attitudes among developers and their own development control officers.

THE INTERDEPENDENCE OF DECISIONS

In the field of planning it is not normally possible to break down policy into independent decision areas. A particular housing location policy, for example, may only make sense when combined with *particular* employment, shopping and school provision policies. Often, in other words, it is the coherence of the overall strategy that matters, and individual policies need to complement the strategy.

This complexity provides an extra headache for the auditor. Straightforward criteria (eg is policy encouraging job decentralization?) are rarely sufficient. Different contexts will call for different strategies. It is also vital to see transport as a function of land use, and vice versa. Given this, the auditing process needs to deal effectively with policy interaction, and needs to take an overview. It is not normally valid, at the strategic level at least, to extract specific issues and leave the generality to look after itself.

In order to grasp the strategy it is necessary to simplify the diverse elements into a manageable number so that the general patterns are clear. Table 8.1 illustrates a possible breakdown into six elements.

There needs to be consistency of approach to policies *within* each broad decision area: for example a similar stance on leisure, retail, educational, health and job facilities – all of which are major generators of trips and are ideally clustered in town and neighbourhood centres.

There also needs to be compatibility and reinforcement *between* each broad decision area: for example the location of jobs/services and of residential development should be closely related so as to minimize the need to travel.

Worked example of consistency analysis

Figure 8.1 takes a set of interacting policies that have been loosely derived from an actual local authority plan. This set was originally introduced in Chapter 2, where the idea of consistency analysis as part of environmental auditing was first advanced. Besides five broad policies the set includes one major site-specific proposal and an overarching environmental goal.

Table 8.1 Key elements of land use/transport decision making

Key elements	*Main related policy areas*
Locational pattern of residential activity (strategic level)	Housing land policies Residential development policies Brown field housing development
Locational pattern of jobs and services (strategic level)	Employment land Job promotion policies Retail development policies Leisure and tourist policies Education, health, social services
Intensity of urban activity (strategic and local)	Residential density policies Commercial density policies Land use zoning policies Energy strategy
Pattern of movement (strategic and local)	Traffic policies Public transport policies Walking and cycling policies Car restraint policies, etc
Pattern of green space (strategic and local)	Recreational provision Nature conservation Water management Energy strategy Pollution and environmental quality
Layout and urban design (local level)	Housing balance and residential environmental policies Local jobs and facilities provision Local circulation and access strategies Heat loss reduction and local energy supply Conservation and aesthetic quality

The degree of inconsistency demonstrated in Figure 8.1 is alarming, but not unusual in evaluating plans that were created in the 1980s when the ethos of planning was different. Figure 8.2 expands on some of the reasons for the judgements made in the matrix.

The auditor may use the compatibility matrix in several ways to achieve greater consistency. The matrix provides a shorthand tool for attempting to get agreement between interests or sections that there *is* inconsistency, and therefore that there is a problem that should be addressed. Recognition is the first essential stage. Once that is established, then prescription follows. Table 8.2 illustrates how conclusions may be drawn out of the matrix and lead on to recommendations for policy review.

The tensions between policies are illustrated further below with a couple of case studies, one from the Taff Valley in Wales, the other from Cornwall.

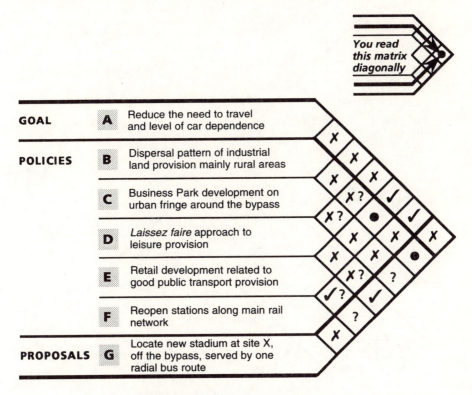

Figure 8.1 Compatibility matrix
(completed version of that shown in Chapter 2 – Figure 2.3)

CASE STUDY: CARDIFF AND THE TAFF VALLEY

This example is chosen to illustrate the environmental impact of land use and transport policies at the strategic level. It also highlights the close relationship to key social and economic issues, and the problems of changing policy direction.

The study of the Taff Valley points up some of the innate conflicts that may occur between established policy and the desire for energy-efficient transport.

At the lower end of the Taff, Cardiff is experiencing rapid growth of car use. The city has a growing concentration of offices in the centre and ambitious plans for the regeneration of Cardiff Bay, dependent mainly on a major pro-gramme of road investments to provide the trigger to the private sector. Economic buoyancy is reflected in high demand for housing, some of which is being met within the built-up area, by reuse of sites and infill. This intensifi-cation of development in Cardiff, raising gross dwelling densities to compen-sate for smaller average household size, is sensible from the energy viewpoint. At the same time however, the restraint of housing development in the sur-

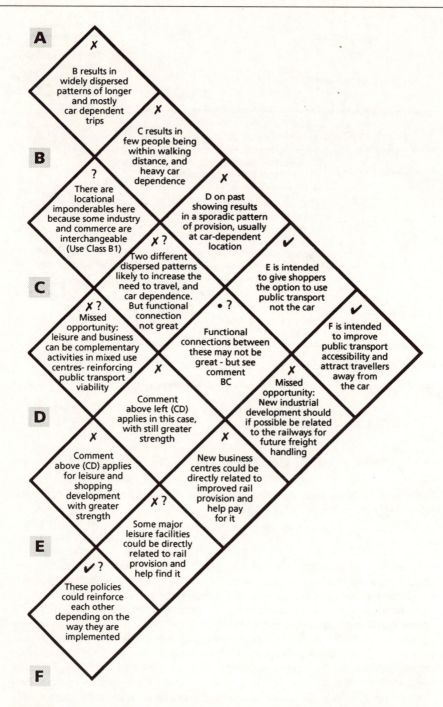

Figure 8.2 Annotated compatibility matrix (explanation of part of Figure 8.1)

Table 8.2 Recommendations emerging from the analysis of consistency

	Conclusions	Recommendations
A	An important sustainability goal not yet reflected in some decision areas	Give greater weight to this goal
B	Inappropriate from the environmental standpoint, leading to reverse car-based commuting *but* does provide rural employment opportunities ... Are they used?	A policy inherited from previous plans, needing to be reviewed. *NB* Study rural employment issue in greater depth
C	Inappropriate from the environmental standpoint, leading to car dependence	Consider a strategy of mixed use centres related to good pt provision
D	Inappropriate from the environmental viewpoint and may hamper 'access to leisure' for the transport poor	Consider a planned strategy of more local provision, with major facilities in mixed use centres
E	Logical from the environmental standpoint, but not reinforced by land use policy	Carry forward, with tight criteria for the quality of pt accessibility
F	Appropriate from the environmental standpoint, but not reinforced by land use policy	Relate station development expressly to the creation of mixed use centres which could help funding
G	Inappropriate from the environmental standpoint, missing the opportunity for association with other activities	Explore other possible sites based on good public transport centrality and mixed use centres

rounding countryside – notably in the Vale – is obliging increased commuting, predominantly by car, from widely dispersed locations. The general pattern of jobs, homes, social and leisure facilities appears progressively less friendly to energy-efficient modes. In theory there is a clear choice: either some of Cardiff's commercial growth should be diverted to the commuting zones or more residential developments of suitable character should be permitted in close-in locations.

The first is problematical from a marketing perspective. The latter is problematical from a political perspective. The poignancy of the situation is increased still further when one realises that, from urban form theory, Cardiff is at or over the threshold at which the economies of scale lead to increased efficiency. Further peripheral growth around the city would just impair the robustness of the city in a hypothetical future situation of punitive pollution taxation. The theory would suggest evolution towards a cluster of semi-autonomous linked towns. Perhaps not a very practical proposition.

The situation further up the Taff is in some way the obverse of that in Cardiff. The overriding priority is to regenerate the hearts of the Valleys. Plans are geared to retaining the valley population, making good use of existing social capital, while attempting to attract new employment where the physical constraints allow. But the strategy has not been entirely successful. The new roads have permitted increased out-commuting, rather than drawing commerce in.

Some valleys now export the majority of their employed residents during the day, and travel has changed from being the historical linear pattern, mainly short distances up and down the valley, to a car reliant web with its heart in Cardiff. So overall, current trends and policies in this area are contributing their fair share to global warming. Redirecting those trends is quite a challenge.

taken from H Barton, 1992

CASE STUDY: CORNWALL

Cornwall has been chosen to illustrate the significance of development policies in a rural county, posing intractable problems, where planning is facilitating energy intensive patterns.

Cornwall presents a knotty problem in relation to sustainable transport ideas. 'Solutions' which are reasonably self-evident (albeit not easy) in higher density urbanized regions do not apply here. The pattern of dispersed settlements and very high car dependence makes Dutch-type public transport strategies impracticable, at least for the present. But this problem does not mean it is valid to accept current Cornish trends and policies. Current trends are energy-profligate and are being reinforced by some key policies – for example, the acceptance of village growth, increased scale and specialization of services (often in non-central locations), and progressive road improvements. In the light of global ecology a decision to carry on as before is a decision to exacerbate a deteriorating situation.

The central issue is: which locational policies could work for energy-efficiency? Urban form theory would indicate that growth should be concentrated in the towns, with jobs/facilities clustered at the town centres. But if that means the local village services die for lack of custom, then rural car-based dependence on the towns would increase yet further. It is probably presumptuous to suggest there are 'right' answers that guarantee 'success', but clearly it is critical to investigate the *actual* affect of current policies before selecting future strategy, for example:

- Do road improvements generate extra trips or not?
- Are village workshops being used by local people or not?
- Does village expansion safeguard local services or do the newcomers choose to rely predominantly on services outside the village?
- Is car ownership use higher in the rural areas than in the towns?
- Do the towns provide most of the jobs/services for most of their inhabitants most of the time, or not?

The experimental approach might also throw light on as yet untried options – for example, would heavily traffic-calmed towns, with greatly increased network provision for pedestrians, cyclists, even buses, reduce car trips?

Reduce the overall level of traffic? Cause real inconvenience? Be welcomed or rejected by people?

Accepting all the caveats, it is still possible to suggest a package of policies that should result in reduced growth in emissions. These could be carefully evaluated during plan preparation. The following list is derived from the *Environmental Audit for North Devon District Council* (Keen, ed, 1990):

1) **Housing location:** concentrate new housing growth in-town, while strongly discouraging rural dispersal except where local low-cost provision is essential.
2) **Service/employment location:** resist the development of isolated/dispersed facilities, most especially car-based retail/tourist proposals. Instead, cluster such activities in town centres or planned public transport nodes, with maximum opportunities for local access.
3) **Small scale job/service provision:** encourage increased small town key village autonomy for local/non-specialized jobs and facilities.
4) **Density:** encourage higher dwelling densities close to town centre by increased proportion of flats/terraces.
5) **Development patterns and layout:** establish design principles that maximize viability of walking/cycling/pt; and encourage energy-efficient development (siting, aspect/orientation, built form, materials, landscaping, local energy and recycling systems).
6) **Parking & traffic calming:** give low energy modes priority within towns and enforce stringent parking maxima to all development, using temporary permissions if conditions not yet right.

Source: Hugh Barton, 1992

CONCLUSION

These two case studies highlight the importance but also the difficulties of establishing consistent planning policies. In the Taff example the desirable strategy (sociably and environmentally) of regenerating the economics of the valley has partially failed and Cardiff's booming economy is not matched by space for people to live. The auditor has the unenviable task of making clear that current policies are tending to exacerbate unsustainability, and pointing to possible alternative ways forward. Unless, however, the planners and politicians who have pursued these policies themselves *own* the process of review, the audit is likely to raise antibodies and a no change result.

In the Cornish case again there is a fundamental tension between established (and accepted) policy and sustainability. Here it is perhaps the case that the original expectations of certain policies (such as the provision of rural workshops) have not been fulfilled in practice. The auditor needs to ensure that the awkward questions are asked.

The commentary in this chapter has concentrated largely on the policy level because the issues there are both important and intractable. It is clear the auditing process, if properly tackled, is bound to cause waves.

Local authorities attempting to respond to PPG12 and the Government's UK Strategy for Sustainable Development will find themselves with very limited scope for policy redirection unless Government converts rhetoric into action, and pursues consistent energy, transport and land use policies in its own sphere of action.

At the same time there are grounds for hope. The Taff example shows that the goal of increased energy efficiency is often compatible with broader social and economic goals, and can reinforce them. It may become possible to put together a powerful coalition of interests in support of sustainable development, and EA could help trigger this.

CHECKLISTS

Review of in-house locational practices
▶ Are local authority facilities:
  - centrally located in relation to their hinterland so as to minimize journey to work and/or client/public visits?
  - located so as to facilitate access by walking, cycling, and where appropriate, public transport from all parts of their hinterland?
  - located adjacent or close to complementary activities (work, retailing, leisure, education etc), facilitating shared trip purposes by employees, clients, or public?
▶ Does the selected unit size of public facilities recognize the social, environmental and economic costs of:
  - excessive centralization which increases the average distance that people have to travel (eg schools, libraries, local housing offices)?
  - excessive segregation which increases the need for trips between facilities by employees or clients?

Note: These two questions apply to all service departments, but particularly **education** *(primary schools, secondary schools, colleges);* **housing** *(housing offices);* **social services** *(local offices);* **engineering** *(waste transfer points, maintenance yards etc);* **leisure** *(libraries, leisure centres, swimming pools);* **chief executive** *(council offices).*

▶ Is council housing located so as to provide varied housing opportunities in each settlement or part of the city?

▶ Do council house/housing association transfer arrangements permit households to move easily, so they have the chance to maximize their level of accessibility and minimize trip lengths etc?

State of the Environment monitoring

▶ Residential location
  - Is the proportion of new housing being built on brown field (or in-town) sites increasing?
  - Is new housing development (market or social) in outlying locations being occupied by commuters or satisfying 'local' need? Is the commuting proportion falling?
  - Are individual settlements retaining and increasing their level of autonomy, ie internal services?
  - Are small settlements or residential neighbourhoods improving their job ratios? (see text for explanation)

▶ Job/service location
  - Are new major employment, retail, educational, health and leisure facilities accessible by public transport from a wide hinterland, ie clustered at public transport nodes?
  - Are new minor facilities (as above) accessible conveniently and pleasantly by walking and cycling, and clustered to allow multi-purpose trips?
  - Are localized facilities (eg corner shops, primary schools, surgeries, post offices) surviving and indeed increasing in provision?

▶ Intensity of activities
  - Are the average net and gross densities of suburban/exurban residential areas increasing? Are inner urban densities being maintained? (Differentiate between household density and population density)
  - Are the average commercial densities in suburban/urban sites increasing?

Is all new higher intensity development (residential/commercial/services) within easy walking distances (ie ¼ mile) of existing or potentially good public transport corridors?

▶ Pattern of movement
  - Is the average length of the 'journey to work' decreasing?
  - Is the average length of shopping, education and service things decreasing?
  - Are modal choices moving away from motorized individual transport?

Note: See also the transport chapter.

▶ Open spaces
  - Have green spaces and corridors within the town been pre-served and, where rare, provided?
  - Is the amount of woodland and the number of trees in town and country increasing?
▶ Urban design
  - Is the proportion of terraces and low-rise flats in new develop-ment increasing?
  - Is new development incorporating principles of solar orienta-tion and aspect?
  - Is new development being planned in terms of siting, planting and layout to minimize wind speeds and avoid frost pockets?
  - Are circulation patterns within new/renewed developments based around walking, cycling and access to public transport, linked in to provision in neighbouring sites?
  - Is new development providing convenient opportunities for growing food locally (eg allotments or back gardens)?
  - Is new development being constructed to facilitate the eventual introduction of district heating?

Land use policy audit

Policy is assessed by several different methods, as described in the text. What is offered here is a 'good practice' checklist derived from DoE policy guidance.

▶ Energy-integrated planning
  - Are energy efficiency criteria used in assessing development proposals?
  - Are policies in place that generally welcome (with safeguards) the development of renewable energy?
  - Is there a coherent strategy for energy supply, and demand management?
  - Are new developments required to minimize heat loss and maximize solar gain through appropriate siting, layout and planting?
▶ Land use/transport integration
  - Is accessibility by foot, pedal and public transport an important criterion in assessing development proposals?
  - Is the layout of new development required to incorporate pro-vision for public transport, cyclists and pedestrians in such a way as to maximize their use?
  - Are settlements being planned effectively so as to reduce the need for travel and reduce car dependence?
▶ Density of development
  - Is density an issue in plans and development control?

- Are low density car-based commercial, institutional and residential developments being deterred?
- Are there explicit density zones in local plans which relate density to the level of access to public transport and local facilities?

▶ Housing development
  - Is a growing proportion of new housing on brownfield or infill sites?
  - Is new housing provision quite widely dispersed in and around the main settlements to maximize locational choice for house hunters?
  - Does policy work to ensure a variety of tenure, house type and affordability in every settlement or suburb?

▶ Location of jobs and facilities
  - Are local facilities in new and old areas being required to cluster (eg on local high streets) on locations that maximize the number of people likely to walk, cycle or use public transport to gain access?
  - Are major employment, retail, leisure and institutional activities being deterred from expanding in car-based locations or local centres with poor district/city-wide public transport connections?
  - Are town centres/district centres being reinforced and diversified in the range of their facilities?

▶ Open space and landscape
  - Is there a strategy for open space?
  - Does this strategy provide a 'network' of linked spaces taking into account recreational need; walking and cycling routes; wildlife corridors and refuges; water management; microclimate management/heat loss reduction; energy supply potential; pollution absorption and noise attenuation; visual quality?

REFERENCES

Barton, H (1990) 'Local Global Planning' *The Planner,* **76**, 42, 26 October 1990, pp 12–15

Barton, H (1992) Seminar for County and District Planners, Truro, Cornwall, March 1992

Department of the Environment (1992) *Planning Policy Guidance Note 12: Development Plans and Regional Planning Guidance* HMSO, London

Department of the Environment (1993) *Environmental Appraisal of Development Plans: A Good Practice Guide* HMSO, London

Department of the Environment (1994) *Planning Policy Guidance Note 13: Transport* HMSO, London

Keen, R (ed) (1990) *North Devon District Council Corporate Environmental Audit* North Devon District Council and Bristol Environmental Audit Unit (BEAU), Bristol Polytechnic, Bristol (now UWE)

Owens, S (1986) *Energy Planning and Urban Form* Pion, London

Planning Week (1994) News: 'DoE puts muscle on framework of PPG6', **2**, 21, 26 May 1994, p 2

CONSERVATION AND AESTHETICS

Richard Guise

While aesthetic and conservation policies overlap and are inevitably linked, it is desirable to treat them separately for the purposes of analysis and undertaking an audit. This chapter concentrates on examining aesthetics and conservation in the built environment, but the approach and structure of the audit checklists could easily be adapted to landscape and country-side.

AUDITS OF AESTHETIC DECISIONS AND POLICIES

We are currently experiencing a cultural climate of aesthetic pluralism, perhaps a reaction against the flawed certainties of modernism. This pluralism is expressed in a diversity of approach to urban art and architectural design: modernism, post modernism, high tech, neoclassicism, neo-vernacular, deconstructivism are only the main branches of aesthetic expression in the built environment.

How then can we make sense of this aesthetic tower of Babel? Government advice through circulars is not particularly illuminating on this matter, emphasizing the need for planning authorities to avoid aesthetic dogmatism (rightly so), as aesthetics are a highly subjective matter. Nevertheless, while encouraging a hands-off approach, it acknowledges that it is the job of planning authorities to reject 'obviously poor design' – especially in protected environments such as conservation areas and in National Parks – where aesthetic judgements hold some power. Thus we have a two tier level of control which is now being challenged.[1] Shouldn't aesthetic considerations also have significance in areas which perhaps need greater aesthetic improvement?

The consistent (if not particularly well developed) aesthetic concept

---

1 See the Royal Fine Art Commission's booklet *Planning for Beauty*, 1990.

which has guided aesthetic decision making within the planning and amenity movement in Britain is that of appropriateness. Does a particular projected development 'fit in' with its surroundings? This concept needs some unpacking. Firstly it assumes that the surroundings are desirable and need little improvement; then it is assumed by too many that to 'fit in' should mean to copy or at least to follow general guidelines regarding scale, bulk and fenestration. Too many aesthetically lazy planning authorities and developers fall back on stereotyped designs which may have proved aesthetically appropriate in specific contexts at a particular time, but are then repeated on a widespread scale, regardless of the character of other contexts. Thus we see the neo-vernacular 'cottage' styles and materials advocated by the Essex County Council's Design Guide for Residential Areas (1973) applied on an almost national scale in urban, suburban and rural situations, completely negating the intentions of the authors.

To make aesthetic judgements based on the concept of appropriateness to specific local identity, in order to maintain or foster a sense of place, it is essential that a local planning authority makes a survey and statement of the character of various areas within its domain. It must be expected that there will be a diversity of character across a district council area, even across a particular town.

Thus the first expectation in an aesthetic audit is that there should be a perceptive appraisal of the existing character of the various areas that comprise the district.

The character of an area comprises not only its townscape and the geology of its local building materials but also the activities which shape and have shaped its sense of place. The character of an area is made up of the layers of evidence it reveals of its earlier existence; there is no such thing as a virgin site in an ancient land. How many planning authorities even begin to possess such statements, yet how many planning authorities exhort developers to reflect the character of the area?

The aesthetic experience of an area is not only visual, but it involves other senses; the sense of excitement in discovery of a place as spaces and activities are revealed as one moves through an area: sounds, smells, tactile experiences. We should be aware of the conditions which contribute to these experiences and the conditions which cause them to disappear (comprehensive redevelopment, change of ownership, gentrification). Kevin Lynch's book *Managing the Sense of a Region* (1980) gives valuable inventories of sensory experiences we should aim to foster or preserve.

We have had the basic guides to the appraisal of our areas for decades now: Brunskill (1971) on vernacular building patterns, Cullen (1961) on townscape, Lynch (1980) on mental maps and sensory places. We have paid lip service to these but basically ignored them in the drawing up of Local Plans and Conservation Area Policies. And yet we need well-expressed aesthetic policies more than ever. We need them to be robust enough for public inquiries and the public looks to planning authorities to be guardians and perhaps promoters of environmental quality.

Aesthetic judgements, however, challenge all who make those judgements to be thoughtful and perceptive. Too many aesthetic pronouncements are made in headline grabbing one-liners of the 'it looks like a...' school of thought. Immediate gut reaction is something we all have, but we need to reflect and ask ourselves is our reaction a response to the immediately unfamiliar, or do we have a well-justified response? We should remember that sometimes the one-off intrusive element, if done with flair and conviction, can have a place. The Eiffel Tower and Sydney Opera House were considered eyesores at first by many and yet they are the very aesthetic symbols of their city – yet many award-winning, uncompromisingly 20th century forms have become social, technical and aesthetic failures almost from the day the award plaque was fitted to them by the local establishment.

Art and music critics can only gain credibility if they know the repertoire – they know comparable works and comparable interpretations of the same work. Similarly if we intend to undertake aesthetic audits we should have knowledge of comparable work in order to assess relative quality.

Figure 9.1 and Table 9.1 (pages 155 and 157) attempt to encapsulate this approach to making aesthetic decisions by emphasizing the appraisal of context and the unpacking of an aesthetic judgement into a series of sub-judgements. In this way perhaps we can make some headway towards what is appropriate in particular situations, rather than acquiescing to stereotyped aesthetic solutions applied to any locality. It is important that aesthetic auditors are able to set criteria for their judgements and can clearly justify their reasons.

It is important that the audit is undertaken with representatives from a wide section of the community, not just the 'aesthetically aware' civic societies and local authority itself. Children, teenagers, disabled people, the elderly and ethnic groups will all have different perspectives. An audit which reflects a range of inputs will have considerably more authority and influence than a purely internal professional one. Audits and appraisals involving the opinions of various groups have been undertaken and can be developed further. The village appraisals of the early 1980s, the Parish Maps project run by Common Ground and the Domesday programme indicate the levels of interest in this work. Similarly urban studies in schools can undertake appraisal.

Finally, it is perhaps worth quoting at some length from Clough Williams-Ellis' book *England and the Octopus*. Published in 1928[2], it eloquently expresses the aims of an aesthetic audit:

---

2 Williams-Ellis, C (1928) *England and the Octopus* Geoffrey Bles, London; new edition (1975) by Golden Dragon.

Needless to say, the good busybody will not plunge ignorantly into criticism and meddling without preparation, but will take the trouble necessary to discover what are the qualities to be looked for in a building, the presence of which will elevate it into the realm of architecture. The great mass of everyday modern building (in England) is, of course, not architecture at all, not because it is small or plain, but because it lacks all sense of coherence, proportion, mass and line, and because the materials are ill-chosen or improperly used.

Decent architecture does not mean any greater expenditure of money – only of thought and skill.

The 'beginner' might find some such catechism as the following helpful in determining whether any particular building is in a state of grace or no.

1) Are you practical – that is, are you an efficient house, shop, school, factory or church? Can a family be brought up in you, or cheese be sold, or children taught, or boots made, or services be conducted in you with convenience?
2) Are you soundly and honestly built and lastingly weatherproof?
3) If you are new, are you going to look (a) shabby or (b) still raw, in ten years time, or have your materials been so wisely chosen and employed that the years will pleasantly mature and mellow you?
4) Are you beautiful, or at any rate to me, or if not, did you seem so to those who built you, and if so, why?
5) Do you express some sort of an idea – are you, for instance, notably restful or vigorous, empathically horizontal or vertical, demure or gay, refined or robust, light or dark, feminine or masculine? Generally, have you 'character', and if so, of what kind?
6) Are you a good neighbour – do you love the Georgian inn next door, or the Regency chemist's shop opposite, or the pollarded lime trees, or the adjoining church and elm grove, as yourself? Do you do-as-you-would-be-done-by? Do the other buildings and the hills and trees and your surroundings near you generally gain or lose by your presence? In short, have you civilised manners?

Those are the sort of questions that a building should be expected to answer and will answer, readily and volubly, to a reasonably skilful examiner.

Such inquiries will naturally lead on to a more detailed and technical analysis of a building's make-up.

Where, for instance, is the proportion between wall surface and window openings, what are the proportions of the windows themselves and even of their panes? Are they successful and pleasant, or is the effect either blank and depressing or distractingly fussy?

How is the roof treated? Does it finish behind a parapet or overhang at the eaves, and if so, too much or too little?

Is the pitch of the roof too high or too low or just right – are its slates or tiles of pleasant colour and texture, soft and 'strokeable', or crude, hard and machine-made-looking?

Are the chimneys tall and important enough, or, on the other hand, top-heavy-looking? If there are mouldings or stone dressings, are they well pro-portioned and well placed, or over-emphatic or overdone?

Finally, is it a decent, sensible, straightforward-looking job, or a brutal, mutton-fisted 'Don't Care' botch, or a silly, dolled-up affair of whim-whams and features that make it a worse neighbour than the downright 'tough' – the frankly blackguard building that has no pretences or illusions about being genteel?

To be able to size up and classify and condemn or approve every building that you come across – as you may soon come to do instinctively – naturally adds prodigiously to the interest of your surroundings, wherever you may be, at home or abroad.

Williams-Ellis (1928)

CONSERVATION

The record of designation of conservation areas and implementation of conservation policies in the built environment reveals considerable dis-parities between the approaches of different local authorities. These dis-parities stem to some extent from the discretion given to local authorities within the framework of legislation and government advice.

While a degree of local discretion is to be welcomed as it allows flexibility and varied approaches to be adopted, it is important for officers, elected members, local civic societies, residents associations and interested indi-viduals to take stock from time to time and consider whether the con-servation work being undertaken in the area

- is what is required in terms of an overall conservation strategy;
- is effective;
- does not have undesirable outcomes (eg displacement of activities/uses);
- is aesthetically pleasing;
- has integrity in terms of conservation aims (eg not bogus histori-cism).

The disparity of policy generation and implementation is probably due to a number of interacting factors, for example:

- level of suitably qualified specialist staff;
- level of financial resources;
- motivation of officers;
- degree of political will by members (conservation might not be regarded as a high priority);
- lack of pressure from residents and civic societies – possibly because the area is *a)* not perceived as particularly interesting, thus no 'need' for conservation; or *b)* is self conserving: no need for intervention.

151

Because of the considerable disparities of approach and in the face of a consistent lack of monitoring by Central Government of listed building or conservation area activity, there have been a number of attempts at auditing performance.

The Civic Trust in the 60s and 70s produced lists of conservation areas by local authority districts, and produced 'blacklists' of those authorities which had not designated a single conservation area. This task was considerably expanded when the English Tourist Board started to produce its annual English Heritage Monitors from 1977. These monitor expenditure on projects, highlight case studies of good practice as well as listing conservation areas and numbers of listed buildings. The Environment Committee of the House of Commons produced its one-off report (DoE, 1987) which also took stock of progress with conservation policy.

The Annual Reports of the Historic Buildings Council, prior to its transformation to English Heritage, were also a source of monitoring progress. Nevertheless this produced only partial snapshots and English Heritage commissioned a Report on the Conservation Areas of England in Regional Volumes (Pearce et al, 1990; DoE 1994). At the same time the Civic Trust published its Environmental Audit (1991). The Royal Town Planning Institute commissioned a study into the reasons for the designation of Conservation Areas and their character (Jones and Larkham, 1993).

The latter report is valuable in looking at the range of authorities and their approaches to conservation area designation and their assessment of the character of areas. It also provides a good background to conservation policy since 1967. While it indicates topics which should be included in a character appraisal it is not wholly comprehensive; perhaps the uses and other non-visual aspects of character need more acknowledgement. 'Character' as a concept is inferred but might need further definition. The Planning Policy Guidance Note No 15 (DoE, 1994) covering conservation areas and listed buildings should also be consulted to build up a knowledge of recommended good practice. Many of the recommendations are absorbed in the checklist for the conservation audit which follows.

The tally of conservation areas is presently around 8,000 and rising, about twice the number envisaged at the outset. Why? Why are they being designated at a time when there is strictly limited money to implement policies except through control? The same can be said of the over half a million listed buildings.

It is likely that we shall experience a continuing trend of designations; it is unlikely that we shall experience an 'end state' of a final inventory of conservation areas and listed buildings. This is due to two main reasons. First, that designation is often seen as the only way to exert some control over inappropriate development, not subject to control under standard planning legislation (ie permitted development).

Secondly, tastes change. A generation ago few would regard Victorian architecture as worthy of protection, yet today it is valued as an important period of cultural and engineering development. Similarly today we seek to protect 'vernacular' buildings (eg cottages and farm buildings) which in the past were taken for granted as they were not threatened with extinction.

CHECKLISTS

Below is a list of suggested criteria against which the work of an authority can be assessed:

Conservation audit

▶ Record of designation of conservation areas

▶ Record of amendment of conservation area boundaries

▶ Published schemes of preservation and enhancement

▶ Implemented schemes of preservation and enhancement

▶ Is the local authority considering further conservation area designations? (Are these based on suggestions from local authority, Civic Society, Conservation Area Advisory Committee, Other?)

▶ Has the authority produced any character statements or appraisals for each of its conservation areas?

▶ Record of additions to the Statutory List of Buildings of Architectural or Historic Interest

▶ Does the local authority analyse its stock of listed buildings (by type, style, material, period etc)?

▶ Record of town schemes, of other conservation programmes and initiatives, eg living over the shop schemes

▶ Record of delisting or consideration of the de-designation of a conservation area

▶ Is there a Buildings at Risk register?

▶ Record of successful/unsuccessful application of Article 4 Directions (covering extensions etc) to protect character of the area's conservation areas

▶ Are there any local authority initiatives to protect areas of residential character by designation of special zones or special design advice?

▶ Record of special policies to protect skylines, infill etc, eg design guides and/or briefs

▶ Record of Tree Preservation Orders

▶ Record of enforcement of Building Preservation Notices, Repairs Notices etc

▶ Evidence of commercial sponsorship of conservation schemes awards/competitions for new development in conservation areas

▶ Existence of Conservation Area Advisory Committee Involvement of Civic Society in conservation schemes

▶ Record of partnership with Utilities on siting, coordination and design of utility works in conservation areas

▶ Amount of conservation budget

▶ Procedure for identifying and saving traditional building and paving materials which otherwise would be lost by redevelopment

▶ Fostering of use of natural building materials – eg encouraging opening up of quarries, local brick and tile works etc

▶ Qualifications status and number of staff allocated to conservation duties.

Aesthetic audit

▶ Does the local authority concentrate its 'aesthetic policies' either on conservation areas and other designated areas or throughout its domain?

▶ Is there an emphasis on aesthetic conformity ('ideal' styles or approaches) or aesthetic diversity (are the aesthetics of various communities acknowledged/celebrated)?

▶ Are aesthetics regarded as visual aesthetic only, or are there attempts to enhance other sensory experiences (eg sounds, smells, levels of vitality)?

▶ Are there published appraisals of the character of areas?

▶ Are aesthetic factors significant and well expressed in the purchasing policy of street furniture, signage, play equipment, landscape, paving etc, both in design and location? How are these decisions made? Who makes them?

▶ Are enhancement schemes planned or in progress
  – in conservation areas?
  – in other areas?

▶ Do Restrictive Covenants/Article 4 Directions exist to 'control' aesthetics?

▶ Is there an urban art policy/programme?
  If yes – does it involve local groups?
        – is there an artist in residence?
        – does it seek to involve the viewer/user (sculpture for blind people, play sculpture)?
        – is there a percentage for art policy for major developments?

▶ Does the local authority encourage local festivals, street theatre, events?

▶ Are there urban trails etc to encourage local awareness?

State of Environment audit

The following figures would form the basis of such an audit – assessing the built outcome of aesthetic and conservation decision making. The two checklists concentrate on organisation management and policy; these being policy impact audits or management audits posing questions of an authority about its structures for achieving quality in the built environment. These audits could be undertaken as part of an in-house appraisal by officers, or by members or by independent lay auditors – they do not need expertise; the questions need to be asked and the answers need substantiating.

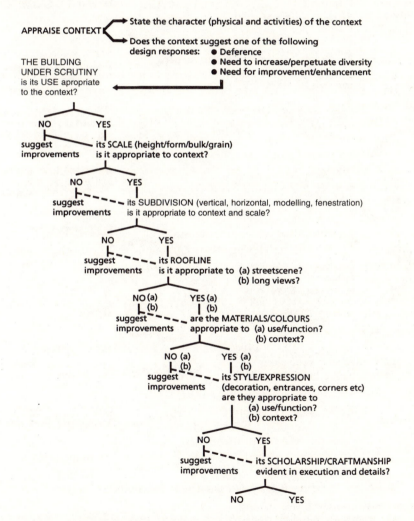

Figure 9.1 A suggested structure for aesthetic assessment of building design

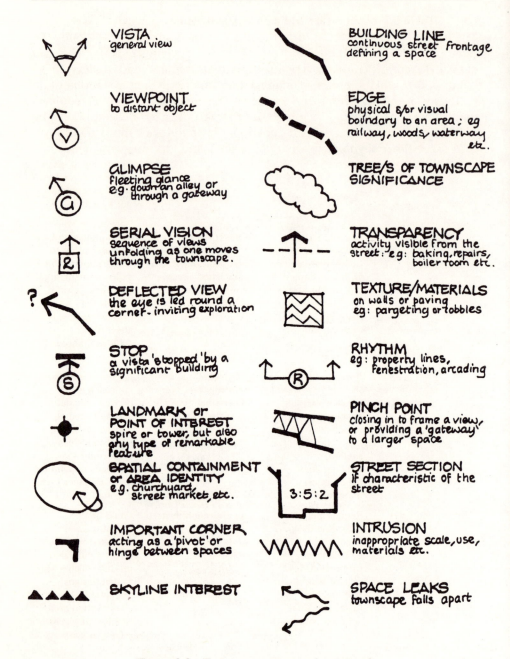

VISTA
general view

VIEWPOINT
to distant object

GLIMPSE
fleeting glance
e.g. down an alley or
through a gateway

SERIAL VISION
sequence of views
unfolding as one moves
through the townscape.

DEFLECTED VIEW
the eye is led round a
corner - inviting exploration

STOP
a vista 'stopped' by a
significant building

**LANDMARK or
POINT OF INTEREST**
spire or tower, but also
any type of remarkable
feature

**SPATIAL CONTAINMENT
or AREA IDENTITY**
e.g. churchyard,
street market, etc.

IMPORTANT CORNER
acting as a 'pivot' or
hinge between spaces

SKYLINE INTEREST

BUILDING LINE
continuous street frontage
defining a space

EDGE
physical &/or visual
boundary to an area; eg
railway, woods, waterway
etc.

**TREE/S OF TOWNSCAPE
SIGNIFICANCE**

TRANSPARENCY
activity visible from the
street; e.g. baking, repairs,
boiler room etc.

TEXTURE/MATERIALS
on walls or paving
eg: pargeting or cobbles

RHYTHM
eg: property lines,
fenestration, arcading

PINCH POINT
closing in to frame a view,
or providing a 'gateway'
to a larger space

STREET SECTION
if characteristic of the
street

3:5:2

INTRUSION
inappropriate scale, use,
materials etc.

SPACE LEAKS
townscape falls apart

Figure 9.2   Townscape appraisal notation*

* R Guise, after Cullen, Lynch, et al
These symbols are intended as an aid to your observation and assessment of an area; it's not an exhaustive
list – add your own symbols and annotations

Table 9.1 Approaches to the design of buildings in infill locations

Infill design options	Characteristics	Context	Comment
Retain facade	Original building gutted, facade retained and tied back to new structure. New structure must relate to existing storey heights on facade.	This option adopted when the facade is recognized as the most important feature of the building, or is crucial to the street scene.	Too often an expedient to maximize site value yet retain familiar facade. Purists (conservation and modernists) concerned at loss of integrity. Often stability problems during conversion.
Copy existing or adjacent	Either on vacant site, or a rebuild of existing unstable building. Adjacent buildings copied in bay widths storey heights. Fenestration, materials, jointing, decoration.	Usually most appropriate in a unified townscape composition eg unfinished Georgian square. Otherwise when a listed building is demolished and required to be replaced.	Deceptively easy option, but requires great attention to detail, supervision and workmanship. Materials (natural) may be very expensive. How is effect of age to be achieved? Should it be?
'Rational' or objective parameters	Basic briefing by planners regarding the new building envelope: includes massing layout, scale, views, heights skyline, proportions, building lines, fenestration, materials, etc	Appropriate in most typical street scenes where maintenance of scale is important, but style could be varied	A 'cool' measurable approach which can be well articulated and defended at appeal, by LA. Can result in lifeless conformity – good solutions depend on good architect/LA negotiation
Neutral/deferential	Requirements regarding the overall effect of the building, eg balanced proportions and regular window/wall relationships. Recessive, low-contrast colours	An approach devised to set off the quality of its (varied) neighbours	Could be monotonous if overused in same street. Could also produce cliché-ridden designs 'acceptable' in conservation areas eg false mansards or reflective glass

Table 9.1 Continued

Infill design options	Characteristics	Context	Comment
Context-expressive	An eclectic approach drawn from an analysis and response to the character style & use of the street or area. Light hearted. Often Post-modern in style	Usually in an area of varied and rich character, not especially of 'High' architecture but mixed use, adapted areas	At best it is both scholarly and witty in its references and adaption of motifs. Relies on choice of good architect. At worst can be glib and can look tatty/ outdated in a short time
Bold contrast/ structure-expressive	A Modernist/high tech approach; an expression and celebration of contemporary technology and building functions	Appropriate a) in confined sites as one-off jewel-like contrast b) in larger cleared or rundown areas where a statement of change and confidence is needed	Appropriate if scale is right. Should be 'friendly' at street level; (transparent, accessible). Could be dull or over assertive if not well designed. What effect if repeated in same street?

REFERENCES

Brunskill, R W (1971) *Illustrated Handbook of Vernacular Architecture* Faber & Faber, London

Civic Trust (1991) *Audit of the Environment* Civic Trust, London

Cullen, G (1961) *Townscape,* Architectural Press, London

Department of the Environment (1987) *Historic Buildings and Conservation Areas* HMSO

Department of the Environment (1994), *Planning Policy Guidance Note No 15: Planning and the Historic Environment* HMSO, London

Essex County Council (1973) *A Design Guide for Residential Areas* Essex County Council Planning Department

Hillman, J (1990) *Planning for Beauty* Royal Fine Art Commission, London

Jones, A and Larkham, P (1993) *The Character of Conservation Areas* Royal Town Planning Institute, London

Lynch, K (1976) *Managing the Sense of a Region* MIT Press, Cambridge, Massachusetts

Pearce, G; Hems, L and Hennessy, B (1990) *The Conservation Areas of England* English Heritage, London

Williams-Ellis, C (1928) *England and the Octopus* Geoffrey Bles, see New edition (1975), Golden Dragon

10

POLLUTION CONTROL

David S Dickerson

INTRODUCTION

The earth could be described as the ultimate waste recycling unit. Many pollutants are present naturally in the environment and while possessing the potential to cause harm, will pass through the environment, life cycles and food chains as valuable nutrients to the benefit of organisms and ecosystems without causing damage or harm to the environment. For example, oxides of nitrogen produced by lightning and washed out as nitrates in rainfall provide a valuable fertilizer nutrient to plants.

It is not until critical concentrations of pollutants are exceeded or the discharge of unnatural compounds which interfere with physical, chemical or metabolic processes that pollution takes place. Discharges of 'natural' compounds from septic tank outfalls into rivers in remote locations can increase the number and diversity of species present whereas a discharge of untreated sewage effluent from a village or town in a similar location could eliminate all aerobic life in the river. Unnatural compounds such as chlorofluorocarbons (CFCs) released into the atmosphere will diffuse into the stratosphere because of their low solubility in rainfall. In the stratosphere, intense sunlight breaks down the CFCs to liberate free chlorine radicals which are responsible for the destruction of the ozone layer with associated risk of skin cancer at ground level. Other unnatural compounds such as DDT or PCBs, when dispersed into the environment, accumulate through food chains until harmful concentrations are reached.

Ecosystems also have the ability to adapt to and recover from the effects of pollutants. Land at Charterhouse on the Mendips was devoid of vegetation at the turn of this century because of high concentrations of heavy metals in surface soils brought about by the mining and smelting of lead. However, leaching of metals out of the surface soils through the action of rainfall and adaptation of a range of plant species have enabled revegetation of the area to take place including a number of species of orchids.

Awareness of these concepts of pollution can be traced through the history of the UK with the earliest statutory controls prohibiting the burning of coal in London in 1273. Penalties were more drastic than today and one persistent offender was beheaded! John Evelyn vividly described the pollution of London in 1661 and proposed practical measures for the

Improvement and melioration of the filthy clowds of smoake and sulphur so full of stink and darknesse over a glorious and antient city.

Evelyn, 1661

Evelyn's recommendations were not adopted and the advent of the industrial revolution greatly increased sources of pollutants in cities and towns leading to a further deterioration of environmental quality. It was not until the early part of the 19th century that Parliamentary committees were set up to investigate and propose statutory measures to control pollution. Early statutory controls such as the Public Health Act 1848 and Alkali Act 1863 have since been developing alongside the common law to protect the rights of individuals and society as a whole against the effects of pollution. These statutory provisions concentrated on individual sectors of the environment with controls that had developed by the 1970s through a range of enforcement agencies including:

- **Local authorities:** Air quality management and air pollution control, control of noise and other nuisances, and control of waste disposal.
- **Alkali inspectorate:** Air pollution control from major industrial plants.
- **Regional Water Authorities:** Water supply, control of discharges into sewers and rivers and sewage treatment and disposal.

However, effective environmental management and pollution control requires an holistic understanding of natural environmental processes and the interactions and effects of pollutants to determine whether environmental pollution is taking place alongside the selection of appropriate levels of control.

This concept was recognized for the first time in legislation in the Environmental Protection Act 1990 (DoE, 1990) with a definition of pollution that embraces the environment as an integrated whole:

Pollution of the environment due to the release [to any environmental medium] from any process of substances which are capable of causing harm to man or any other living organisms supported by the environment.

The environment is defined as consisting of:

All, or any of the following media, namely, the air, water and land; and the medium of air includes the air within buildings and the air within other natural or man-made structures above or below ground.

The interpretation of harm is crucial to the definition of pollution and is taken to mean:

Harm to the health of living organisms or other interference with the ecological systems of which they form part and in the case of man includes causing offence to his senses or harm to property.

In addition, integrated pollution control was introduced for major industrial plants where the best practicable environmental option is used to prevent or minimize pollution. The concept of 'Best Practicable Environmental Option' was introduced in the 5th Report of the Royal Commission on Environmental Pollution in 1975 (RCEP, 1975) and was the subject of the 12th Report in 1988, (RCEP, 1988) (see Box 10.1). In the 12th report, BPEO was defined as: 'The optimal allocation of the waste spatially; the use of different sectors of the environment to minimise damage overall'.

Future controls over all sources of pollution should encompass the concepts of the best practicable environmental option.

THE ROLE OF LOCAL AUTHORITIES IN POLLUTION CONTROL

The historical role of local authorities in pollution control has been divided between district and county councils. District councils have been responsible for monitoring levels of air and noise pollution in addition to a range of activities that may be prejudicial to health or give rise to a nuisance. Powers to control or prevent risks from these activities are exercised through planning or pollution control legislation. For effective environmental con-

---

Box 10.1 Best Practicable Environmental Option

In establishing the best practicable environmental option, the disposal route (air, water or land) must be selected only after a detailed analysis of options has been made including steps necessary to reduce waste to the minimum practicable. BPEO should be considered at the initial stages of the development of projects. It need not be complex but should be comprehensive, dealing with the whole environment, anticipating effects of discharges on the environment and considering the control of pollution by a range of technologies, recycling and waste disposal. The preferred option should be examined in detail and the cost of pollution control balanced against the protection of the environment. An audit trail should be used to record the decision process and decisions should be open to scrutiny. Finally, the selection of BPEO should be kept under review as circumstances change.

Source: 5th Report of the Royal Commission on Environmental Pollution, 1975

---

trol, knowledge and understanding of the local and regional environment is necessary to assess the effects of current and proposed development. County Councils were responsible for waste disposal but this role has been transferred with extended powers under Part 2 of the Environmental Protection Act 1990 to Waste Regulation Authorities. For example, the duty of care under section 34 of the Act can be used to prevent contamination of land from the storage, handling or transport of waste. The Waste Regulation Authorities will merge with Her Majesty's Inspectorate of Pollution and the National Rivers Authority in due course to form the UK Environmental Protection Agency.

Control of pollution by agencies such as Her Majesty's Inspectorate of Pollution and the National Rivers Authority is by national organization administered through regional offices. Local authorities have a valuable role to play in association with the national authorities in relaying information about the local environment or pollution incidents. Local authorities can also provide the local base through which the public can gain access to pollution monitoring and control information from other pollution enforcement agencies.

The policies and activities of the local authority will also have an impact on pollution of the environment, for example transport, energy and employment policies. Local authorities therefore have a vital role to play in the control of pollution and any environmental policy of the authority should embrace strategies and initiatives to address both local and global pollution issues.

POLLUTION POLICY ISSUES

The policies of local authorities to control pollution in a manner appropriate to sustainable development should encompass the global issues of UN Agenda 21 and the EU Action Programmes on the Environment within the philosophy 'Think globally, act locally'. Such policies will be revised and updated in the light of new findings. A summary of current issues follows.

Air quality

The EU has set air quality standards through a number of Directives for sulphur dioxide and particulates, nitrogen dioxide and lead; ozone is the subject of a Draft Directive. These standards are being restructured and extended under a Proposed Framework Directive on the assessment and management of air quality with Sectoral Directives for individual pollutants (EU, 1994).

These standards are being set to protect human health, the environment and sensitive ecosystems and World Health Organisation (WHO) Air

Quality Guidelines for Europe are likely to be applied (WHO, 1987).[1] Long-term limit values and short-term alert thresholds will be set for each pollutant. Where limit values are exceeded, measures must be taken to reduce concentrations which must be reduced to within the limit within 10 or 15 years. Where alert thresholds are exceeded, the public must be informed.

Standards for sulphur dioxide, nitrogen oxides, black smoke, suspended particulates, lead and ozone will be established before the end of 1996. Standards for carbon monoxide, acid deposition, benzene, aromatic poly-cyclic hydrocarbons (APH), arsenic, fluoride and nickel will be established before the end of 1999.

Local authorities have powers under the Environmental Protection Act to investigate circumstances that may be prejudicial to health or a nuisance. In addition, powers are available in the Clean Air Act 1993 to undertake or fund research relevant to the subject of air pollution. Monitoring should be undertaken to ascertain compliance with air quality standards and guidelines, to identify particular sources of air pollution and to assist in the development of control strategies through a range of measures such as location, process controls and emission controls.

Volatile Organic Compounds – VOCs

VOCs represent a wide range of organic compounds from many sources such as combustion, transport, incineration and use of solvents in industrial processes. Certain VOCs are toxic or carcinogenic while others are involved in the formation of ozone through complex reactions between oxides of nitrogen and sunlight.

The EU has set targets for a 10 per cent reduction of man-made emissions of VOCs by the end of 1996 and a 30 per cent reduction of 1990 levels by the year 2000 (EC, 1992). This will be achieved by tighter controls on emissions from industry through the proposed Directive on VOCs by December 1996 and by additional controls on transport. Emphasis should be placed on reduction and elimination of compounds which are classified as carcinogens, mutagens and toxic to reproduction, as well as those that are chlorinated (known as Article 7 compounds). Local authorities should be monitoring ambient air quality to identify where air quality guidelines and standards are being exceeded.

Heavy metals

The EU has set a target of at least a 70 per cent reduction from all pathways of cadmium, mercury and lead emissions by the end of 1995 (EC, 1992). This will be achieved by control of emissions at source by substitution (eg lead-

---

1 See Appendix 1.

free petrol) or by more stringent controls on emissions (eg improved arrestment plant).

Local authorities should investigate all sources of heavy metals in their area and establish the best practicable environmental option to control releases. Where metals are released, monitoring should be undertaken to ensure air and water quality standards are not exceeded.

Dioxins

Dioxins and furans have been subjected to stringent controls because of evidence of harm to life at extremely low concentrations. These compounds could be produced during the combustion of chlorinated compounds in municipal, clinical or hazardous waste incineration processes in addition to cremation. The EU has set targets for a 90 per cent reduction of 1985 levels of dioxin emissions from identified sources by 2005 (EC, 1992).

Local authorities within a region should cooperate to establish a policy that embraces the best practicable environmental option on the disposal of such wastes. This may involve a rationalization of incineration facilities and pretreatment of wastes to ensure that incinerators under their control are provided with the best available technology and are operated under optimum combustion conditions to ensure the destruction of these compounds. Alternatives to such incineration should also be considered, eg the sterilization of certain clinical wastes with disposal by landfill (Smith, 1994).

Acidification

Combustion of fossil fuels and agricultural practices are changing soil pH causing mobilization of toxic metals into surface and ground water. Critical loads have been calculated for the deposition of acid (sulphates or nitrates) or alkali (ammonia) to identify soils that are at risk.

The EU has set the aim that critical loads should not be exceeded; to achieve this aim, emissions of NO_x should be stabilized at 1990 levels in 1994 with a 30 per cent reduction in 2000, while emissions of SO_2 should be reduced by 35 per cent of 1985 levels in 2000 (EC, 1992).

Local authorities should assess their areas to ascertain whether critical loads are being exceeded or whether emissions from their area are causing critical loads to be exceeded in other areas. Policies for controlling such emissions should be developed, eg transport, the nature of industrial development, energy efficiency and the use of appropriate fuels.

Climate change

Releases of greenhouse gases could pose problems through global warming which may affect meteorological patterns, climate, flooding and agriculture.

Targets have been set within the EU to stabilize 1990 levels of CO_2 emission by the year 2000, to phase out CFCs and other ozone-depleting substances by 1996 and to gather information of releases of methane and nitrous oxide (EC, 1992).

Many authorities have set targets to reduce energy consumption and CO_2 emissions which can be achieved by improved insulation of buildings, combined heat and power and district heating schemes. However, little is known about actual CO_2 emissions within the boundaries of local authorities from industry, transport, domestic and commercial sources. Emission inventories should be established alongside other atmospheric pollutants and control strategies devised.

Noise

Complaints about noise to local authorities from all sources continue to increase, placing heavy demands on the resources of authorities. EU targets for night-time exposure to noise are to phase out exposures above 65 dB(A) L_{eq} and prevent any increase in noise exposure below this level (EC, 1992).

Effective control of noise by local authorities will involve liaison between Planning and Environmental Health Departments to separate noise sensitive developments from noise generating activities. In addition, sufficient resources must be available to establish current background noise levels and control existing noise sources by a range of educational, legislative and technological approaches.

Contaminated land

Government policy in dealing with contaminated land is as follows:

- Prevention or minimization of new pollution with the polluter paying for any damage or necessary controls.
- Dealing with existing contamination which poses actual or suspected risks to health or the environment.
- Improving sites to a level suitable for the proposed land use.
- Encouraging the development of land subject to potential or actual contamination provided appropriate investigations and remediation work are carried out.

District Councils have an important role to play in controlling the redevelopment of contaminated land and in preventing new developments that may contaminate land. Proposals for the possible reclamation and use of contaminated land can be included in development plans and Government grants may be available for the cost of investigations and remediation. In 1992/93, a total of £157 million was awarded for investigations and remediation of derelict land in England and Wales.

Controls on the redevelopment of contaminated land depend on identification, and the remediation appropriate to the proposed land use, or restrictions on land use dependent upon the level of contamination.

Section 143 of the Environmental Protection Act 1990 enables the Secretary of State to make regulations requiring local authorities to compile and maintain registers of land which is being or has been put to contaminative use and would assist in the identification of such contamination. However, the term 'contaminative use' does not necessarily indicate *actual* contamination and the proposed regulations met with considerable opposition because of the potential blighting of properties on or near to land on the register. It is therefore likely that section 143 will be withdrawn. Nevertheless, information held by local authorities in relation to contaminated land should be made available to the public under the Environmental Information Regulations 1992.

Local authorities should continue to gather information on the historical use of land as an indication of whether contamination may have taken place. Where such evidence exists, appraisals of the risk to health and of damage to the environment should be carried out with appropriate site surveys (vegetation surveys can provide an initial indication of the location and extent of contamination). Priorities should be set for making contaminated sites safe and remediating sites to a level appropriate to current or proposed use with the onus on polluters, owners or developers to undertake the work. Where contaminated land is in public ownership, funding should be sought to enable remediation and beneficial development of the land to take place in preference to new development on green field sites.

Water

The control of water in England and Wales is exercised by the National Rivers Authority and private water companies. Nevertheless, local authorities have roles to play in the control of drinking and bathing water quality, in the prevention of pollution of fresh and marine surface waters and ground water, the restoration of natural ground water and surface waters to an ecologically sound condition, and in ensuring that water demand and water supply are brought into equilibrium on the basis of more rational use and management of water resources.

Local authorities are also users of water and through their activities will contribute to the overall load on sewage treatment works as well as surface runoff into water courses. The use of biocides is also likely to cause a deterioration of water quality.

Planning controls over the use of land for the purposes of housing, tourism, roads, industry or agricultural use will affect the demand for water and the nature and quality of discharges into the aquatic environment. The establishment and achievement of statutory water quality objectives for improvements in ground and river water quality will require cooperation between the various pollution enforcement agencies coupled with pollution control strategies establishing the best practicable environmental option.

Overall

As a basis for the Pollution Policy, priorities should be set for relevant issues with objectives, targets and timescales depending on local conditions and circumstances. Proper resources and personnel must be provided to implement the pollution control policies having regard to the best practicable environmental option. The responsibility and relationship of key personnel must be defined and documented. There should also be effective communication with staff, councillors and the public coupled with training programmes for relevant personnel.

POLLUTION CONTROL AUDITS

1) **State of the Environment Audits:** To assess information on the natural environment alongside pollutant emissions and the achievement of environmental quality standards
2) **Pollution Management Audits:** To review and assess the effectiveness of policies of the authority in relation to initiatives tackling pollution and the enforcement and effectiveness of legislation controlling pollution.

STATE OF THE ENVIRONMENT AUDIT

Effective pollution control and environmental management requires an understanding of the natural environment alongside the interactions and effects of pollutants on human beings and other living organisms supported by the environment. Detailed information on the nature and quantity of pollutants emitted is also necessary to assess likely environmental levels and trends in emissions. Modelling of emissions can be carried out in association with meteorological, hydrological or geological data to predict the dispersion or propagation of pollutants in the environment. Resultant environmental levels will also depend on removal mechanisms and other interactions such as solubility, adsorption, biodegradation, and chemical and photochemical reactions which can be incorporated into the models. Local environmental monitoring should be used to validate the models as well as establishing compliance with environmental quality standards and guidelines. Environmental risk assessment incorporating the Best Practicable Environmental Options should also be incorporated into the setting of environmental targets and objectives in the management of local environmental quality. Examples of the application of this information includes:

- establishing the source of industrial emissions causing a nuisance in the neighbourhood;
- determining appropriate levels of control in existing pollution problems such as high concentrations of oxides of nitrogen from motor vehicles;
- response to accident situations with the release of hazardous material into the environment at potentially harmful concentrations;
- the appraisal of proposals for new development in relation to the effects on the environment; and
- epidemiological investigations to establish links with pollution sources.

Most Environmental Health Departments of local authorities provide annual reports on air and water quality, noise and contaminated land. An increasing number of authorities are extending these reports to include meteorological data alongside the development and use of air quality dispersion models (meteorological stations gathering detailed weather data can be linked by modem to the authority's offices for under £1000). This information should be extended to incorporate environmental risk assessment and the rationale for setting priorities for action.

Powers of local authorities to gather such information in relation to air pollution originated in the Public Health Act 1936 but are now contained within the Clean Air Act 1993. The Environmental Information Regulations 1992 implemented the requirements of the EU Directive EC 313/90 requiring public authorities to provide environmental information to the public.

On the national level, the annual Digest of Environmental Protection Statistics (HMSO, 1978) provides an excellent overview of the state of environmental quality in the UK which could be replicated at the local level. Furthermore, as part of the 5th Action Programme on the Environment, the EU has published a general overview of the state of the environment and natural resources in the Community, of the damage and pressures to which they are exposed and of the changes and trends observed (EC, 1992). The UK Government has also published pollution control policies within the Strategy for Sustainable Development (DoE, 1994a), and the UK Programme for Climate Change (DoE, 1994b). These documents provide the basis from which environmental policies can be made and targets set. A similar approach should be adopted at the local level with local authorities continuing to develop their role as custodians of the local environment.

Information that should be collected, evaluated and appraised to provide an effective pollution control and environmental management service is indicated in Box 10.2 (see Checklists). Expert advice may, however, be necessary to establish the location, nature and extent of environmental data that should be gathered, processed and evaluated.

Box 10.2   Information necessary to provide an effective pollution control and environmental management service

WEATHER DATA

To be used for air pollution dispersion models, energy demand and water quality models:

- Wind speed and direction
- Rainfall
- Temperature
- Humidity
- Atmospheric pressure
- Stability class
- Solar radiation including UV-B

AIR POLLUTION

Sources

To prepare emission inventories and predict ground level concentrations through dispersion modelling:

- Authorization
- Emission limits
- Chimney heights
- Discharge parameters:
    - temperature
    - volume
    - efflux velocity
    - concentration of pollutants
    - mass emission

Environmental levels

To ascertain compliance with air quality standards and guidelines, to investigate and establish sources of air pollution and to gather data for epidemiological studies:

- Total particulates
- Respirable particulates (PM10)
- Oxides of sulphur
- Oxides of nitrogen
- Volatile organic compounds (VOCs)
- Heavy metals
- Radon and other gases
- Odours

Dispersion models
To predict the likely effects of proposed developments or accidents on environmental quality.

- Point source
- Line source
- Area source
- Ambient air quality

NOISE POLLUTION

Sources
To monitor compliance with standards and establish measures to remedy any nuisances or excessive levels:

- Domestic
- Commercial
- Industrial
- Motor vehicles
- Railways
- Airports
- Leisure activities

Environmental levels
To establish background levels and prevent any deterioration in environmental quality with respect to noise.

Models
To predict the likely effects of proposed developments on environmental quality by noise propagation and attenuation:

- Construction
- Industry
- Roads
- Railways
- Airports

WATER POLLUTION

To provide information on resources, water quality and sources of pollutants:

- Natural river water quality
- Natural ground water quality
- Sources of pollution:
  - domestic
  - agricultural
  - industrial
- Discharge consents:

- location
- discharge parameters
  temperature
  volume
  concentration of pollutants
- River water quality
- Ground water quality
- Bathing water quality
- Drinking water quality

Models
Dispersion in ground water, rivers and estuaries.

LAND POLLUTION
To provide information on ground water resources, quality and flow, contaminated land and suitability of land use.

- Natural geology
  - characteristics
  - permeability
  - ground water flow
- Contaminated land:
  - location
    type of industry/activity
    date/duration of activity/contamination
    significance of contamination (low/moderate/high)
  - nature of pollutants
    asbestos
    metals and metalloids
    inorganic anions
    organic compounds/material
  - properties of pollutants
    pH/solubility/redox potential
    chemical reactions – synergism/antagonism
    persistence
    evaporation/dust potential
    adsorption/absorption
    degradation/production of methane and other gases
  - likely effects
    air quality
    fire/explosion risk
    water quality
    damage to materials
    bioaccumulation
    toxicity to humans and ecosystems

POLLUTION MANAGEMENT AUDIT

Pollution management audits should review and assess the effectiveness of policies of the authority in relation to initiatives tackling pollution and the enforcement and effectiveness of legislation controlling pollution. The British Standards Institute document BS7750 (1994) provides a specification for environmental management systems to demonstrate compliance with a stated environmental policy (BSI, 1994a).

The elements of the environmental management system under BS7750 (1994) can be applied to the enforcement activities and initiatives of local authorities related to pollution control providing an indication of policies, procedures, activities and actions to be audited. The objectives, scope and execution of the audit should be clearly defined (BSI, 1994b). Areas likely to be covered by the audit include:

1) **Organization:**
   - Organization structures and responsibilities to implement pollution control policies and initiatives including relationships between different departments, committees and agencies.
2) **Knowledge:**
   - Knowledge and understanding of legislative controls, standards, guidelines and targets.
   - Knowledge and understanding of the environment, ecosystems and the interactions between individual sectors.
3) **Human, physical and financial resources:**
   - Sufficient staff, training and qualifications.
   - Monitoring and control equipment, access to information and databases, office/work facilities, communications.
   - Sufficient provision for current and anticipated legislative requirements and other environmentally friendly initiatives.
4) **Administrative and operational procedures:**
   - Management procedures and manuals, operational controls, production of records and reports and quality assurance.
5) **Environmental performance:**
   - Compliance with legislation, emission and environmental quality standards and targets.
   - Effectiveness of surveys, assessment and evaluation of monitoring data.
   - Use of environmental models in pollution control and environmental quality management.
   - Enforcement action, response to complaints and incidents including emergency situations.

The main function of the audit is to identify difficulties or deficiencies in implementing the Pollution Management System or in gathering, assessing and evaluating environmental information. The audit may simply note problems, or may suggest remedial measures.

The Pollution Policy will have to be reviewed to establish its continuing effectiveness. Matters to be addressed as part of the review process include:

- Any recommendations which have been made in pollution management audit reports, and how these should be implemented
- The continuing suitability of environmental policy, and whether it should be revised in the light of, for example:
  - growing environmental concerns in specific areas;
  - developing understanding of environmental issues;
  - potential regulatory developments;
  - concerns among interested parties;
  - market pressures;
  - changing activities of the authority; and
  - changes in sensitivity of the environment.
- The continuing suitability of environmental targets and objectives, and any revisions to the environmental management programme.

CHECKLISTS

The checklists form the conclusion and summary of this chapter. The first section presents some 'general' principles from the EU action programmes relevant to pollution control, and could be used as an aid in gauging the performance of the authority in relation to pollution control issues:

- ▶ Are the principles of 'Prevention is better than cure' and 'Any damage should be rectified at source' being applied?
- ▶ Is the precautionary principle being applied?
- ▶ Are environmental effects being taken into account at the earliest possible stage in decision making?
- ▶ Is the exploitation of nature or natural resources which cause significant damage to ecological balance being avoided?
- ▶ Is scientific knowledge to enable appropriate action to be taken being improved?
- ▶ Does the polluter pay?
- ▶ Is protection of the environment a matter for everyone?
- ▶ Is training and education on environmental issues and pollution control taking place?
- ▶ Is environmentally relevant data readily available?
- ▶ Is the appropriate level of control being applied?
- ▶ Is sustainable growth respecting the environment being promoted?

POLLUTION CHECKLISTS

Air Quality

▶ Is monitoring being undertaken to ensure compliance with EU air quality standards (see Box 10.3) for sulphur dioxide, particulates, nitrogen dioxide and lead?

▶ Are World Health Organisation (WHO) guidelines being applied for organic and inorganic compounds (Box 10.4), as well as considering implications for sensitive ecological ecosystems?

▶ Have all sources of heavy metals such as cadmium, mercury and lead been investigated and monitored (Box 10.4)? Has the 'Best Practicable Environmental Option' been considered where metals are released?

▶ Are there policies to monitor and control emissions of toxic metals caused by the combustion of fossil fuels (eg transport, industrial developments) and agricultural practices causing acidification (Box 10.2)?

▶ Is detailed information collected, including weather data, to assess the nature and quantity of pollutants emitted and to consider potential trends for epidemiological studies (Box 10.2)

Noise

▶ Have all the potential sources of noise pollution been established and monitored to conform with EU targets (Box 10.2)?

▶ Is sufficient liaison carried out between the planning and environmental health sections to ensure that noise sensitive developments are separated from noise generating activities (Box 10.2)?

Water Pollution

▶ Is consideration given to the local authority role in water consumption and management through its own activities, and as a role model for reducing consumption?

▶ Is sufficient information provided to the public on the quality and control of water sources (Box 10.5) in liaison with the NRA and water companies?

Land Pollution

Ensure that all proposals for new development are appraised in relation to possible effects on the environment: this may include groundwater resources, natural geological factors and existing soil contamination (Box 10.5).

Box 10.3   Air quality standards and guidelines

Current EU air quality standards
The adoption of the Directive EC/80/779 on sulphur dioxide and suspended particulates introduced the first air quality standards to the UK. This was followed in 1982 by Directive EC/82/884 on air quality limit values for lead and in 1985 by Directive EC/85/203 on nitrogen dioxide.

These standards are now applied in the UK through the Air Quality Standards Regulations 1989 and are as follows:

Smoke:
Annual median   80 ug/m3

SO$_2$:
Annual median   120 ug/m3   if smoke < 40 ug/m3
                       80 ug/m3   if smoke > 40 ug/m3

Smoke:
Winter median   130 ug/m3

SO$_2$:
Winter median   180 ug/m3   if smoke < 60 ug/m3
                       130 ug/m3   if smoke > 60 ug/m3

Smoke:
Annual peak   250 ug/m3   (98th percentile of daily
                                          values)

SO$_2$:
Annual peak   350 ug/m3   if smoke < 150 ug/m3
                       250 ug/m3   if smoke > 150 ug/m3

NO$_2$:
Annual peak   200 ug/m3   (98th percentile of hourly
                                          values)

Lead:
Annual mean   2 ug/m3

A Draft Directive on air pollution by ozone (COM(92) 236 final) sets the following standards:

Ozone:
8 hour mean   110 ug/m3
1 hour mean   360 ug/m3 health protection warning
1 hour mean   200 ug/m3 vegetation protection threshold

Box 10.4   WHO air quality guidelines for sensitive ecosystems

The WHO Air Quality Guidelines for Europe are divided into organic compounds, inorganic compounds and guidelines for sensitive ecosystems. Where the carcinogenicity of the substance has been evaluated the substance is also classified and the risk estimated. The classification of carcinogens is as follows:

Group 1:   Proven human carcinogen
Group 2:   Probable human carcinogen
        2A: Proven evidence in animals
             Limited evidence in humans
        2B: Sufficient evidence in animals
             Inadequate evidence in humans
Group 3:   Not carcinogenic in humans

Acrylonitrile:
Group 2A Carcinogen, no safe level
$1 \text{ ug/m}^3 = 2\,2 \times 10^{-5}$ lifetime risk

Arsenic:
Group 1 Carcinogen, no safe level
$1 \text{ ug/m}^3 = 3\,2 \times 10^{-3}$ lifetime risk

Asbestos:
Group 1 Carcinogen, no safe level
$1000 \text{ fibres/m}^3 = 10^{-6}$ to 10^{-5} risk of lung cancer
                       10^{-5} to 10^{-4} risk of mesothelioma

Benzine:
Group 1 Carcinogen, no safe level
$1 \text{ ug/m}^3 = 4\,2 \times 10^{-4}$ lifetime risk of leukaemia

Cadmium:
Group 2B Carcinogen
1–5 ng/m^3 in rural areas, no increase
10–20 ng/m^3 in urban and industrial areas, no increase

Carbon disulphide:
24 hour mean   100 ug/m^3 (adverse effects)
                          20 ug/m^3 (1/10th odour threshold)

Carbon monoxide:

15 min mean	100 mg/m^3 (86 ppm)
30 min mean	60 mg/m^3 (52 ppm)
1 hour mean	30 mg/m^3 (26 ppm)
8 hour mean	10 mg/m^3 (9 ppm)

Chrome VI:
  Group 1 Carcinogen, no safe level
  1 ug/m^3 = 4 2 10^{-2} lifetime risk

1,2 Dichloroethane:
  24 hour mean   700 ug/m^3 (adverse effects)

Dichloromethane:
  24 hour mean   3000 ug/m^3 (adverse effects)

Formaldehyde:
  30 min mean   100 ug/m^3

Hydrogen sulphide:
  24 hour mean   150 ug/m^3 (adverse effects)
  30 min mean   7 ug/m^3 (1/10th odour threshold)

Lead:
  Group 3
  annual mean   0.5–1 ug/m^3

Manganese:
  annual mean   1 ug/m^3

Mercury:
  annual mean   1 ug/m^3

Nickel:
  Group 2A Carcinogen, no safe level
  1 ug/m^3 = 4 2 10^{-4} lifetime risk

Nitrogen dioxide (NO$_2$):
  1 hour maximum   400 ug/m^3 (0.21 ppm)
  daily maximum   150 ug/m^3 (0.08 ppm)

Ozone (O3$_3$):
  1 hour maximum   150–200 ug/m^3 (0.076–0.1 ppm)
  8 hour maximum   100–120 ug/m^3 (0.05–0.06 ppm)

PAN:
  1 hour maximum   300 ug/m^3
  8 hour maximum   80 ug/m^3

Particulates:
  24 hour maximum   125 ug/m^3 (smoke stain)
  24 hour maximum   120 ug/m^3 (gravimetric)
  24 hour maximum   70 ug/m^3 (PM$_{10}$)
  annual maximum   50 ug/m^3 (smoke stain)

Polycyclic aromatic hydrocarbons (PAHs):
  No safe level
  1 ng/m^3 = 9 2 10^{-5} lifetime risk

Radon:
  annual average   < 100 Bq/m^3 EER in new buildings
                       > 100 Bq/m^3 EER – remedial work in existing
                       buildings
                       > 400 Bq/m^3 EER – urgent action in existing
                       buildings

Styrene:
  Group 3
  24 hour mean   800 ug/m^3 (adverse effects)
  30 min mean   70 ug/m^3 (1/10th odour threshold)

Sulphur dioxide (SO$_2$):
  10 minute maximum   500 ug/m^3 (adverse effects)
   1 hour maximum   350 ug/m^3 (adverse effects)
  24 hour maximum   125 ug/m^3 (adverse effects)
  annual maximum   50 ug/m^3 (adverse effects)
  H$^+$ ion activity   10 ug/m^3 H$_2$SO$_4$ or equivalent acidity

Tetrachloroethylene:
  Group 3
  24 hour mean   5000 ug/m^3 (adverse effects)
  30 min mean   8000 ug/m^3 (1/10th odour threshold)

Toluene:
  24 hour mean   7500 ug/m^3 (adverse effects)
  30 min mean   1000 ug/m^3 (1/10th odour threshold)

Trichloroethylene:
  Group 3
  24 hour mean   1000 ug/m^3 (adverse effects)

Vanadium:
  24 hour mean   1 ug/m^3

Vinyl chloride:
  Group 1 Carcinogen, no safe level
  1 ug/m^3 = 1 2 10^{-6} lifetime risk

Nitrogen:
  annual deposition   < 3 g/m^2

Nitrogen dioxide (NO$_2$):
  4 hour maximum   95 ug/m^3
  annual average   30 ug/m^3

Ozone (O$_3$):
  annual average   60 ug/m^3

Sulphur dioxide (SO$_2$):
  4 hour maximum   95 ug/m^3
  annual average   30 ug/m^3

REFERENCES

British Standards Institute (1994a) *Part I: Auditing of Environmental Management Systems* Guidelines for environmental auditing – Audit Procedures, ISO/CD 14011/1, Document 94/400414DC, BSI, London

British Standards Institute (1994b) *Environmental Management Systems* BS7750, BSI, London

Department of the Environment (1978–) *Digest of Environmental Protection Statistics* HMSO, London

Department of the Environment (1990) *Environmental Protection Act 1990* Part 1, HMSO, London

Department of the Environment et al (1994a) *Sustainable Development – The UK Strategy* Cm 2426, HMSO, London.

Department of the Environment et al (1994b) *Climate Change – The UK Programme,* Cm 2427, HMSO, London

European Commission (1992a) *A European Community Programme of Policy and Action in relation to the Environment and Sustainable Development* Commission of the European Communities, COM (92) 23 final vol II, EC, Brussels

European Commission (1992a) *The State of the Environment in the European Community* Commission of the European Communities, COM (92) 23 final vol III, EC, Brussels

European Union (1994) *Proposed Framework Directive on the assessment and management of air quality* COM (94) 109, Commission of the European Union, Brussels

Evelyn, J (1661) *Fumifugum – The inconvenience of the Aer and Smoake of London Dissipated*

Royal Commission on Environmental Pollution (1975) *5th Report of the Royal Commission on Environmental Pollution* HMSO, London

Royal Commission on Environmental Pollution (1988) *12th Report of the Royal Commission on Environmental Pollution* HMSO, London

Smith, J (1994) *The Safe Handling and Disposal of Clinical Waste: Alternatives to incineration of clinical waste: Sterilisation* Joint Seminar organized by Safety and Environmental Management Consultants and Environmental Toxicology Centre, Bristol University, Clifton, Bristol

World Health Organisation (1987) *Air Quality Guidelines for Europe* Regional Office for Europe, European Series No 23, WHO

11

Waste and Recycling

Bob Keen

ORIENTATION

Wastes dealt with in this chapter are those which, in a domestic setting, would be consigned to a dustbin, or in a typical factory removed in a skip or road tanker. Industry's other gaseous and liquid effluents are discussed in the chapter on pollution control. The basic administrative pattern (at least as far as England was concerned) of District Councils operating as Waste Collection Authorities with County and Metropolitan Councils controlling waste disposal has been significantly altered by the Environmental Protection Act 1990 (EPA) which includes requirements for setting up of 'arm's length' companies and the transferring of supervision to the new Environmental Protection Agency.

Auditors working on waste and recycling should be prepared for difficulties. Some of these arise because recycling issues are dominated by short-term economics, therefore some attractive scenarios just won't work. Other difficulties are, because there are no binding definitions of categories, inter-authority comparisons can be meaningless. Finally as producers of waste, most people regard themselves as experts, hence there is an amazing amount of rubbish talked about rubbish!

Many local authorities (LAs) have in the past regarded waste management as a Cinderella topic, and also had very public disagreements about it. County Councils (as Waste Disposal Authorities) have been in direct conflict with Parish and District Councils and some of the most vitriolic examples of this NIMBY (not in my backyard) syndrome have arisen in disputes between councils over the siting of waste disposal facilities near to residential areas. In practice, much of the criticism levelled at LAs has been unjust, as they have sought to be responsive to the wishes of their own electorate while being very much bound to the apron strings of central government (notably by the *ultra vires* doctrine).[1] Auditors can consider encouraging local councillors to follow the traditions established by many of their Victorian forebears of pioneering the use of novel waste disposal techniques.[2]

Nowadays, activities of local councils in regulating waste management are increasingly dictated by central government[3] (notably by stressing 'arm's length' activities), leaving LAs virtually acting as agents. However the House of Commons Select Committee on the Environment has criticized the Government for lacking an overall recycling strategy. For example, when the concept of recycling credits was recently introduced, local authorities were unable to give much in the way of guidance, as the information was slow to emerge from the DoE. Protracted confusion has also existed over the changes in disposal site licensing procedures. Hence councillors and officials may be wary of doing much more than putting a superficial veneer on the practice of waste management, as they are unable to promote radical solutions. On the recycling front one collection authority has even publicly complained that its refusal to submit a recycling plan emerged from its inability to find the money to undertake the activities for which it was required to plan.

PLANNING ISSUES

Nowadays there is a trend for the more hotly disputed planning and licensing applications to end up on the desk of the Secretary of State, and because the Minister can generally be expected to take the wider view when

---

1 The *Ultra Vires* doctrine derives from local authorities being creatures of statute who can only act when they have explicit (or clearly derivable) legislative authorization provided by parliament. Mrs Thatcher's administration used the courts to clearly define the limitations on LAs' freedom of action.

2 Local government's practical involvement in environmental issues predates the initiation of positive action on the part of central government. Despite the appearance of Chadwick's classic report in 1842 and the Royal Commission which followed, it was local initiatives in the cities and large towns (some of which were still being administered as if they were villages) which actually pioneered the sanitary movement in the UK. Developments such as the *Liverpool Sanitary Act 1846* began to create a healthy and tolerable life style out of the dangerous chaos which had resulted from the industrial revolution.

3 By using one (or a combination) of the following methods:
- Introducing legislation which sets specific environmental objectives.
- Issuing circulars and guidance notes which specify environmental criteria (for instance appointing specific officials such as local government commissioners for administration (ombudsmen) and audit commissioners, to police both performance and financial parameters).
- Most commonly by strictly controlling the purse strings so that central funding is only available for approved schemes.
- In the specific area of waste disposal by the creation of 'arm's length' companies.

weighing national needs against local considerations,[4] auditors should be aware that it may be necessary to pursue their enquiries all the way to Whitehall if they really wish to get to the root of specific disposal policies (such as the lack of any real commitment to sustainability).

In the 1990 White Paper *This Common Inheritance* (DoE, 1990) the government undertook to

> consider the need for ... guidance on the relationship between planning and pollution control in the light of new measures in the Environmental Protection Bill.

They have subsequently commissioned a specific report on the topic (Planning, Pollution and Waste).[5] Auditors need to uncover the extent to which there has been a real commitment to a radical change of direction presaged in the European Commission's 5th Environmental Action Programme and the EPA.[6]

CURRENT ATTITUDES IN LOCAL AUTHORITIES

Although the proportion of the UK's total annual waste tonnage which is collected or disposed of by LAs is small (see pie diagram Figure 11.1), concerns over the management (and recycling) of these 20 million tonnes currently enjoys a high priority among the environmental concerns exhibited by local residents.[7]

Whether or not LAs are really willing to acknowledge the highly significant institutional changes which a full commitment to achieving the (much tougher!) goal of sustainability actually requires, is a much more fundamental point.

WASTE AND LITTER MANAGEMENT

Even allowing for the significant changes brought about by the EPA in the separation of executive and supervisory roles, LAs still have an important role to play in the management of solid wastes and the cleansing of streets and public places. They are responsible for ensuring that over twenty million tonnes of waste (99 per cent of the total generated) are collected from dwellings in the UK per year, a service mostly funded by central government grants, augmented by local council tax income. Besides paying

4 Conclusion reached in the report *Planning, Pollution & Waste Management* published by the Department of the Environment (page 13) (see References).

5 ibid, page iii.

6 EC Directive EEC/85/337 on Environmental Assessment.

7 Data on the generation of wastes are published annually by the DoE.

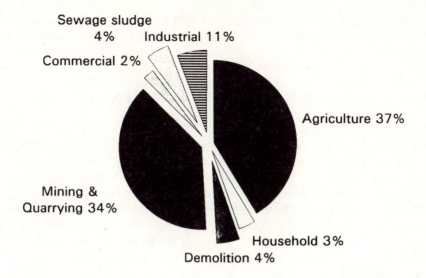

Figure 11.1 Estimated total annual waste arising in the UK in the late 1980s

the lion's share of the bill, central government also is beginning to take seriously its role in imposing legal standards for the performance of the service, and becoming increasingly involved in setting standards, notably with regard to high profile activities such as litter collection (see page 186).

Much amenity damage results from litter and roadside dumping. Auditors can ascertain whether the obligations set out in Civic Amenities legislation[8] to provide facilities for bulky domestic discards and garden waste are being met and the removal of dumped vehicles such as MOT test failures from the streets, receive appropriate priorities and whether the policy maximizes recycling opportunities (but see notes below on recycling).

REFUSE COLLECTION

The routine by which refuse is put out by householders in dustbins, collected by teams of dustmen and manually thrown into dustcarts is so time honoured (not to say old fashioned) that it would be very familiar to Eliza Doolittle's father, save only for the fact that the vehicles are no longer horse-drawn and also are provided with mechanical assistance for refuse compaction and increasingly for actually lifting of the bins. The domestic refuse collection routines often require dustbins (and sacks) to stand in the

---

8 Mainly the Refuse Disposal (Amenity) Act 1978.

streets ahead of the collection vehicles, and the consequential activities of scavengers[9] have often resulted in the scattering of waste around pavements.

THE USE OF PLASTIC RUBBISH SACKS

There is no doubt that plastic sacks offer significant advantages in ease of handling refuse and breaking the life cycle of the housefly (which will otherwise breed in dustbins in warmer months), but some three million of these can be used by a typical District Council in the course of each year's collection routines. Plastic sacks are not inherently environmentally friendly as they consume non-renewable resources, are not reusable or readily recyclable and they may also have disadvantages within a landfill once tipped. Bio- and/or photodegradable sacks which break down more readily in the environment are available, and although these may create some marginal improvements in alleviating certain disposal problems they still use non-renewable resources.[10]

A good alternative to the plastic sack is the wheeled bin which can be mechanically loaded into the collection vehicle. Although this carries an extra labour cost penalty (because the empty bin has to be returned to the property), it does offer solid environmental advantages, such as the diminished use of a non-renewable resource and the recycling of plastic from scrapped bins. While benefits also arise from reductions in street litter (from burst sacks) and improvements for the health and safety of the refuse collectors, the generous capacity of the 'wheelie bins' chosen by most LAs has led to criticism that they encourage profligacy in domestic waste production.

Pipeline systems for solid waste collection have been available for several decades,[11] but they are relatively uncommon even in modern high-rise congested urban developments. Auditors should ask whether the council has a policy on the use of electric sink waste ('garbage') grinders. If used in large numbers, these latter devices not only consume extra energy in the grinding process, but also contribute to the loading on domestic sewage disposal works to the detriment of local watercourse quality.

---

9 Besides human scavengers (theoretically prohibited by the Control of Pollution Act 1974) and wildlife such as foxes, seagulls and rats, some domestic livestock and pets can be incriminated.

10 Many studies have been published. See for example Keen and Lee's work listed in the Bibliography.

11 Garchey, a French invention, was installed in several 1950s high-rise developments in the UK. Solid domestic waste was removed with kitchen sink waste water.

GARDEN WASTE

The extent to which households are provided with a collection service for garden waste varies between authorities, and of course a totally free service does act as a disincentive to composting by householders. It has been suggested that the amount of composting could be increased if LAs educate householders,[12] and councils are well advised to set a good example by composting within parks and public pleasure grounds. Widespread publicity should then be given to the use of such compost in every municipal application. Several authorities provide free communal facilities for overcoming the problem of quickly producing compost from the tough woody waste arising from the seasonal trimming of trees and shrubs. Such facilities can help with the recycling of Christmas trees and at least one County council also runs a 'chip don't tip' campaign throughout the year.[13]

COLLECTION OF INDUSTRIAL AND COMMERCIAL WASTES

Most industrial and commercial wastes are collected by private enterprise with local authorities collecting only nominal amounts. Due to the lack of direct interest from municipal authorities, facilities for disposal of such wastes have been limited and a tradition of unlicensed dumping has arisen (particularly among smaller companies). Auditors should enquire into the extent to which local authorities are enforcing the duty of care provisions imposed under the EPA on waste producers. These duties include taking all reasonably applicable measures:

- to prevent the escape of the waste;
- to prevent any unlawful disposal of the waste by any other person;
- on the transfer of the waste, to secure:
  - that the transfer is only to an authorized person
  - that there is transferred such a written description of the waste as will enable other persons to dispose of the waste lawfully and to comply with the duty to prevent the escape of waste.

Many environmental problems caused by waste arise from simple carelessness and casual storage or thoughtless disposal of waste. In fact, education is necessary to ensure that the packaging is good enough, not merely for the next link in the disposal chain, but for the entire process up

---

12 Recommendation made in Corporate Environmental Audit of North Devon District Council (see References).
13 Cambridgeshire County Council has teamed up with some of its constituent District Councils and obtained a £3500 grant from the environmental group UK2000 to provide ten free shredders for villages.

to delivery at the point of final disposal. Such obligations already exist in a similar form in the regulations governing the carriage of dangerous substances by road.

The EPA provisions have now enhanced the powers of councils to prosecute offenders who dump wastes otherwise than on licensed sites (and officers might need reminding that clues to the origin of waste which has been dumped can often be found among the discarded material itself).

DISPOSAL OF WASTE

Introduction

The potential for the development of acceptable disposal facilities within the local authority's own district is usually limited and the long-standing controversy over the relative merits of the two main disposal methods still continues. Possible landfill sites within most urban areas will have already been utilized or rejected as unsuitable, and the high costs and great air pollution potential of small-scale incineration plants both militate against such developments (waste heat regeneration is also technically more difficult to achieve). Accordingly the long distance transportation of waste seems set to increase, even though at the end of the journey the waste may be simply placed in a hole in the ground (or burnt without heat recovery).

Although there is no statutory restriction on the distance that waste can travel for disposal, auditors can usefully probe into the environmentally unfriendly act of using the heavy domestic refuse collection vehicles for anything but the very shortest of journeys (because the restricted payload means that this is inherently wasteful of fuel and these vehicles also increase traffic congestion when they are fully loaded). Transfer loading, where specialized long-distance transport (using road vehicles, barges or rail freight trains) is employed to move the waste from a suitable collection point to the disposal site, can help to alleviate these problems. Clearly the use of the most fuel efficient transportation (railroad or waterways) is the most environmentally acceptable option.

Landfill

The introduction of disposal site licensing under the Control of Pollution Act 1974 (and its strengthening under EPA) has done much to disperse the adverse publicity left from the days when irresponsible operators (and several local authorities) left the operation of their landfill sites to the whim of the driver of the site bulldozer. Some sites did not even boast a bulldozer and simply burnt the rubbish as it arrived. Given the greater involvement of central government and the imminence of the arrival of a draconian new EU

Directive on landfill, auditors should find it easier to ascertain the extent to which resources are devoted to the monitoring of conditions on site for the suppression of nuisance from smell, dust, airborne paper and various pests, as well as checking on the fate of landfill gas and leachate[14] generated on the site.

They should also enquire whether the authority has undertaken feasibility studies on the utilization of methane generated during the landfill decomposition process as an alternative energy source. That such exercises can be financially viable on many (not always larger) sites is demonstrated by the success of the schemes listed in Box 11.1.

Incineration

Incineration is a concept which has undergone a significant metamorphosis from the days when every large city possessed several rather smoky and smelly manually fired 'destructors' (which were thought to be necessary to sterilize domestic rubbish). Today's incinerator is likely to be a sophisticated continuous grate type, which may boast heat recuperation, even electricity generation, and incinerator manufacturers extensively promote this expensive hardware. However certain technical difficulties militate against easy access to the considerable heat potential of burning domestic refuse. These difficulties centre on the fact that its heterogeneous nature makes it a far from ideal fuel, with corrosion and slagging of the heat exchange surfaces also imposing significant cost penalties.

Several combined heat and power from incineration initiatives are currently in the pipeline which, aided by the Government's Non-Fossil Fuel Obligation (a provision of the Electricity Act 1989), promise to achieve significant amounts of waste heat recovery. SELCHP's £90M plant will produce 31 MW (enough for 50,000 homes) from a 58 tonnes/hour input. Objections due to public disquiet over possible dioxin contamination from incinerator chimneys will have been somewhat enhanced by a recent report from the US EPA.[15]

Auditors should satisfy themselves that any authority using or considering incineration is being totally frank about the real costs, especially the relative costs of incineration compared with other waste disposal alternatives.

---

14 Leachate is the offensive liquid which escapes from landfill sites due (in the main) to rainfall washing out organic pollutants and metals from the wastes.
15 *Waste Management Research* published by The Waste Management Information Bureau, who also produce a CD-ROM which can be searched to yield references to the world's literature on waste (see item in **Useful Contacts**).

Box 11.1   Landfill gas utilization projects

Date: **1981** *Location:* **Stewartby** *Operators:* **London Brick** *Output:* **300 cubic metres gas per hour**
Gas from a landfilled claypit used to fire housebricks and power 1MW generators via spark ignition engines. Set up with an Energy Efficiency Demonstration Scheme (EEDS) grant.

Date: **1983** *Location:* **Aveley** *Operators:* **Aveley-Purfleet Board Mills** *Output:* **3500 cubic metres gas per hour**
Joint venture between National Smokeless Fuel Ltd and the old GLC to create the scheme in which gas originally powered a boiler which was raising steam for energy hungry cardboard manufacture.

Date: **1985** *Location:* **Birkenhead** *Operators:***Premier Brands Ltd** *Output:* **1000 cubic metres gas per hour**
Gas piped 3km from large county council site to Cadbury Typhoo factory where it is raising process steam. EEDS grant aided.

Date: **1986** *Location:* **Brodsworth** *Operators:* **Bilham Grange Landfill Site** *Output:* **20 cubic metres gas per hour**
Nursery developed close to a small landfill to demonstrate the feasibility of small scale operation using gas to heat greenhouses in Yorkshire.

Date: **1986** *Location:* **Dartford** *Operators:* **Blue Circle** *Output:* **5000 cubic metres per hour**
5km pipeline links Stone landfill with Swancombe works where gas is used as fuel supplement in cement manufacture.

Date: **1987** *Location:* **Packington** *Operators:* **Peel** *Output:* **3400 cubic metres of gas per hour**
3.7 MW of electricity exported to the local grid in the vicinity of the NEC Birmingham.

Date: **1992** *Location:* **Mucking** *Operators:* **Cory Environmental** *Output:* **4200 cubic metres of gas per hour**
Gas (collected by a grant-aided pipeline system), generates 3.8 MW of electricity via Centrax gas turbines which is supplied to Eastern Electricity in a £3 million scheme located on the North bank of the Thames.

Other options

Auditors need to be mindful that although many ingenious (and sometimes outrageous) alternatives to the landfilling and incineration of domestic waste have been tried, almost every attempt to scale up such processes from pilot plant to workable proportions seems destined to throw up a host of technical and economic difficulties. The production of refuse-derived fuel (with a nuisance free, transportable product) and the destruction of waste by pyrolysis (which yields a rich hydrocarbon feedstock) both provide recent examples of promising ideas which have not yet achieved commercial success. Hence no panacea is in immediate prospect while short-term market considerations continue to predominate the decision making process.

HAZARDOUS WASTE MANAGEMENT

The NIMBY syndrome will usually mean that any disposal site which treats 'special' wastes[16] tends to arouse fears in the minds of local residents, these (sometimes irrational) fears often being expressed via virulent public protest campaigns. Hence applications for planning permission are often refused or (like many other waste disposal site licence applications) have to be settled on appeal by the Secretary of State for the Environment.[17]

Although the appalling record of some hazardous waste operations has quite properly been a historical cause for concern, vastly improved standards of regulation and handling do now allow a more rational analysis of the dangers. This should facilitate the making of decisions based on an objective assessment of the hazards from such an undertaking alongside the risks from other companies which, for example, may be handling virgin hazardous chemicals. The current economic situation is forcing communities to become more objective about their fears; nowadays the fact that a regional disposal facility might help to attract much needed industrial development to an area of high unemployment may induce a groundswell of support for the proposal.

---

16 Special waste is a term coined by the Government to include all categories of hazardous waste (except radioactive). It is clearly less emotive than calling it poisonous (as the Deposit of Poisonous Waste Act did in 1972). In practice the environmental impact of leachate from household refuse can result in an equally significant environmental burden as that from an industrial waste landfill.

17 Environmental Protection Act 1990, Section 91.

RECYCLING OF WASTE MATERIALS

The fact that many of the earth's resources (notably minerals and metals) are demonstrably finite, should mean that it is easy to convince people that it is imperative that they prioritize their own consumption patterns to take account of this fact. Unfortunately a whole panoply of forces constrain this noble goal (not the least of which is the short timescale on which most politicians operate). Hence, certainly within local government, sustainable economics (and even waste minimization) excite much less attention than recycling of wastes.

Surveys of public opinion on green issues show that matters related to waste (and especially recycling) are now perceived to be of significant importance. The concept of credits claimable by the recycler (introduced in the EPA) should help to focus attention on these topics, and few authorities are nowadays ignoring the opportunities which exist for obtaining media coverage for their latest recycling activity, however inconsequential this may be. The lack of real interest by LAs in sustainability has been a common focus of discontent amongst green groups (but auditors should note that Local Agenda 21 initiatives are beginning to alter this).

Local authority recycling targets

Recycling is mentioned many times in representations made by the public to any auditors and although certain LAs are currently seeking a high recycling profile, councils are frequently still criticized for failing to take an adequate lead in this respect. Indeed the record of the UK is often cited in unfavourable comparisons with our European neighbours. The Secretary of State for the Environment promised in 1989 that the record of UK local authorities on recycling would dramatically improve by the year 2000 (reaching a target of 25 per cent of collected tonnage).

More recently his department has found it worthwhile to publish an 86 page guidance memorandum on the topic addressed to LAs (in the Waste Management Paper Series)[19] (DoE, 1991). Although several councils have publicized their ambitions to achieve (and better) the target (99 per cent recycling is the target identified by Halton DC), authoritative comparisons recently published[20] suggest that the current average is no better than 5 per cent.

---

19 *Recycling* – memorandum 28 in the Waste Management Paper Series which carried a number of very informative appendices with useful addresses and a comprehensive bibliography.
20 Review of the Recycling Credits Scheme commissioned by DoE from MEL Research 1994.

Auditors should note that at least one district council has refused to publish its plan on the grounds that the resources were not available to implement it. It also makes little sense to devote extensive resources to recycling if this merely results in householders loading their estate cars with piles of Sunday supplements and empty Chianti bottles and taking a long drive to the recycling centre to assuage their consciences (especially if the paper or glass is being collected to court favourable publicity and still ends up in a landfill site!).

Few Rural District Councils have a history of publicly encouraging recycling activities and even wastepaper collection faces greater logistical problems in the countryside than in a densely populated urban centre. Transportation costs may pose particular problems in promoting recycling in rural communities of course, but these difficulties are not unsurmountable. Some councils (such as North Devon) have encouraged, and even subsidized, recycling organizations.

Education regarding recycling

Media campaigns can change people's attitudes – during World War II the Government sponsored a successful 'waste not, want not' campaign in which food scraps were collected for animal feed, hence reducing food imports. However it is significant that market mechanisms proved incapable of supporting the same service in peacetime (although Government farming subsidies also upset the picture). The recycling of ferrous and certain non-ferrous metals such as copper and brass are very well served in the UK by an extremely sophisticated recycling service provided entirely by private enterprise. LAs are unlikely to find room for the development of any significant recycling schemes which show a sensible return on investment, as all materials which can be profitably recycled (such as ferrous and precious metals), will already be being collected by the private sector. In this connection the Aluminium Foil Recycling Campaign aims to reduce the £15m worth of foil which is lost to landfill annually by linking charities to metal merchants, and Intercity has introduced a Save-a-Can scheme on the London to Sheffield line to recycle drinks cans from train buffets.

Although it is unrealistic to assume that it is feasible to return to the feeding of domestic kitchen scraps to livestock (eg the domestic fowl), the cessation of this practice has obviously increased the waste of these valuable resources, and also contributed to the worsening of the nuisance inherent in landfilling or incinerating waste (which nowadays has a higher proportion of putrescible domestic discards). Hence auditors should encourage authorities to minimize the output of decomposable waste from all houses by encouraging those with gardens to compost such wastes along with garden trimmings, and assisting others to use small domestic wormeries (or slug bins) into which kitchen food scraps can be placed for recycling.[21]

Examples of recycling

Certain LAs have had a long commitment to recycling and the last few years have witnessed a rapid expansion of interest on the part of LAs in the topic of recycling. The UK Recycling Directory (1992) lists some activity at virtually every LA in the UK (see Box 11.2).

LAs are responding in some fashion to the statutory imperative for recycling. It is the task of the auditors to ascertain the extent to which this commitment is really productive.

Box 11.2   Old and new recycling practice in LAs
(based on UK Recycling Directory)

- Birmingham City Council originally introduced a policy to maximize recycling of domestic waste more than half a century ago. In the 1930s it was burning domestic refuse to generate electricity which then powered its refuse collection vehicles.
- Leeds City Council had a Save Waste and Prosper (SWAP) programme run by the Environmental Health Department for several decades, which collected from 12,000 properties.
- Greater London Council operated a municipal waste incinerator at Edmonton which currently generates electricity to a value of £1.4M per month. It will soon be expanded to 90MW capacity.
- Kingswood Borough Council has sponsored a composting wormery trial at 100 homes.
- Milton Keynes Borough Council has a door to door collection scheme for all recyclables at 61,000 properties, with the sorting and baling being undertaken by CROP.
- Westminster City Council are using goats to help to keep Paddington recreation ground clear of refuse and promote recycling.
- Tonbridge and Malling DC are collaborating with SCA Recycling and Biffa to provide some of the 420,000 tonnes pa throughput paper recycling mill operating at Aylesford in Kent.

---

21 Slugs or worms will turn waste food into an excellent compost and excess worms can be culled for use as fish bait.

CHECKLIST

Attitudes to waste disposal
▶ Has waste disposal been taken into account in development control by the planning authority?
▶ Have environmental assessments been required for all major waste disposal applications?
▶ Are environmental auditors pressurizing politicians and officers to think more radically than simple waste management and recycling schemes?
▶ What steps are taken to counter NIMBY and also the 'not in my term of office' (NIMTO) syndrome, which refers to the activities of councillors who seek to veto developments which might damage their own interests?

Refuse collection
▶ Are the LA's obligations under Civic Amenities Legislation fully discharged?
▶ Has the council debated the environmental impact of any plastic bin liners which they purchase and what would be the cost benefit aspects of switching to the wheeled bin?
▶ Do they have policies on sink waste grinders?
▶ Have they examined pipeline removal from their urban centre?

Garden waste
▶ How much advice is given to householders on composting?
▶ Has the LA a policy of encouraging composting?
▶ Is finance being sought to follow examples of the 'chip don't tip' type?
▶ Have the authorities, by the addition of wood chips to compost, been able to completely eradicate their own use of peat?

Industrial and commercial waste
▶ Is the new duty of care with respect to waste being enforced rigorously?
▶ Are waste production volume and composition criteria used by planning officers when vetting proposals for new industrial developments?
▶ Do authorities assist local skip handling firms in the establishment of transfer facilities (thereby permitting the more efficient transportation of wastes to environmentally acceptable locations)?
▶ Are local Councils engaging in 'Waste Awareness' programmes to

draw the attention of the public and industry to the need to minimize waste production?

Incineration

▶ Have all the disposal options been objectively compared using cost benefit analysis?

▶ Is methane capture being practised on landfill sites?

▶ Does a liaison committee exist to facilitate the County and District Councils getting together at the operational level to review the availability of disposal facilities in their area and the implications for recycling practice?

Hazardous waste

▶ Are there advantages in having a local special waste facility which avoids the necessity of transporting wastes over unacceptably long distances?

▶ Has the question of a regional special waste disposal facility been fully explored?

▶ Are the media fully briefed and using objective criteria as to the actual extent of the hazard from special waste disposal?

Attitudes to recycling

▶ Is the Council being put under pressure to be proactive regarding sustainability?

▶ Is it using every opportunity for achieving improvements on the personal and institutional front?

▶ Can more be done to increase the extent of recycling by schools, uniformed organizations, churches etc?

▶ Does the LA encourage (or provide) wormeries?

General considerations

▶ Have all of the key issues identified above been properly examined?

▶ How can local authorities cope with the global dimension inherent in questions related to sustainability and waste management?

▶ Is the political dimension being fully explored, *viz* are local councillors fully alive to the national dimensions of local decisions on waste disposal and recycling?

▶ Is recycling viewed as salvation or just a smokescreen?

▶ Are local authorities able to persuade local industrialists to take their own wastes seriously?

▶ Is the Council fully complying with the various performance standards specified in legislation and ministerial edicts (these include litter removal and recycling targets)?

▶ Does the Council undertake the statutorily prescribed 'duty of care' regarding its own wastes?

REFERENCES

Department of the Environment (1990) *The Environmental Protection Act* HMSO, London

Department of the Environment (1990) *This Common Inheritance: Britain's Environmental Strategy* HMSO, London

Department of the Environment (1991) *Waste Management Paper No 28* a Memorandum Providing Guidance on Recycling, HMSO, London

Department of the Environment and Environmental Resources Ltd (1992) *Planning, Pollution and Waste Management* in association with Oxford Polytechnic School of Planning (now Oxford Brookes University), HMSO, London

Keen, R C (ed) (1990) *Corporate Environmental Audit of North Devon District Council* BEAU, Bristol Polytechnic (now UWE), Bristol

Keen, R C and Lee, L Y (1990) *A Study of the Weathering and Accelerated Light Degradation of Photodegradable Polymers* IUAPC, Montreal

UK Recycling Directory 1992–1993, *Recycling and Resource Management* magazine

THE PURCHASE AUDIT

Dominic Stead

INTRODUCTION

> The state of the environment, whether on a global or local level, is now such
> that everyone must participate if we are to halt and reverse its decline. Con-
> sumers have a vital role to play in that process.
>
> Carlo Ripa de Meana, then European Environment Commissioner (McBratney, 1990)

Today there is more environmental information than ever before about the
products we buy. There are environmental claims attached to almost all
modern goods: less packaging, low energy, biodegradable, recycled, CFC
free and so on. In spite of this amount of information, however (or maybe
because of it), purchasers often find it difficult to make choices between the
environmental impact of one purchase against another. Information is often
presented in so many different ways that comparisons between purchases
are at best difficult and at worst, impossible. Identifying goods with the
minimum environmental impact is therefore not easy.

No manufactured goods are without an environmental impact. Conse-
quently, the purchase of products and services is an important part of an
environmental audit. Purchasing is one of the key issues addressed by
many local authority audits (Bruder, 1995). Local authorities purchase
large quantities and many types of products and services in the course of
their activities and therefore have the opportunity to reduce their environmental impact across many different types of goods and services.[1]
This chapter is concerned with the process of evaluating and comparing
the environmental impact of goods and services purchased by local
authorities, and identifying ways of reducing these environmental

---

1 Expenditure by local authorities on goods and materials was more than £47,000 million in
1992 (CSO, 1993). This includes the purchase of building materials, food, energy, vehicles, road
materials, school and office supplies, street furniture, cleaning materials and horticultural
products.

impacts. It is divided into four parts, dealing in turn with the methodology of the purchase audit, the principles for developing environmental purchasing policies, the effect of green consumerism on purchasing and the environment, and the terms of reference for a purchase audit (including a checklist).

PURCHASE AUDIT METHODOLOGY

The purchase audit provides a way of assessing and implementing environmental checks and controls on goods and services. The process can also assist the development of environmental purchasing policies and raise awareness about the environmental impact of purchases in the organization.

The purchase audit is a key part of the internal audit and involves the assessment of the environmental impact of all the organizational policies and practices that relate to the purchase of goods and services. The purchasing audit has two aims:

1) to assess the environmental costs and benefits of each discrete policy and practice (but not to place monetary values against these);
2) to provide a comprehensive source of quantified environmental data and analysis to guide the development or revision of policy and practice.

(FoE, 1993).

All purchases should be itemized and the ones with significant environmental impact should be identified. Significance of environmental impacts may be measured in terms of environmental importance or volume (DoE, 1993). Thus, a purchase has a significant environmental impact if the environmental effect is important even if the volume of purchasing is small (such as products containing CFCs), or if the volume of purchasing is large even if the environmental effect is less important (such as paper products). Purchases of goods made through contracts for services should also be identified (such as aggregates for road building or maintenance contracts).

For each environmentally significant purchase, the following measurements should be made in the internal audit:

- the quantity/volume of products purchased (tonnes, reams, litres, etc);
- the amount of money spent on these products; and
- the proportion of less environmentally damaging ('environmentally friendly') products purchased.

With periodic assessment, these measurements allow the examination of purchasing trends over time, and can form the basis of targets for the absolute reduction in consumption of damaging products and targets for the proportional increase in consumption of less environmentally damaging products.

Purchasing responsibilities should also be established as part of the purchasing audit. This involves identifying for each environmentally significant purchase the person(s) responsible for the following tasks:

- deciding on the type, quantity and source of products purchased;
- researching and identifying less environmentally damaging products; and
- measuring, monitoring, enforcing and reporting on any purchasing policies and targets.

In some local authorities, responsibility for purchasing is split between operational units and departments. The following issues affecting the management and control of purchases in an organization should also be examined in the purchase audit:

- the level of centralization over purchasing decisions about the type, quantity and source of products – the more decentralized the decisions, the more difficult it is to control purchasing according to environmental (and other) criteria;
- the number of people with the authority to make purchasing decisions – the greater the number of people involved, the more difficult it is to monitor and enforce purchasing policies; and
- the role of any central supplies department (or equivalent) and how proactive it is in researching and promoting the purchase of less environmentally damaging products.

These issues influence the way in which the organization is able to deal with environmental issues related to purchasing. They are also important issues when developing environmental purchasing policies, and are discussed in more detail in the next section.

PRINCIPLES FOR DEVELOPING ENVIRONMENTAL PURCHASING POLICIES

Introduction

An environmental purchasing policy addresses two key issues: minimizing the depletion of non-renewable resources, and avoiding the creation of pollution. Effective environmental purchasing policies should be based on an effective environmental strategy and sound environmental objectives, and should take into account the purchasing process of the local authority. Policies should be applicable to all purchasing activities in the organization and should draw on the responsibility of everyone involved with the organization, and emphasize the contribution they can make to the improvement of the environment on both a local and a global scale. The main role and the objectives of an environmental purchasing policy are summarized in Boxes 12.1 and 12.2 respectively.

Purchasing process

There are a number of key questions about the purchasing process to be asked before developing an environmental purchasing policy.

- Are there already any environmental policies relevant to the purchasing process?
- How aware are personnel of existing environmental purchasing policies?
- Who has the responsibility for purchasing and product specification?
- What is the organizational purchasing structure?
- Are there information sources held about environmental purchasing (internal or external to the organization)?
- Are specialist officers (such as trading standards, environmental health, legal or health and safety personnel) involved in the purchasing process?

Policy content

Because a number of local authorities already have environmental purchasing policies (such as Birmingham City Council, London Borough of Merton, Oxfordshire County and Woking Borough Council), a look at some of these may provide a guide for policy development. Regional or organizational variations mean that policies should not simply be copied, how-

---

Box 12.1   The main role of an environmental purchasing policy

- To discourage unnecessary purchasing and consumption of products and services
- To discourage the use of goods and services that heavily deplete non-renewable resources (either in their production, distribution, use or disposal)
- To encourage the use (and reuse) of goods and services that minimize the depletion of non-renewable resources
- To discourage the use of goods and services that cause excessive pollution (either in their production, distribution, use or disposal)
- To encourage the use (and reuse) of goods and services that minimize pollution.

Box 12.2 Objectives of the environmental purchasing policy

- Reduction in consumption wherever possible
- Use of products more intensively
- Purchase of products manufactured from recycled or renewable materials
- Replacement of more environmentally damaging purchases with least environmentally damaging purchases
- Purchase of products without unnecessary packaging
- Purchase of long-lasting, durable, reusable, refillable, repairable or recyclable products in preference to short-life, insubstantial, disposable alternatives
- Active search for the least environmentally damaging purchases
- Promotion of the use of the least damaging purchases
- Reduction in waste arisings
- Recycling and reuse of waste arisings wherever practicable

---

ever – the language and form of the policies should reflect the particular authority. Woking Borough Council's Purchasing Policy document presents for each of eight product groups (chemicals; construction materials; energy; peat; plastics; stationery; vehicles and fuels; and woods and metals) an inventory of the products purchased, the environmental issues associated with them, the relevant council objectives, policy recommendations, a good practice guide and an action plan for implementing and monitoring the policies (comprising recommended action, lead officer(s), implementation timetable and performance indicators).[1]

Compulsory competitive tendering

A number of local authority activities are now subject to compulsory competitive tendering (CCT). While local authorities have restricted powers to impose environmental conditions on contractors, they nevertheless have a general duty to set standards for products under consumer legislation. They also have a general duty to take reasonable care and apply expertise to ensure that goods are fit for their purpose and that services conform to the customer's requirements (LGMB, 1992). Department of the Environment Circular 7/90 advises local authorities that Article 30 of the EEC Treaty applies in this area and states that tender documents must avoid naming particular products and avoid descriptions or specifications which point to or favour a particular supplier (DoE, 1990). The use of

---

1 Woking Borough Council, 1994.

technical specifications which mention articles of a specific make or source, or produced by a particular process, and which therefore favour or eliminate certain alternatives, is also prohibited. It is, however, possible to specify compliance with British or European Standards. Section 17 of the 1988 Local Government Act prohibits the inclusion of 'non-commercial matters' in contracts. Many environmental criteria, however, may legitimately be described as commercial (DoE, 1993). A number of local authorities have established environmental criteria in their purchasing policies. Barnsley Metropolitan Borough Council and West Sussex District Council, for example, require compliance with British Standards 5750 (Quality Assurance) in all tendering applications and many authorities are intending to introduce a similar requirement for British Standards 7750 (Environmental Management Systems).[2]

Life cycle analysis

Environmental purchasing policies should be based on the selection of products with the least environmental impact during the entire life cycle of the product. This approach, known as life cycle analysis (LCA), is used to assess the environmental impacts of products for the EU ecolabel (see Box 12.3).

Management issues

Developing an effective environmental purchasing policy may involve the creation of a small interdepartmental team whose responsibility it is to

---

Box 12.3   Definition of life cycle analysis

Life Cycle Analysis (LCA) involves carrying out an inventory of the main impacts associated with the manufacture, use and disposal of a product, from the mining of the raw materials and energy used in its production and distribution, through to its use, possible re-use or recycling, and eventual disposal. A study would normally ignore second generation impacts, such as the energy required to fire the bricks used to build the kilns used to manufacture the raw materials.

Most LCAs are simply inventories of materials consumption and releases to the environment: emissions to air and discharges to water and the level of solid waste generated. Carrying out an LCA is a relatively straight-forward exercise, *provided* the boundary of the study has been clearly defined, the methodology is rigorously applied and the data are accessible.

Source: Flood, 1992

---

2 Woking Borough Council, 1994.

identify problem areas within the authority, to give guidance and to be responsible for the implementation of new purchasing policies. Individual members should be able to provide expertise in matters such as the safety, legal and technical aspects of products (LGMB, 1992). Purchasing officers also have a key role to play in the successful implementation of an environmental purchasing policy. Environmental criteria can be written into purchasing contracts by purchasing officers (for details refer to the final part of the chapter), in addition to the other purchasing controls at their disposal, such as the Trade Descriptions Act, the Food Safety Act and the Consumer Protection Act.

Implementation

The successful implementation of environmental purchasing policies depends on education and training to encourage all personnel to think and act critically in terms of the environmental impacts of products purchased to assess whether:

- purchases are really necessary – is their purchase essential (rather than borrowing, sharing or hiring)?
- they are the most suitable for the purpose they are intended;
- their quantities can be reduced;
- they present a hazard to health or the environment.

A selection of important elements for the successful implementation of an environmental purchasing policy is presented in Box 12.4.

Cost implications

Specifying environmental criteria in purchasing policies may not necessarily impose extra costs – some less environmentally damaging products may actually save money (such as certain types of paper or low energy products). There will, however, be other less environmentally damaging products which cost more than the 'usual' ones. It is therefore recommended that the implementation of an environmental purchasing policy proceeds first with cost saving products. The money saved by these products may then be used to offset the extra cost of purchasing other less environmentally damaging products which do not compete in price with the 'usual' ones.

GREEN CONSUMERISM AND ITS EFFECT ON PURCHASING AND THE ENVIRONMENT

Green consumerism is the basis of environmental purchasing policies. This section takes a critical look at the effect of green consumerism on pur-

---

Box 12.4   Successful implementation of the purchasing policy

The successful implementation of an environmental purchasing policy in the organization involves:

- promotion of education and the dissemination of information concerning environmental purchasing policies and initiatives in the organization;
- production of publicity concerning environmental purchasing policies and initiatives to inform members of the organization and the general public;
- cooperation with unions, local interest groups, other public authorities, environmental groups, educational establishments and businesses in achieving environmental objectives;
- consultation with all involved in the organization's activities during the development and implementation of environmental policies and initiatives;
- encouragement of all members of the organization to react appropriately and concertedly to the environmental challenge;
- adoption of an environmental policy statement of intent;
- nomination of an environmental contact in the organization, preferably a member of the management team, supported by key personnel with power to change environmentally damaging activities where necessary;
- identification of principal environmental action areas;
- formulation and implementation of an action plan based on the above principal environmental action areas;
- and monitoring and periodic review of environmental strategy.

---

chasing and the environment and, in particular, the extent to which green consumer guides and ecolabels can affect purchasing patterns and environmental impact.

Green consumer guides

Of the variety of green consumer guides, one of the most well known is *The Green Consumer Guide* (Elkington and Hailes, 1988). Others include The Ethical Consumer Research Association's magazine, *The Ethical Consumer*, which reports on the ethical issues (including environmental concerns) behind brand name products; and The New Consumer organization's green purchasing guides including *Shopping for a Better World* (Adams et al, 1991) and *The Global Consumer* (Wells and Jetter, 1991). All these consumer guides cover a wide range of general purchases. There are also other guides that have been produced for a more specific range and type of purchases, such as *The Good Wood Guide* (FoE, 1990) or *The Universal Green Office Guide* (Elkington and Hailes, 1989).

These guides have a positive role to play in reducing the environmental impact of purchases. They allow purchasing practice to be aligned so as to minimize environmental impacts, maximize consumer benefit and exert pressure on manufacturers and suppliers to provide goods with a less detrimental environmental impact. It could be argued that additives, whether colour in food, lead in petrol, phosphates in washing powder, or chlorofluorocarbons (CFCs) in aerosols, are now found less in goods as a result of purchaser and legislative pressure. Using green consumer guides, consumers can encourage manufacturers and/or suppliers to provide goods with less of an environmental impact in two complementary ways: by supporting the manufacturers or suppliers of the least environmentally damaging purchases, and by avoiding the manufacturers or suppliers of the most environmentally damaging purchases. Green consumer guides are also useful for raising awareness about the environmental impacts of purchasing.

On the other hand, however, certain criticisms are levelled at green consumer guides. Firstly, it is argued that the term 'green consumerism' tends to imply environmental benefit or sustainability, but *all* manufactured goods ('environmentally friendly' or not) have an environmental impact. Green consumer guides do not begin by first identifying the necessity or suitability of products. Often they do not question the need for consumption or purchasing. Secondly, it is argued that green consumerism has little effect on the way in which goods are produced. Pearce et al (1989) argue that the production process is unlikely to be significantly altered as a result of green consumerism, since the consumer is generally less well informed about these processes and less able to impact on the choice of process. Process changes will only occur if industry also becomes environmentally conscious, and/or the cost signals to industry alter. Thirdly, green consumerism requires money to change patterns of consumption. Some goods may be both less environmentally damaging and less expensive than their alternatives, in which case a switch in favour of the less damaging goods has both economic and environmental benefits. However, other goods may be less environmentally damaging but more expensive than their alternatives, in which case a switch in favour of the less damaging goods has economic costs. The choice of these goods relies on the willingness to pay for less environmental damage. With limited finances, such a decision is not often easy or obvious. Fourthly, the effect of green consumer guides depends very much on accurate and up to date information. With changes in manufacturing processes, for example, such guides may become outdated and obsolete.

In summary then, the purchase of *all* manufactured goods entails environmental impacts, so green consumer guides do not identify products without any environmental impacts. The effect of green consumer guides is limited in terms of the production processes of products, and they may be limited in terms of the accuracy and currency of information. The guides have a role in reducing the environmental impact of purchases but can at best only partially reduce environmental impacts, or switch one impact for another.

Ecolabels

A number of ecolabelling schemes have been developed in countries such as Canada, the United States and Germany as a way of informing consumers about the environmental impact of products.[3]

A Europe-wide ecolabelling scheme was launched more recently in October 1992, following the introduction of the EU Regulation on ecolabelling. At the launch, labelling criteria for two product groups (washing machines and dishwashers) were announced, with criteria for several other product groups promised at a later date: product groups ranging from shampoo to shoes and packaging products to paints and varnishes (ENDS Report, 1993). Manufacturers of these products are able to apply for the ecolabel once the relevant environmental criteria for each product group are established (see Figure 12.1).

The EU labelling scheme takes into account all the environmental impacts of purchases from manufacture through reuse and recycling to final disposal (or 'cradle to grave') using standardized environmental criteria. The ecolabel can therefore be used to compare the impacts of similar purchases and identify the least environmentally damaging product. It provides information to consumers on the environmental impacts of goods and allows purchasers to make direct comparisons of environmental impacts between similar goods. It also raises organizational and individual awareness about the wider environmental impacts of their purchases.

There are also, however, criticisms of this and other ecolabelling schemes:

1) Products without ecolabels are not *necessarily* environmentally worse than those with ecolabels: they may just have not been submitted for accreditation.

2) Ecolabels are not a sign of zero environmental impact: manufactured

---

3 One of the oldest and most well established schemes is the German 'Blue Angel' scheme which has been in existence since 1978 and covers around 2000 products (Dadd and Carothers, 1991)

Figure 12.1   The EC ecolabel

goods, whether accredited by the ecolabelling scheme or not, have an environmental impact (no manufactured product can claim to be free of environmental impacts).
3) Ecolabelling schemes are limited in their scope. The EC scheme will never cover a complete range of product groups. Ecolabelling criteria had been developed for only two product groups (washing machines and dishwashers) 18 months after the launch of the scheme.

In summary then, ecolabelling schemes represent a way of assessing the environmental impacts of goods. The schemes offer a comprehensive and standardized approach to labelling and enable purchasers to assess and compare the environmental impacts of similar goods. Purchasers should also, however, be aware of the limitations of such schemes. Like green consumer guides, ecolabelling schemes have a role in reducing the environmental impact of purchases but should not be seen as a single solution to the environmental problems associated with the consumption of goods.

PURCHASE AUDIT TERMS OF REFERENCE

Box 12.5   The environmentally benign product –
an Extremely Rare Beast!

- It is durable and reusable, or recyclable and truly biodegradable
- It is responsibly and minimally packaged
- It is not obnoxiously frivolous, like a new electric pepper mill
- It releases no persistent toxins into the environment during production, use or disposal
- It is made from recycled material or renewable resources extracted in a way that does not damage the environment
- It includes information on manufacturing, such as location, labour practices, animal testing, and the manufacturer's other business.

Source: adapted from Dadd & Carothers, 1991

The terms of reference of the purchase audit should encompass all the organization's policies and practices that have an influence on purchasing. The terms of reference of the audit should be applicable to all the organization's different sections or departments. This section describes some commonly used terms of reference for purchase audits. It also summarizes the main environmental impacts of a number of different product groups commonly purchased by local authorities. At the end of the following section there is a corresponding checklist for each product group containing indicative questions for use in the purchase audit process (and also for use in the development of environmental purchasing policies).

Products containing paper

Large quantities of paper and paper products are consumed by most organizations. The main environmental advantages of recycling paper and using recycled paper concern issues of energy use and waste disposal. The energy required to produce recycled paper is up to 50 per cent less than that required to produce new paper. Waste disposal and its environmental impact can be relieved by recycling paper and using recycled paper products, thereby reducing the amount of waste paper for disposal.

There are many uses where recycled paper can be substituted for virgin paper. The quality of some recycled paper may be high enough to be used in printing and reprographic processes. Suitability requires tests to establish information such as dust generation, temperature sensitivity and paper stability (during multiple processes). At the moment the major obstacle for recycled paper use is cost but there are now certain types of recycled paper products which can compete with virgin paper equivalents on a quality and cost basis. These include products such as envelopes and high quality papers. A feasibility study into the use of recycled paper should be made at an early stage of purchasing policy review.

As with all products, the purchase of paper and paper products should be examined such that consumption is minimized wherever possible. This then reduces costs and lessens the environmental impact. It is also necessary to evaluate the appropriate grade of paper to be used for particular uses: certain applications may not require expensive, high grade or pure white papers. Lower grade paper is produced with less environmental impact. Unbleached paper is better for the eye: more eye strain results from reading dark printing on a bright paper background, rather than on a less bright background.

There are a number of ways of reducing the consumption of paper and paper products in organizations. These include the reuse of scrap paper on which only one side has been printed (for jotter pads for example), wipeable notice boards in place of information circulars, reuse of envelopes, double-sided rather than single-sided letters and photocopies, and recycling of waste paper.

Energy and products consuming energy

Energy management is a means of saving money and reducing the environmental impact associated with energy production. It is essential that energy demand is minimized if fuel resources are to be conserved and pollution controlled. Current UK energy generation contributes to approximately 70 per cent of sulphur dioxide and 30 per cent of nitrogen oxide emissions (responsible for acid rain), and 30 per cent of carbon dioxide ('greenhouse gas'). It is possible to make energy savings in purchases such as building materials, electrical appliances, heating systems and motor vehicles.

Products containing CFCs and other ozone-depleting chemicals

Chlorofluorocarbons (CFCs) are a group of chemicals which have in the past been widely used in aerosols, refrigerators, solvents, cleaning materials, insulating and structural foams. These chemicals are particularly damaging to the Earth's protective layer of ozone in the upper atmosphere. Eliminating their use and the safe disposal of wastes containing CFCs can help to reduce the impacts of the greenhouse effect.

Products containing lead

Lead is a toxic metal which can accumulate in the environment and in the body. Small quantities absorbed by the body over time may be sufficient to cause serious health effects. Steps should be taken to reduce the amount of lead in the environment to an absolute minimum. It is also necessary to ensure the safe disposal of wastes containing lead.

Products containing unsustainable materials

The production of certain products involves the use of environmentally unsustainable materials, thus causing serious environmental destruction and irreversible harm. It is therefore essential that alternatives to such products are purchased. The effects of tropical deforestation, for example, threaten biodiversity and, in some cases, release carbon dioxide stored in organic material (with consequent implications for the greenhouse effect). The quarrying of material may involve the removal of natural features from an area as well as noise, vibration and dust nuisances, traffic generation and interference with the water table. The production of peat involves the destruction of scarce wetland habitats.

Products containing asbestos

Asbestos fibres are carcinogenic and pose a threat to health. Steps should be taken to reduce the amount of asbestos in the environment to an absolute minimum. It is also necessary to ensure the safe disposal of wastes containing asbestos.

Water and products consuming water

Conservation of water is necessary to avoid depletion of supplies and the environmental effects of lowered water tables in areas of water abstraction. Metered water supplies mean that savings in water consumption can be equated to financial savings.

Products containing bleaches and phosphates

Certain cleaning chemicals may be produced by environmentally unacceptable means or pose a threat to health or the environment in their use. Bleaches and phosphates may have significant environmental effects on water courses. Bleach is an acute poison and phosphates can be responsible for eutrophication (algal bloom). Such materials should be avoided and acceptable alternatives found. COSHH regulations may also apply to some of these materials (see next section).

Products containing substances hazardous to health

The Control of Substances Hazardous to Health (COSHH) regulations affect the storage and use of certain office and workplace substances. Many substances including cleaning products, laboratory chemicals, office products, gardening and grounds maintenance chemicals are included in the regulations. If they are labelled as toxic then certain written procedures need to be adhered to. Education and training should be given to those persons working with these substances. It is essential that all persons concerned are made aware of this procedure. Each department or section should have a nominated COSHH coordinator who can be consulted on purchases covered by the COSHH Regulations. Reports suggest that there may be up to 4000 acute poisonings from pesticides each year (AMA, 1993). Pesticides may have deleterious effects on health and the environment. It is recommended that purchasers seek alternatives to UK red list and EU black list pesticides, and avoid wood preservatives containing pentachlorophenol, lindane and tributyltin oxide (FoE, 1989).

CHECKLIST

Products containing paper
▶ Are recycled paper products purchased whenever practicable?
▶ Is waste paper reused and recycled?
▶ Are the appropriate grades of paper purchased according to their use?

Energy and products consuming energy
▶ Are low energy light bulbs and tubes purchased?
▶ Are energy efficient appliances purchased?
▶ Are low fuel consumption vehicles purchased?

Products containing CFCs and other ozone-depleting chemicals
▶ Are products made with or containing CFCs (solvents, refrigerants, foams, aerosols) purchased?
▶ Have fire extinguishers containing CFCs been replaced?
▶ Is the use, servicing and disposal of existing products containing CFCs controlled?
▶ Are non-pressurized pump-action reusable sprays or non-spray products purchased in preference to pressurized aerosol products?

Products containing lead
▶ Are products containing lead (paints, building and plumbing materials, fuel) purchased?
▶ Is lead-free fuel purchased?
▶ Have petrol-fuelled devices been converted to use lead-free petrol?

Products containing unsustainable materials
▶ Are tropical hardwood products purchased?
▶ Are quarried materials purchased?
▶ Is peat purchased?

Products containing asbestos
▶ Are products containing asbestos (insulation and building materials, clutch linings) purchased?

Water and products consuming water
▶ Are low water consumption appliances purchased?

Products containing bleaches and phosphates
▶ Are cleaning materials without phosphates or bleaches purchased?
▶ Are environmentally suitable, biodegradable cleaning materials purchased?

Products containing substances hazardous to health
▶ Are purchases for COSHH regulated substances compulsorily ratified by department or section COSHH coordinators?

REFERENCES

Adams, R; Carruthers, J and Fisher, C (1991) *Shopping for a Better World* Kogan Page, London

Association of Metropolitan Authorities (1993) *Purchasing Power: A Green Purchasing Guide* AMA, London

Bruder, N (1995) 'Developing an Auditing Strategy' in Barton, H and Bruder, N (1995) *Local Environmental Auditing* Earthscan, London pp 226–56

Central Statistical Office (1993) *United Kingdom Accounts* HMSO, London

Dadd, D and Carothers, A (1991) *in* Plant, C & Plant, J (eds) (1991) *Green Business: Hope or Hoax?* Green Books, Bideford

Department of the Environment (1990) *Circular 7/90* HMSO, London

Department of the Environment (1993) *A Guide to the Eco-Management and Audit Scheme for UK Local Government* HMSO, London

Elkington, J and Hailes, J (1988), *The Green Consumer Guide* Gollancz, London

Elkington, J and Hailes, J (1989) *The Universal Green Office Guide* Universal, London

ENDS REPORT (1993) 'Eco-Labelling Scheme Launched Amid Widespread Criticism', *ENDS Report* **203**, pp 18–19

Friends of the Earth (1989) *The Environmental Charter for Local Government – Practical Recommendations* FoE, London, p 11

Friends of the Earth (1990) *Environmental Audits of Local Authorities: Terms of Reference* FoE, London

Friends of the Earth (1990) *The Good Wood Guide* FoE, London

Flood, M (1992) 'Life Cycle Analysis' *Warmer Bulletin* **34**, pp 14–15

Gray, R; Bebbington, J and Walters, D (1993) *Accounting for the Environment* Paul Chapman Press, London, p 100

Local Government Management Board (1992) *Environmental Practice in Local Government* LGMB, Luton

McBratney, K (ed) (1990) in preface to *You and the Environment* Consumers Association/Hodder & Stoughton, London

Pearce, D; Markandya, A and Barbier, E (1989) *Blueprint for a Green Economy* Earthscan, London

Wells, P and Jetter, M (1991) *The Global Consumer* Gollancz, London

Woking Borough Council (1994) *Purchasing Policies and Good Practice Guides* Woking Borough Council, Woking

13

COMMUNITY AWARENESS

Jane Stephenson

INTRODUCTION

The successful accomplishment of local government policies and programmes regarding sustainability can only be fully achieved through individual and community action at home and at work. While there are some
areas in which local governments can enforce action, for example in the
field of environmental health, there are many others where their role is
rather one of enablement. Thus the local authority can encourage recycling
through the provision of facilities, or the greater use of public transport and
cycling by the introduction of parking restrictions and cycle lanes. However, it does not have any powers of enforcement in these areas. Clearly the
success of initiatives will depend on the willingness of individuals to participate. Such participation will in turn depend upon their understanding of
the issues and how proposed measures relate to their own environmental
priorities in their neighbourhoods and workplaces.

Community awareness is thus important to policy and programme
makers who need to engage people in change. It is important too, to the
community itself, so that it is better able to articulate its needs and
priorities, and so influence decision makers. The auditor will need to assess
measures that are being taken to incorporate community views into policy
and programme design as well as actions taken to increase community
awareness about issues of sustainable development in the context of Local
Agenda 21. This chapter will examine the options open to local authorities
to increase community awareness and action and suggest ways in which
auditors can assess their impact and effectiveness. The issues will be
addressed under the following sections:

- taking stock of local opinion
- environmental awareness/education
- staff training and involvement
- coordination and partnership.

TAKING STOCK OF LOCAL OPINION

Auditors will need to assess the effectiveness of local authority initiatives to incorporate local opinion into policy development and implementation. Several steps will need to be taken in this assessment.

Consultation – with whom?

Local authorities are ostensibly democratic, with local councillors accountable to the electorate, and the first route many people will take to try and influence local programmes will be through their own councillor. However, relying totally on councillors to reflect local opinion is clearly not satisfactory. A relatively small number of people, usually those who are articulate and vociferous, use councillors in this way. Clearly other representative bodies such as tenants associations, community associations as well as other voluntary groups, and environmental groups, will need to be targeted as part of any consultation exercise. If the local authority does not itself keep a comprehensive list of such groups one should be available through the local Council for Voluntary Service or Rural Community Council. Views of members of the public other than those involved with local community groups also need to be taken into account and mechanisms set up to solicit these. In addition elements of the community which are perhaps not represented by a local group, for example ethnic minorities, the disabled etc, should also be consulted.

Consultation – how?

The mechanisms used to conduct a consultation exercise are numerous and those which are employed clearly depend on its purpose and the budget available. A summary of some of the methods available and their relative advantages/disadvantages is given in Table 13.1.

In practice the best way of eliciting a good cross section of views will be to employ a number of the methods shown in the table. Where resources are limited it may be possible to use students or members of community organizations to conduct local residents' surveys.

CONSULTATIVE COMMITTEES

Having taken account of the public's views in assessing areas of environmental concern in the locality, local authorities will need to address how to ensure that these concerns are translated into policy development and practice. Many councils have, over the last few years, established environmental forums or liaison groups at which officers, councillors and

Table 13.1 Undertaking a consultation exercise

Method	Advantages	Disadvantages
Sample survey of residents	A good cross section of views can be sought Easy to collate responses	Time consuming and therefore relatively expensive Style and range of questions may be restrictive
Specific manned contact point in the authority coupled with local media coverage	Relatively easy to establish and resource Respondents not restricted by scope of a survey form/questionnaire	Relies on public taking the initiative More difficult to collate responses
Leaflets/questionnaire distributed through libraries etc	Easy to administer	Relies on public taking the initiative
Meetings in each area	Allows for full discussion of the issues	Many people feel inhibited at meetings
Inviting comments from community groups	Easy to administer	Responses don't necessarily reflect concerns of the public at large

selected representatives from local environmental groups meet to discuss council policies and programmes. Where these do exist they could be given the remit to take on the broader agenda of sustainability. If so it could be argued that their membership should be expanded to include a broader range of community groups to reflect the social welfare aspects of sustainability. However such forums are made up, it is critical that those organizations who are invited to participate feel that their views are really being taken into account and that the spirit of consultation is genuine. In reviewing their effectiveness auditors should be aware that the existence of such consultative bodies does not necessarily mean that community views are being incorporated into policy development. Auditors should be encouraged to question participants, not just council employees, as to the effectiveness of the group. The role of an environmental forum is described in more detail in Chapter 15, page 275.

LIMITATIONS

Devising means of involving the community in the planning and delivery of sustainability plans is obviously crucial to its success. However it must also be recognized that there are limitations inherent in this process as community views are more likely to reflect parochial problems such as litter and dog mess as opposed to factors affecting global warming. There will also be conflicts where local concerns are out of tune with the general aims of sustainability, for example public demands for more car parking when Council policy is to restrict town/city centre parking. How these limitations and conflicts are overcome will depend largely on an effective environmental awareness/education programme.

EXAMPLE OF A CONSULTATION PROCESS

Some local authorities, notably Birmingham, Bradford and Islington have been developing models for 'neighbourhood forums', as a means of decentralizing Council services and providing a forum for resident groups to articulate local needs and participate in the planning of Council services. Such initiatives would be well placed to assist in devising methods for the delivery of Local Agenda 21. As the forums are locally based they are more likely to be accessible to local people and their opinions and members could be used to conduct local surveys of residents.

ENVIRONMENTAL AWARENESS/EDUCATION

In order that individuals and communities can develop their own strategies for achieving sustainable development they need to have an understanding of the issues involved and the Council's own policies and planned programmes. In particular people need to recognize what sustainability means to them and their neighbours as well as understanding how this relates to national and international objectives. All too often information about sustainability, Agenda 21, state of the environment reports, local environmental indicators and so on is presented in such a way as they appear remote, full of jargon and an intellectual rather than a practical issue. The marrying of environmental and social welfare goals within the concept of sustainable development should mean a greater relevance to local communities who may well have been put off the environmental movement in the past as it was perceived as putting greater emphasis on planting trees and recycling than poor quality housing.

This section will look at the scope of local authorities to promote a greater community awareness and the means of achieving this.

Scope

Local authorities have, through their varied responsibilities, many points of contact with the general public, institutions, community groups and local businesses. Although now diminishing, their role in the provision of education services is still important and one which should be utilized while it is still there. Maximizing the potential for developing community awareness through the channels which already exist implies a degree of inter-departmental cooperation and coherence in approach. Auditors should examine whether or not policies developed in this field are promoted by the Council as a whole. Thus for example there may be a programme for increasing awareness about energy efficiency within the home; in this case it would be necessary to ascertain what the Council was doing with its own housing stock and what information and advice was promoted through tenants associations and its own housing office.

Means

There are a number of means through which local authorities can promote environmental awareness:

- Making use of existing publications, newsletters, leaflets, mailings. Thus, leaflets giving dates for bank holiday arrangements for the refuse collection may also include details of local recycling facilities. Another example might be distributing information about car-sharing together with pay slips. The auditor should investigate whether all Council publications are being used effectively to promote awareness of sustainability.
- Maximizing the use of the media, not only the local press, radio and television but also community newsletters etc.
- Events – for example exhibitions touring local libraries and other Council-owned property, public meetings etc.
- Major projects such as environmental centres (see page 218).
- Working with existing environmental and community groups – these may be more effective than the Council itself in raising community awareness of the issues. Groups such as Friends of the Earth, local Wildlife Trusts etc have for a number of years produced information and advice on environmental issues. The Council could use its powers as a grant-giving institution to fund existing groups with particular skills in this area to run awareness-raising campaigns.
- Developing programmes aimed at reducing a household's impact on the environment. These would include basic information about what householders can do to reduce waste, improve energy efficiency, minimize car use etc, with follow up questionnaires to ascertain whether participants have pursued any of the options open to them.
- Working with the private sector, through bodies such as the Chamber of Commerce, to promote environmental awareness in the business sector.
- Working with schools to build in environmental issues into cross-

curriculum activities; encouraging schools to undertake practical environmental projects, for example energy efficiency programmes, a wildlife area etc.

It will be important when deciding what avenues to pursue that local authorities make assessments as to what is the most cost-effective means of raising awareness. It may be that launching a major project, without private sector support, may be less cost effective and certainly involve more risk than working through existing structures, and community and business links, to promote a greater awareness of the issues.

It is also important for auditors to make some assessment of the accessibility of the Council's publicity material. At its most fundamental level it is clearly important that in areas where English is not the first language of people within the community any literature is made available in all appropriate languages. It should also be accessible in style and give examples as to how the issues discussed are relevant to that particular community.

EXAMPLES OF AWARENESS-RAISING INITIATIVES

Major project – CREATE centre, Bristol

The CREATE (Community Recycling, Environmental Action, Training and Education) project is being developed by Bristol City Council in a refurbished Edwardian warehouse. The aim of the project is to provide a stimulating and imaginative environment where people living or working in Bristol, and visitors to the city, can experience and learn about a variety of environmental issues and ideas. The centre is to have three functions:

1) **Visitor centre:** providing easily accessible information on general and specific environmental issues for the general public. The centre will be dynamic, educational, experimental, interesting, and above all, fun.

2) **Training and Education Centre:** providing a range of flexible spaces designed to facilitate the promotion of detailed awareness of environmental issues to individuals and organizations. These will include a 'one-stop' business advice centre and environmental information facility.

3) **Accommodation:** for appropriate environmentally sensitive organizations.

While the project is now being led by Bristol City Council, the concept has been developed in close collaboration with the community and business sectors.

Programme to encourage greater awareness of and participation in environmental improvement measures – Richmond Ecofeedback Scheme

Ecofeedback began in the Netherlands in 1979 when 18 households took part in a scheme to reduce their energy consumption. Householders were given a target for energy reduction and were asked to report progress to the authorities running the scheme. The scheme has spread and now more than one quarter of the households in the Netherlands take part, reducing gas consumption by an average of 10 per cent. The London Borough of Richmond was the first local authority in the UK to take the principle of Ecofeedback and apply it to waste minimization. The scheme was launched during the 1992 National 'Watch Your Waste' week and participants were given information about ways of reducing their waste and asked to record their weekly waste arisings. The majority of participants reduced their waste by over 10 per cent.

STAFF TRAINING AND INVOLVEMENT

It is clearly important that if local authority staff are to be responsible for policy development, evaluation and monitoring that they themselves should have a firm understanding of the issues. Auditors should examine staff training programmes to assess whether this matter is being addressed. There are often within local authorities pockets of specialized knowledge and experience and where this is found, for example in energy efficiency measures, such staff should be involved in devising training for other staff. It may be that people with suitable skills exist outside of the local authority, in the local community, who could provide training on particular issues. For example many grassroots environmental groups have built up expertise in certain areas which could be utilized in Council training programmes.

It is clear that sustainable development cannot be achieved by local authorities acting in isolation. It is thus important that local authority staff are given appropriate training in working effectively with other bodies.

While this section has focused on local authority staff, there is also a need for councillors to be better informed about the issues surrounding sustainable development. Councillors are themselves very busy people and need concise and relevant information upon which they can make decisions.

COORDINATION AND PARTNERSHIPS

Coordination within local authorities

Coordination across departments of council programmes and policies for sustainable development is clearly important if progress is to made. This is not always easy; while environmental issues may be high on the agenda in Planning and Environmental Health departments, this will not always be the case in other departments. Clearly councils need to adopt a corporate view on the priority given to issues of sustainability and develop a strategy for progressing programmes across the council as a whole. In some areas this has been achieved by creating a new committee, reporting to the main policy and resources committee, drawing representatives from each department to progress the council's environmental policies and programmes. This topic is expanded further in Chapter 15.

Partnership with private/community sector

Sustainability can only be achieved through cooperation between the three sectors involved: public, community, private. In their role as enablers it is often the local authorities who take the lead in developing partnerships as a means of effecting change. Successful partnerships need all parties to recognize their relative strengths and weaknesses, to make the best use of existing resources and thus avoid duplication of effort. Successful partnerships, especially across different sectors, each with their own cultures, require commitment and time if they are to reach their full potential. Auditors should examine the ways in which local authorities are working with other sectors and assess how effective such partnerships have been in initiating local programmes for change. As more and more Council services are contracted out to the private sector, it is clearly important that as far as possible contract specifications take account of measures to further sustainable development (see Chapter 12 for further details).

Example of partnerships

BEET (The Bristol Environment and Energy Trust)

BEET is an initiative to bring together the public, private and community sectors to further sustainable development policies and programmes in the Bristol area. The Trust draws its trustees from the three sectors and has established four action groups (Energy, Waste and Recycling, Natural Environment, and Transport) to identify new programmes and ensure effective coordination of existing programmes for environmental improvement. BEET has organized a successful public environmental festival and runs an Environment Club for local businesses. The Environment Club is aimed particularly at small- to medium-sized business and involves a monthly meeting at which an invited speaker addresses a specific environmental theme and members are encouraged to share ideas and experiences.

CONCLUSION

Community awareness is arguably the most important area to be tackled if sustainable development is to be achieved. Local environmental groups such as Friends of the Earth, Wildlife Trusts and Energy Action groups have done a great deal to promote community awareness of environmental problems and promote practical solutions. Since environmental issues have become mainstream, and have through the concept of sustainable development been broadened to include social objectives, it is now the responsibility of all sectors and interest groups to become involved in the process of promoting awareness. Local authorities need to be imaginative in their approach and show a willingness to work closely with others in order to achieve their objectives in this field.

CHECKLISTS

The consultation process – involving the public
▶ What contacts does the council already have with community groups?
Is this list comprehensive?
How are these contacts spread across the various departments?
Is there any coordination between different departments regarding community contact?
▶ What mechanisms have been used to elicit local opinion?
How effective have these been in terms of
– response?
– ensuring local views are incorporated into policy/programme development?
▶ At what stage of policy/programme development are local views sought?
▶ Is best use made of local community groups/environmental groups and their specialist knowledge?
▶ Has the Council established any liaison group?
How is the membership of such groups drawn up?
Is the membership representative of the various interest groups?

How effective is the group
- from the Council's point of view?
- from the participant's point of view?

▶ How are Council services organized – centralized or decentralized? Is there scope for decentralizing services to encourage greater community participation in planning and development?

The local authority role in environmental awareness

▶ Does the Council have a coherent corporate approach to promoting environmental awareness?
Who is responsible for developing a strategy?
Do they have access to facilities across all departments?

▶ Is there a budget available?
Who is responsible for it?

▶ What means have been employed by the Council to promote environmental awareness?
Has the Council investigated all available options?

▶ Does the Council work with existing community and environmental groups to promote awareness?

▶ Is care taken to make publicity material relevant to the particular local situation, eg use of appropriate language, illustrative local examples etc?

Developing expertise – training for staff and councillors

▶ Is awareness of sustainability built into staff training?
How is this done?
Does it maximize the use of expertise within and outside the Council?

▶ Is training provided on the concept and practicalities of developing partnerships with outside agencies?

▶ Are councillors aware of the issues of sustainable development?
Have steps been taken to inform them?
How successful have these been?

The corporate approach to sustainability

▶ Is the Council aware of the importance of developing partnerships?

▶ Is there a corporate view on how such partnerships should be developed or has the lead been taken by individual departments?

▶ Is there a high level of cooperation between departments towards achieving sustainable development?

▶ What experience has the Council had of developing/taking part in partnership projects?
How successful have these been?

▶ Where Council services have been contracted out, has the contract specification taken into account environmental objectives?

Part III

ANALYSIS OF CURRENT PRACTICE

INTRODUCTION

From here to eternity

Much of the work that has been produced about environmental auditing to date has fallen into two main categories. Firstly, there are those studies that have examined current practice in a limited number of cases and on the basis of this have propounded a range of advice. This is sometimes to do with content (for example what to look at when studying a particular issue), and sometimes advice on approach (procedures, methodologies or management strategies).[1]

Secondly, and much less obviously, there have been some studies on the philosophy and institutional agenda of auditing. Institutional agenda refers to the political scene (in its widest sense) both within and outside of local authorities, the influence of global, European and national policies and guidance, and the organizational and community setting for the audit. Work in this category has generally been of an academic nature or has investigated environmental initiatives more widely. This has only been of limited usefulness to local government environmental auditing.

This book aims to remedy this situation by combining a range of advice and information that addresses both of the categories mentioned. Part III, in particular, takes a hard look at the way the EA process is managed and operated in local government. It focuses on the themes of process and institutional change, exploring why things happen the way they do and what the possible consequences are. In order to help clarify what can sometimes be very complex issues, the 'technical' tasks of developing a process are separated out from the 'management' tasks of coordination and implementation. This should allow a deeper investigation of the different elements in the process.

The discussion is in three chapters. After this brief introduction, Chapter 14 presents a strategic framework for EA. This is based on an examination of current practice and should help clarify some of the elements in a successful approach to EA. Chapter 15 then explores the other side of the EA coin, addressing issues of individual motivation, corporate commitment, management mechanisms and organizational change. Finally, Chapter 16 is an attempt to take stock of this dynamic subject and to thereby assess its impact to date and prospects for the future. In addition to tying together the strands of thought from throughout the book this concluding chapter provides an opportunity to explore the future agenda of EA.

---

1 The guides to best environmental practice in local government (ACC, ADC, AMA, 1990 and ACC, ADC, AMA, LGMB, 1992) and many of the LGMB publications are prime examples of this type of advice.

The research project

Part III is based on the results of a four-year investigation into environmental auditing in UK local government. This research has been undertaken at the University of the West of England by Noel Bruder and is the basis of a doctoral dissertation. This section briefly explains the aims and methodology.

The research project has investigated EA in local government with the aim of trying to see what works and what does not. In particular, the issues surrounding the identification of elements or criteria for effective implementation have been examined. Besides literature sources and personal contacts, the research data were collected in two main ways:

1) A comprehensive postal survey was carried out on all English and Welsh local authorities in 1992 (see Appendix 7). The main part of the survey sought to collect first-hand data on why authorities have become involved in EA, what assessment and management procedures are being used and what tangible results are emerging from the process. A second part of the survey was for those authorities not yet involved in EA. The purpose of this was to provide comparative material and to provide an insight into why certain authorities felt they could or would not benefit from auditing. A response rate of 51 per cent (226 authorities) was achieved, of which 24 per cent completed part 1 and 27 per cent completed part 2. This level of response is extremely high for a detailed survey of this kind and is considered to be a fairly balanced breakdown of the level of involvement at the time and thus provides a sound basis for analysis.

2) Following from the analysis of the survey findings, a number of local authorities were chosen for more detailed investigation. These local authorities represent different tiers of local government, different locations throughout the country and different political constituencies. They all, however, shared a belief in the effectiveness of their approaches to EA. Elements drawn from the case studies help liven up the presentation of survey data by illustrating issues of importance and by grounding the discussion in the realities of local authority management.

In addition to the general overview of strategic and management issues there will also be detailed discussion of the more important elements in the auditing process. These extra insights will hopefully help to portray EA for what it is – a dynamic, synergistic and ultimately political process.

14

DEVELOPING AN AUDITING STRATEGY

Noel Bruder

INTRODUCTION

This chapter focuses on the technical tasks of developing an EA strategy. The discussion starts by looking at the overall makeup of a strategy and then examines specific stages which can help in developing a coherent approach. How EA is managed within the organization is addressed in Chapter 15. Both Chapters 14 and 15 should, however, be read in conjunction because the discussion on strategy will only make sense if it is related to its institutional context.

The chapter is in three main parts. The first section examines the background and evolution of approaches to EA. The middle section then builds on this by identifying the different tasks involved in EA and how these may be combined into a strategic process. The aim is to arrive at a coherent and manageable framework for achieving quick but lasting progress. The final sections elaborate on the specific requirements of each of the stages in the strategic process.

AN AUDITING STRATEGY – BACKGROUND

One of the most important tasks of the survey was to find out what types of audits were being undertaken by authorities. There is now a much clearer picture of what constitutes EA, whereas at the time of the survey the purpose and extent of the processes involved was not self-evident, even for many of those involved. Chapter 2 explained the types of audits, with the major distinction being between internal auditing (IA) and state of the environment (SoE) reporting. A process combining IA and SoE reporting is referred to as a **full audit** (SoE/IA). Although these distinctions are now becoming dated and the elements of what may be considered to be an EA process have evolved and fractured (see Chapter 16), the basic components can still be viewed as internally focused (IA) or externally focused (SoE). Where necessary in this chapter IA will be divided into PIA, RIP and MA. This applies particularly where issues of scope are being discussed.

Figure 14.1 shows the percentage of respondents engaged in the different types of EA.

There is a clear preference for IA over SoE reporting. This conforms with most of the advice given by the local authority associations and is also in keeping with the most recent developments, specifically with respect to environmental management systems. The emphasis is very much on putting one's own house in order before spending time and money examining the detailed nature of the environmental problems. There is a very pragmatic logic behind this approach which is undeniably attractive in these times of financial restraint. It is also supported by the imperative to begin reducing unsustainable behaviour even though the exact direction of sustainable development policies has not yet been worked out. So, the evidence is that given a choice between internal and external auditing a local authority is most likely to go down the path of IA.

Combining the auditing tasks

An interesting finding is the number of authorities who identified themselves as conducting a full audit. Once again, there are clear advantages from pursuing this combined approach. The data from the SoE can help inform policies and practices in the IA and these can then be subsequently monitored and their progress assessed by referring back to the quality of the environment data.

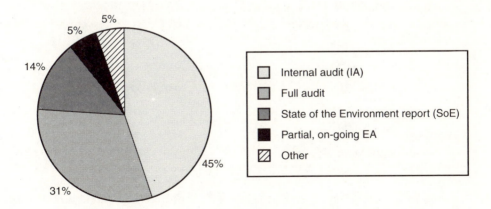

Figure 14.1   Type of audit

The important thing is not to get tied up in terminology and typology. If the basic purpose of an SoE is seen to be gathering information on the state of health of environmental features, then it follows that all audits will to some extent involve an SoE component. The issue then becomes one of degree. The amount and focus of information collection will vary depending on the tasks for which it is intended. This can be most clearly illustrated by discussing the various tasks within the context of an overall environmental strategy. Figure 14.2 presents two quite standardized approaches to developing an EA strategy.

Approach A is based on the premise, as outlined above, that it is better to begin the process of change as soon as possible. The most accessible issues and probably the most amenable to change are therefore those related to internal practices (this would include management systems). These practices are intimately linked to the authorities' policies, so once the process of practice review has begun the audit will inevitably also draw in some policy areas. For instance, aiming to raise internal environmental awareness should lead to the generation of ideas and the production of materials which can then be used in a community awareness programme. Another example is where changes in internal purchasing arrangements can result in amendments to contracting policies (to include environmental criteria) and perhaps even changes in investment strategy (stressing ethical and environmental provisions). Thus a RIP and a PIA are to a large extent overlapping processes or tasks.

The product of the internal audit will be some sort of action plan, which

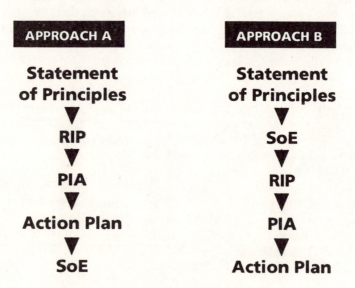

APPROACH A	APPROACH B
Statement of Principles	**Statement of Principles**
▼	▼
RIP	**SoE**
▼	▼
PIA	**RIP**
▼	▼
Action Plan	**PIA**
▼	▼
SoE	**Action Plan**

Figure 14.2   Basic approaches to EA

sets out for internal and/or external consumption what the authority intends to do as a result of the audit findings. However, somewhere along the way it should become clear that assessment and decision making can only ever be limited unless more information is brought into the system. This realization might occur while still in the process of producing the first action plan or perhaps during a subsequent review. It will certainly soon be apparent that only a very limited system of monitoring will be possible without some sort of SoE process. Judging the effectiveness of many of the policy recommendations, for example in the area of pollution control or awareness raising, will involve environmental surveys.

Approach B, though less often chosen, has an equally sound logical basis. For some authorities, there is considered to be little point in assessing policies and practices and recommending a set of actions without first taking stock of the detailed nature of the issues being addressed. Most authorities recognize that although they have a direct influence within their region, for example as a resource consumer and potential polluter, they have an even greater indirect role to protect the quality of life of the region's inhabitants. This reflects the often-vaunted position of local authorities as stewards or guardians of the local environment. Authorities pursuing this approach would therefore conduct some sort of SoE survey either before or in conjunction with an IA and would use all this information to produce their action plan.

These approaches, though representing divergent positions, can be equally successful. They have been presented as processes which happen within the bubble of an enclosed local authority. This is clearly not a realistic scenario. Many external factors will impact on every stage of the process. The principles will, for instance, have been framed by officers and members and will be based on their perceptions of the environment. These perceptions will naturally be greatly influenced by the quality of the local environment as they see it themselves and as it is portrayed by various interest groups. Similarly, the RIP and PIA each address issues which on one level are internal to the authority but are ultimately about the authority's impact on the wider environment. Both the purpose and consequences of the internal assessment are therefore inextricably linked to a consideration of this wider environment. In the same way, no SoE can be conducted in isolation from its policy context. This may be most clearly evident in the standards by which the quality of the environment is judged, in terms of legislation and local authority policies. The SoE will at the very least require an evaluation of the environment in relation to these standards and the results of the evaluation will be a series of recommendations for what the authority, among others, needs to do to improve matters. Clearly, therefore, the terms of reference and the output of the SoE link directly to the IA.

These points should serve to illustrate that eventually all audits combine elements of both IA and SoE. The difference between the approaches is in timing and emphasis. Evidence for this appears in the discussion which follows.

Taking the process forward

Before going on to look in more detail at auditing strategies, there is one more finding in Figure 14.1 which is of note. In 5 per cent of cases authorities felt that a partial, ongoing process was a more realistic description of the way they were approaching the issues involved. In fact, subsequent investigations show that this number is much higher because many other authorities clearly view EA as a continuing process to be tackled in stages.

When one thinks about the range of issues involved – the number of practices and policies that impinge on the environment, the interlinkages between all of these, the amount of change required within the organization to take these into account, the complex web of social, economic as well as environmental factors, etc – then the logic of a staged approach becomes unavoidable. Apart from the scope of issues, EA in order to operate as an ongoing process, must have a system of feedback and review whereby success can be evaluated and new issues brought on board. The shape of this process is addressed later in the chapter. The next section will explore how EA can be taken forward on a staged basis, keeping the tasks manageable while still maintaining the essential overview.

BUILDING A SUCCESSFUL AUDITING STRATEGY

A strategy is largely about getting the right elements into the right order. The difficulty is in knowing what is 'right' for each particular circumstance. Whereas a clearly identifiable set of procedures with formal decision points may suit one authority, it may be totally inappropriate in the context of an authority exploring alternative processes or seeking to accommodate wide-ranging involvement. The discussion in the remainder of this chapter proposes a set of elements which, when combined, represent a strategic framework for EA. The recommendations that are made are not intended to be prescriptions suited to all authorities but rather suggestions which will hopefully provide a starting point for developing a strategy suitable to its particular setting.

The framework proposed draws on three main factors:

1) Over the last few years a clear pattern has emerged from experience of the elements that should be in an auditing strategy if it is to have a good chance of success.

2) Many of these elements have been crystallized in the EMAS scheme,

which presents an excellent framework approach likely to become the standard against which audits are judged in the future.

3) Over and above everything else, what really matters in a successful audit is the degree of commitment there is to bring about real change. A robust strategy can aid this commitment but it can not replace it. So, to a degree, any strategy which suits the authority and focuses on engendering commitment has a good chance of success.

The final point is an issue for Chapter 15. The remainder of this chapter will first examine some general issues on developing a strategy and then look at each of the stages proposed in turn.

Initial thinking

Figure 14.2 outlined two very basic approaches to EA. The features from these approaches are recreated in Figure 14.3 but this time the emphasis is on a strategic process which involves interlinked activities and feedback.

Simplified as this model is, it provides a reasonable representation of the stages in the process and is generally applicable to all audits. It is just this type of model that has informed the initial thinking of many authorities engaged in EA. A more detailed analysis of the stages of the process will follow, but first the relationship between the main assessment elements (RIP, MA, PIA, SoE) is discussed.

Figure 14.3 A simplified strategic EA process

Prioritizing the tasks

It was noted in the previous section that all audits combine these assessment elements to varying degrees and to do so, while still maintaining a manageable process, necessitates adopting a staged approach. This in turn requires a strategy for ensuring that continual progress is actually achieved and managed within the authority, while at the same time an overview of the entire process is maintained. The key to this is to focus the objectives of the audit so that the emphasis is always on the design and implementation of actions. This might sound like an obvious point but it is actually at the core of the problems encountered in a number of authorities (see Box 14.1).

Box 14.1   The implications of not keeping the audit action-orientation

■ 'West Country' CC was one of the first counties to get involved in a detailed audit, with the focus predominantly on internal practices and some areas of policy. Much of the analysis was very perceptive and the process was conducted in a reasonably open and participatory fashion. Although the final report contained some recommendations for action, these were not worked out very comprehensively and the action phase was in many ways considered as a separate process. The result was that an action plan did not emerge until well over a year later, by which time much of the impetus had faded. In hindsight, the initial audit assessment might have been overambitious or perhaps the process was not managed well. What is certain is that the implementation or output phase of the process received too little attention early on and the audit was not driven by the imperative of action.

■ 'East Country' DC was also one of the first authorities to see the potential of EA, this time with a focus on SoE reporting as a stage before IA. Consultants were hired to produce the initial audit report and, although it took much longer than originally expected, the results were very encouraging. However, while the scope of the audit spanned the whole gambit of internal and external issues, it did not have a specific brief to produce a comprehensive set of recommendations. This was to be a follow-on task for an internal steering group. For various reasons the action proposals did not emerge for nearly a year and when they did it was not as detailed recommendations but as compromise, no-cost, solutions. The process had to all intents and purposes broken down and despite an impressive assessment of issues the auditing effort bore little fruit.

Listed below are a number of suggestions to help achieve this action orientation:

- Avoid trying to be too comprehensive. Accept that the issues can be extremely complex and will require detailed assessment. Therefore, narrow down the scope right from the start.
- Focus on those issues where there is the greatest opportunity to bring about change. The issues of relevance will vary for every authority, depending on location, tier of government, knowledge, expertise etc. This does not mean avoiding SoE issues but it does mean that any environmental assessment must be tied in with internal mechanisms.
- Remember that successful change is as much about manageability as about direction. There is little point in producing a strategy for sustainable development, for example, if the institutional mechanisms and resources are not capable of delivering it.
- Don't allow the process to become top heavy. Defining principles, setting aims etc can be very difficult and engrossing tasks. The time spent on them should initially be deliberately limited to allow progression to assessment and action. Later in the audit cycle, principles and aims can be returned to and if necessary refined.

If these few suggestions are taken on board the priorities for the audit should become much clearer. The exact sequence of issues to be addressed is largely a matter of choice for those directing the process. In deciding, they should have regard to the views and aspirations of the Council personnel (through, for example, staff representatives and an internal survey of attitudes) and of the community (through perhaps a public opinion survey and a forum of interested parties). Mechanisms for wider involvement will be addressed in Chapter 15. Box 14.2 expands on this issue in the context of the approach adopted by the LB Sutton, whose EA process was outlined more generally in Chapter 4. This is one approach that seems to work quite well but is by no means the only way to proceed.

The final point to make in relation to developing a strategic EA process is that it must be manageable on a corporate level. Mechanisms to achieve this will be discussed later but from the outset the process should be designed with this overview in mind.

On a practical level this will be facilitated by a clear statement of principles and aims but also by explicitly addressing the interrelationships between issues and levels of impact. Box 14.2 showed how LB Sutton maintained an overview through a complete annual review of the aims while at the same time conducting a very detailed analysis of selected topics through the issue-based audits. Another way to achieve this is to resolve, right from the beginning of the process, to consider the environmental impact of all new policies and council decisions, perhaps as a paragraph in committee reports. This relatively simple act of notification could have tremendous benefits in terms of raising awareness and ensuring that the

---

Box 14.2   LB Sutton approach to scoping issues of concern

Sutton's auditing process (though not originally called that) began as far back as 1986, when they adopted an 18-point environmental statement. Four interlinked approaches emerged from these aims. First, there have been a series of annual reviews which have taken each of the aims, elaborated on the themes, assessed the council's performance and recommended a strategy for action. The amount of detail in each review has varied but there has never been an attempt to be all-inclusive. This part of the process is intended to achieve a broad overview of issues and progress. Recognizing that this approach was inadequate for some quite complex topics, another element has involved a more analytical evaluation of selected issues. Each year between four and six aims are chosen from the original set of 18. This has allowed efforts to be concentrated and enabled special attention to be paid to pursuing specific actions.

Yet another strand has involved an on-going series of issue-based audits. These have been chosen partly because of their importance in terms of environmental improvement and partly because they constitute manageable areas of Council interest. The assessment for these issues is not confined to internal policies and practices but has also involved a consideration of the wider environment and a more far reaching evaluation of what the authority could do to bring about positive change. Chapter 4 showed how three such issue-based audits had been completed, on transport, waste and energy.

A final element of note has been the identification of 'strategic priorities' which are designed to help achieve a set of corporate goals. Two out of six of these priorities relate directly to areas of auditing interest and the reports that have been completed are comparable to the issue-based audits.

All four approaches in Sutton are interlinked and complementary. They have operated within a strategic framework which is now also seeking to incorporate Eco-Management and Audit and Local Agenda 21. This exact combination of elements might not be suitable to all authorities but it does demonstrate the range of possibilities that are available for designing a staged and manageable process.

audit does not become a dislocated or sectoral initiative but is amalgamated within the entire workings of the authority.

TOWARDS AN ORGANIC MODEL OF THE AUDITING PROCESS

The framework presented below is a development of the basic strategic process outlined in the previous section. The same elements are there, but now they are amalgamated into a unified representation of the auditing process. It is a reformulated version of a basic rational (or normative) approach to planning and decision-making. Here lie its strengths and its potential weaknesses. It is this type of approach that has informed much of the plan formation and policy development in the last few decades. It facilitates logical analysis, sequential progress and should provide clear information to aid decision-making and guide action implementation. This, at least, is the theory! The reality is naturally a bit messier. Without entering into the larger debate, suffice it to say that in practice the conditions of the rational process are rarely fully met. Analysis is only ever partial, progress occurs more cyclically and erratically than can be planned for and, most importantly, decisions are not based on clear and full knowledge. These weaknesses in the rational approach suggest three ameliorative solutions:

1) An attempt should be made to amend the model to take account of these factors.
2) The elements in a model should only ever be adopted if it suits the interests of those using it to do so. Flexibility and adaptability are essential, so a model must only be a starting point for a process and not viewed as a blueprint.
3) The policy process, as represented by the model, should be recognized for what it is – simply an aid to help those who are actually managing the process. Another focus of attention should therefore be the organization, management mechanisms and individuals involved in EA.

It is around the first two points that the remainder of this chapter is presented. It will examine each stage in the auditing model to seek a rational but realistic explanation for how to proceed. The approach to doing this has already been largely outlined in the introduction. Basically, it involves looking at past experience and combining the findings of what has happened with what could and should happen, if the conditions are right. There is a danger that these recommendations will come across as prescriptive statements but they are not meant to be viewed in that way. Figure 14.4 simply represents a set of logical stages while the discussion of each of these stages tries to produce some informed advice. Limitations are highlighted but the emphasis is on practical steps for making progress with EA.

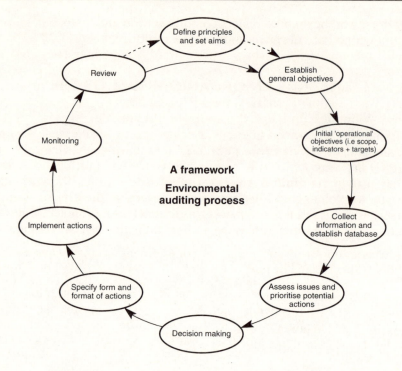

Figure 14.4   Stages in an environmental auditing process

Following this, Chapter 15 will present and evaluate a management framework that takes account of some of the realities of policy development, decision-making and action implementation and tries to direct these towards producing change in the right direction.

DEFINE PRINCIPLES AND SET AIMS

This is often considered as a rather vague and slightly abstracted stage from the rest of the process. Principles and aims are often set out at an early stage, sometimes in a separate 'Environmental Policy Statement' or 'Green Charter'. As such they obviously represent some of the initial thinking on EA and can not be expected to be a totally accurate representation of what will follow. This does not necessarily matter. There will be plenty of time later in the process, or in a subsequent review, to amend and update these initial statements. This does not, however, mean that how they are set out originally is unimportant. Their influence lies not in their exactness but in the expression of commitment. In fact, they are the very foundation stone for the entire process. Their importance centres around the following points:

■ **They represent the authority's commitment to act**
They incorporate the inspiration for the auditing activities and the set of beliefs around which these activities are developed. As such they will largely determine the type of audit, the scope, the resources made available and the sort of output expected. In other words, they characterize the entire auditing process.

■ **They define the direction the audit should take**
In particular, the aims are the starting point for all the assessment and review stages which follow. It is against these that the audit will ultimately be judged.

■ **They provide the initial strategic framework**
A working framework for all the other stages in the process and for management is often developed at this time. While this should be flexible and adaptive, it will certainly be a major influence on what follows.

A discussion on the importance of commitment and of ways to help engender it forms a major part of Chapter 15. This is because commitment is to a great extent an issue of individual beliefs and perceptions. While framing the statement of principles and aims this must be kept in mind. Apart from this, the only advice that can be offered is that the statements should be as open and honest as possible and that they should result from a truly in-depth exploration of what is hoped for from the process.

Box 14.3 lists a sample of the sort of principles and aims that often appear in audits. The key phrases, as such, are:

■ local action
■ participation
■ environmental protection and enhancement
■ institutional change
■ sustainable development
■ balance and harmony.

These give a reasonable indication of what EA is all about.

A final point to make about this stage is that the thorny issue of resources should be squarely faced. One of the greatest determinants of the type of process that will evolve is the amount of resources (both time and money) that can be made available. There is no point in ignoring this issue until, say, the decision-making stage because much of the assessment will require a knowledge of the potential resource input (see Chapter 15).

ESTABLISH GENERAL OBJECTIVES

Principles and aims do not in themselves provide sufficient direction for what can be a complex and multi-levelled process. They must be taken and

Box 14.3   Samples of statements of principles and aims

Principles

■ *'Think Globally, Act Locally'*
This is probably the most commonly quoted principle of EA.

■ *The council 'is committed to the protection and enhancement of the local and global environment. To achieve this, policies, institutions and day to day practices will have to change.'*
(Clwyd County Council, Environmental Policy)
Clwyd's statement both elaborates on the 'thinking globally, acting locally' axiom and mentions some of the other key ingredients of what should be in an audit.

■ *'This authority will seek to promote the conservation and sustainable use of natural resources and to minimise environmental pollution in all of its own activities, and through its influence over others. The authority will review all of its policies, programmes and services and undertakes to act wherever necessary to meet the standards set out in the charter.'*
(Friends of the Earth, Declaration of Commitment)
A highly influential statement of principles (and some broad aims) which has either been adopted directly or in an amended form by many authorities.

■ *'The council through its actions and enabling powers needs to seek to achieve sustainable development of resources in order to help prevent ozone depletion, tropical deforestation (and) global warming.'*
(Wansdyke District Council, Environmental Strategy)
The imperative of sustainable development rarely achieves such explicit recognition but is in fact integral to most audits.

Aims

In practice aims and principles are quite difficult to untangle. Aims should, however, be slightly more focused than principles and should point in a general direction rather than represent a set of beliefs.

■ *'Assembling data about the state of health of the local environment and the authority's impact upon that state of health on a regular basis.
Using the data to increase understanding and awareness to fulfil the public's "right to know", and to generate action to sustain and improve the environment.'*
(The Local Authority Association's 'Environmental Practice in Local Government' Guide (1990))
These were the main aims identified by a local authority association survey in 1990. The first statement clearly relates to SoE and the second to IA. By and large they are still applicable today.

refashioned into a coherent and pragmatic set of objectives. At this stage the objectives should still be quite general but must focus the aspirations in such a way that the aims are kept in sight while the process of change is kept manageable.

Figure 14.5 illustrates in descending order of importance the general objectives, based on categories suggested by the 1990 'Environmental Practice in Local Government' guide.

A number of key issues arise from an examination of this data:

1) The majority of authorities endorsed at least nine objectives. This makes it clear that most authorities have a range of quite broad and diverse objectives for their EA process. It could also suggest a certain vagueness as to what exactly is to be achieved, the audit perhaps being viewed as a potential panacea for a wide variety of environmental ills.

2) It suggests a laudably pragmatic approach. Given the evolutionary nature of the process and the lack of experience with handling the type of change involved, most authorities are initially quite tentative and concentrate on the process itself rather than some of the longer term aims.

3) Most fundamentally, there appear to be two levels of EA active at the same time. The first is an inductive process, which is tuned to gathering information in order to formulate strategies and define aims. This is suggested by the top three objectives in Figure 14.5, which shows the audit to be a first attempt at a comprehensive and corporate environmental strategy for the vast majority of councils. The second level of EA is that of normative process. As suggested by the theory, it is seeking to satisfy prescribed aims and to guide actions towards their fulfilment. Figure 14.5 shows that the pursuit of stated principles and aims (participation, environmental enhancement, resource conservation etc) is generally given a low priority.

The contradictions raised by this dual purpose are quite fundamental; not least in deciding towards which objectives efforts (and in particular resources) should be directed. The solution lies, as suggested earlier, in the development of a strategic process. Within this process the two levels become eminently compatible. The objectives can be pursued in stages, with feedback from the assessment and review directing the priority to be assigned to each. In this way, establishing a firm auditing process will facilitate some immediate, though probably short-term, actions while at the same time paving the way for the more long-term changes which will be required.

INITIAL OPERATIONAL OBJECTIVES

Gathered together in this stage, under the term 'operational' objectives

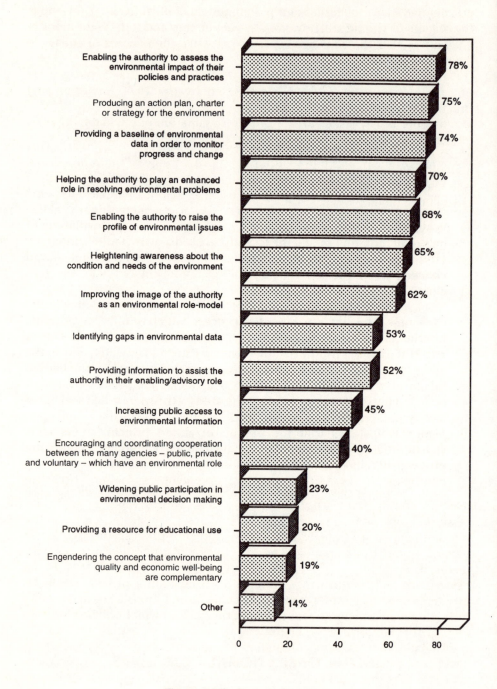

Figure 14.5 Stated objectives

are some of the most important components of an audit. This refers specifically to the tasks of scoping, setting targets and identifying suitable indicators. These tasks represent the worked-through details of what is to be achieved in the EA process.

Scoping

Defining the scope of the audit has already been discussed in a number of respects, particularly in relation to how comprehensive or partial the initial approach should be (page 230). Taking on board the recommendation that a staged and strategic process is the most appropriate way forward, the issue then becomes one of prioritizing areas of concern. The following three criteria can be employed:

1) **Scale of concern:** A local authority will inevitably focus on issues of local concern, but should do so with an eye to other scales of impact. This is what is meant by 'Thinking Globally, Acting Locally' – local change is part of a cumulative and large scale process.

2) **Status of issue:** Sometimes scope is decided purely on the basis of whether the issue involves statutory duties or not. Such a bland distinction is rarely helpful, however. There are no wishful 'add-ons' in EA; whether the issue is statutorily defined or not does not necessarily reflect its merit in the eyes of those conducting the audit. There are many instances where a new agenda can and has been set. In a sense this is what EA is all about. So, begin by looking at duties but always keep in mind the responsibilities the authority has in respect of other issues.

3) **Area of influence:** Strictly speaking the planned influence of the audit will be defined by the emphasis given to the different tasks in the process (RIP, PIA, MA and SoE). At the same time, all of these tasks are interlinked. In the area of recycling, for example, an internal scheme might overlap with a community-wide scheme, both could be supported by an awareness raising campaign, reducing waste and pollution would have positive effects on the quality of the environment and could lead to reduced council expenditure in these areas. While internal change might be the primary initial focus of an audit, opportunities for expanding the area of influence should be sought.

Another element in prioritizing areas of concern, but of a different order, is to define the *subject areas* or environmental topics that are to be addressed. The relative importance of different categories is shown in Figure 14.6.

Although there is some difference in emphasis between the auditing 'tasks', the data are even more remarkable from the degree of overlap. This supports the assertion made earlier that EA is more of a combined process than is commonly thought, more distinguishable by emphasis than by any

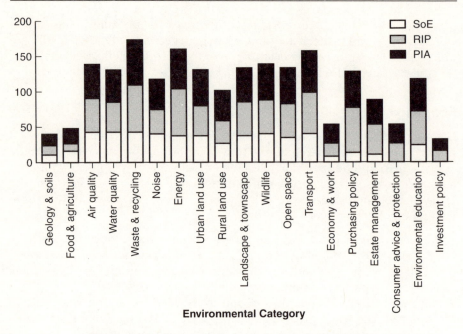

Environmental Category

Figure 14.6 Scope of the audit/areas of assessment

simple definition of 'type'. There is a core of a dozen or so issues which receive much attention, with waste and recycling, energy, transport and purchasing standing out, particularly with regard to RIP issues.

Pages 237–9 highlighted the preference that has been demonstrated for short-term, small-scale objectives. This is reflected here too, with the least popular IA issues being those associated with longer term change. This includes investment policy, economy and work, and consumer advice and protection. These are key areas of interest and must surely receive more attention in the future. Box 14.4 illustrates the status of financial issues in the definition of scope. Chapter 15 explores the broader resource implications of EA.

Indicators and targets

As the degree of rigour demanded from EA has increased over time, the issue of assessment criteria has gained prominence. While an audit undertaken in 1990 might have got away with a relatively descriptive evaluation of policies, practices and environmental quality, one undertaken now would need to include a more objective analysis in terms of how the authority performs against a range of measurable targets and standards. In a sense, the balance is swinging away from an inductive and more towards a normative process. At the moment, however, authorities are left in a kind of

---

Box 14.4   Thorny economic issues

Two of the least popular issues that are covered in EA relate directly to the economic policies and practices of a local authority. Given the widespread endorsement of sustainable development, which is substantially an economic concern, this lack of attention is particularly worrying.

The issue of 'investment' is illustrative of a number of underlying economic factors which define scope. It is potentially a major tool for achieving environmental goals – through fund management, capital building programmes, provision of loans and grants, etc.... Reasons why investment has been largely ignored range from claims that to include environmental factors in financial decisions would be precluded on legal grounds (not altogether true), to difficulties in finding suitable companies and funds to invest in (hardly an insurmountable problem). A more realistic explanation probably has to do with the underlying economic interests dominant in local authorities. In a number of cases that were examined the section of the authority responsible for economic development viewed the audit with suspicion and where possible avoided participation in the process. This stance was tolerated because of the powerful backing for economic interests within the organizations. This simply highlights the point that environment and economy are still regarded as strange bedfellows and wherever conflict occurs it is inevitably the economic interest that wins out.

While the issue of investment is peculiar in that it introduces economic factors at an early stage in the EA process, the paramount importance of these factors often surfaces at the stage when resources must be allocated in order to pursue recommended actions. As the sustainable development debate gathers force, particularly with the production of Local Agenda 21s, there is hope that the weight assigned to environmental and social, as opposed to purely economic, factors will increase in local authority decision making. This will inevitably involve a challenge to many traditional assumptions and powerful interests in local government.

'wilderness'. While the demands of EA are increasing, particularly with respect to EMAS and Local Agenda 21, the guidelines on targets and indicators are still being developed. This section seeks to explain the role of targets and indicators in helping define local authorities' operational objectives for EA.[1]

---

1 Refer to Chapter 3 for a discussion of targets and carrying capacities, and Appendix 6 which explores environmental indicators in more depth.

An ideal sequence of activities is that, in relation to a particular environmental subject area (eg transport or energy), the authority should set a range of carrying capacities that reflect the limit of justifiable human impact on the environment. With these capacities as the template, objectives can be defined in terms of targets which are precise statements of what is to be achieved and within what timescale. Progress can then be monitored using different types of indicators of performance. Naturally the sequence never runs quite so smoothly. There are as yet no universally agreed carrying capacities and it is doubtful if there ever will be, given the scientific uncertainties and political exigencies (see Chapter 3). This makes defining targets an often impossible task, which in turn leads to indicators becoming redundant. The solution, as you might expect, is to concentrate on what you know and on what you can do. Thus, for example, the precise limits of water pollution that can be tolerated might not be known but there are minimum standards defined by legislation and the damage that is resulting from what is known should indicate what action is necessary. In effect this is putting into practice the principle that until sustainable development can be more clearly defined, action should be directed towards reducing *un*sustainable development.

It is just this type of pragmatic approach that is being adopted by some authorities. Figure 14.7 shows some of the sources identified in the survey that have been used to help define targets and choose appropriate indicators.

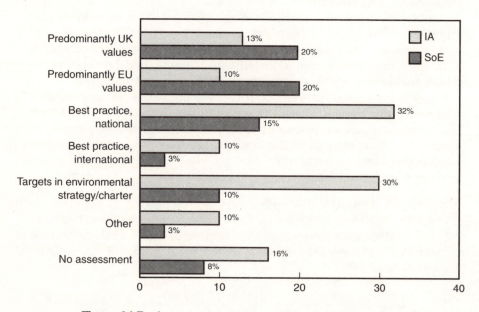

Figure 14.7 Assessment criteria – targets and indicators

Clearly, standards derived from UK and EU policy and legislation are the most accessible and useful, especially in terms of ensuring compliance. It is also encouraging to see the number of authorities that are seeking to go beyond minimum standards, towards identifying best practice elsewhere. This could be of particular relevance in areas where no legislative or policy guidelines yet exist. Thus while there are agreed standards for some aspects of environmental quality (ie the indicators used for SoE) this is not the case for many areas of policy and internal practices. For these, Figure 14.7 shows that best practice emerges which then helps set new standards. The Checklists in Part II are a useful set of targets and indicators for both SoE and IA. They could form the starting point for an authority to develop their own assessment criteria.

The dissemination of best practice knowledge is dependent on an effective information network. The sources and form of information in EA are discussed in the next section.

COLLECT INFORMATION AND ESTABLISH DATABASE

Information is the raw material of an audit. The quality of what comes in will greatly determine the level of assessment and ultimately the standard of decision-making that results.

The key characteristics for the information are **relevance** and **reliability**. Both will be greatly facilitated by the definition of operational objectives. An early scoping of the issues allows effort in collecting information to be clearly focused, while the establishment of targets and indicators points the way towards the type of data required. The alternative, of launching in with ill-defined objectives, risks the problem of information overload, where the direction is lost under the weight of too much data.

Reliability simply means ensuring that the information is up-to-date and accurate. Efforts should be made to substantiate findings and to ensure that all useful sources are investigated and a variety of collection methods employed. The methods, being inextricably linked with the assessment procedures, are discussed in the next section. Potential information sources may be looked at in four categories:

1) **Data already existing within the authority:** These are the most accessible, locally relevant and perhaps the most useful data available. Figure 14.8 shows that practically all authorities have made use of them. Indeed the missing 10 per cent must be a statistical anomaly because all auditors, even consultants, draw heavily on internal data. The figures were equally high for SoE as for IA, once again suggesting that there is significant overlap between the tasks and that there is obviously a deep well of information that can be drawn on internally.

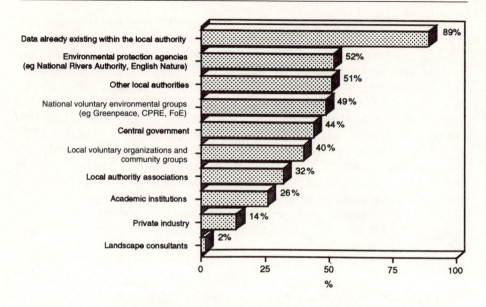

Figure 14.8 Information sources – agencies

2) **Agency sources:** Figure 14.8 also illustrates a whole range of other agencies which can and should be investigated. It reveals that the potential of these agencies has not yet been fully realized but contacts and networks are certainly expanding all the time.
3) **Environmental forum:** An excellent way to harness the cooperation of both other agencies and the wider public is through an environmental forum. This will act as a two-way conduit for information.
4) **Documentation sources:** There is a whole host of literature now available to help in developing the EA process. Some of the earlier reference documents are shown in Figure 14.9; the bibliography will update this list. The number of authorities who have used the FoE 'Charter' is extremely revealing of the influence this has had. Also of interest is the process of information exchange that clearly goes on directly between local authorities and more indirectly through best practice guides such as 'Environmental Practice in Local Government'.

Establishing a **database** at an early stage in the process allows the data that are collected to be stored in an accessible manner and subsequently facilitates monitoring and updating. Undoubtedly the most useful but also the most expensive option is a Geographic Information System (GIS). However only 2 per cent of those surveyed had an established GIS (Lancashire County Council being the most notable). Most opted for a manual approach, which is naturally cheaper but is possibly only delaying the

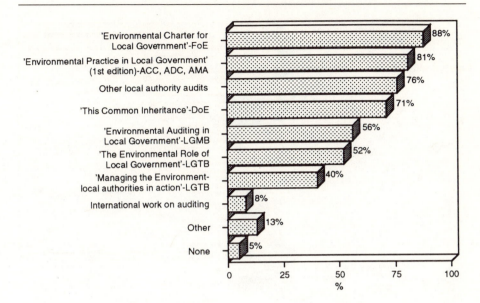

Figure 14.9 Information sources – reference documents

inevitable requirement for a computerized database. The merits of different systems are discussed in Chapter 2. Failure to establish some sort of system has led in more than one case to contacts having to be retraced and a whole new body of base data reassembled – definitely an unenviable and superfluous task.

ASSESS ISSUES AND PRIORITIZE POTENTIAL ACTIONS

Assessment procedures represent the point of praxis where the information that has been collected must be evaluated against the objectives in order to aid decision making and ultimately facilitate the implementation of actions. Attempts so far at introducing technically objective procedures have not been entirely successful. It is not only that the tools for such an assessment are not developed but many of the issues involved simply do not lend themselves to the analytic evaluation which this implies. As a result, many audits have tended to be of a descriptive nature (see Figure 14.10), more compilations of issues than review of performance. The recommendations in this section are an attempt to make the most of the skills and resources currently available rather than trying to introduce a spurious objectivity through a supposedly scientifically objective process. It involves a four-step assessment, as follows:

247

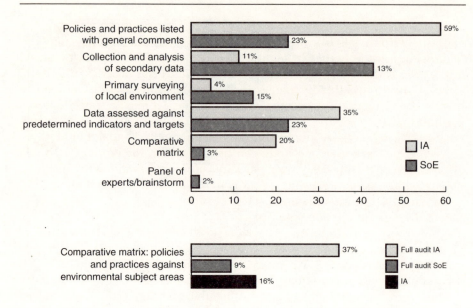

Figure 14.10   Procedures for data collection and analysis

Step 1: Test significance of the data
This follows-on directly from the need to ensure that relevant and reliable data have been collected. The key test is that the information is appropriate to help meet the set objectives and ultimately help advance change in the 'right direction'. A checklist or a simple matrix can certainly help in this respect, to ensure that information is adequate for the task in hand.

Step 2: Choose assessment methods
The degree to which targets and indicators have been defined will determine the nature of this assessment. If, for example, the authority has set a target for itself to convert all council vehicles to unleaded petrol, then the assessment can clearly see the proportion that are converted and recommend a programme for phased conversion in the future. This is perhaps an overly simplistic example, but the lack of a target would in this case probably result in a descriptive treatment of the pros and cons of unleaded versus leaded petrol and would lead to difficulties in recommending a way forward. Although many authorities had regard to predetermined indicators and standards, Figure 14.7 shows that the majority still had not.

As stated in the previous section, the methods for data collection and analysis are inextricably linked, particularly when the form of the data input predetermines the level of analysis that is possible. Figure 14.10 indicates the choice of methods.

The data clearly show that the preferred approach to assessment was to describe rather than evaluate impacts and performance. As for the form of data, SoE tasks obviously involve a wider trawl for information but the majority of this is still from secondary sources. By implication, the majority of data input for IA comes from internal sources. There is an obvious need in EA to introduce a greater degree of rigour into the process. Chapter 2 attempts to do just this by suggesting a number of techniques which can help in objectifying the assessment. In using these it must always be borne in mind that they *aid* the political process but should not be used to supplant it. The subjectivity involved should be highlighted and not hidden. So, while the best practical methods can be employed, the emphasis should always be on maintaining transparency and participation. In this way, debate will be generated, and it is this debate that will ultimately lead to more effective decision making.

Step 3: Decide on appropriate format

The most appropriate format is obviously dependent on a wide range of factors, but Box 14.5 below presents a simplified approach that has proven quite popular in practice. With varying emphasis on the different elements it can be made to apply equally well to SoE and IA tasks.

This type of format highlights the subjectivity and uncertainties involved in the assessment. If based on a reasonably comprehensive knowledge of the issues, it should aid participation and provide a clear basis for decision making.

Step 4: Prioritize options for action

Within the sequence presented in Box 14.5, the 'options for action' represent a quite discrete element of the assessment. Issues identified as being of greatest concern need to be further prioritized so that the choice of and basis for recommendations is made more explicit. The following three criteria should be of use:

–   *Cost* – This is probably going to be the overriding factor. All the implications of proposed actions should be investigated so that the nature and scope of the resource commitment is fully known in advance. Staff

---

Box 14.5   A simplified approach to the assessment

For each set of issues (policies, practices or environmental topics) tackle the assessment in the following sequence:

1) General introduction and review
2) Current status of the issue with regard to the local authority
3) Statutory obligations; best practice elsewhere; possible standards, targets and indicators
4) The assessment of 2 in relation to 3
5) Options for action
6) Conclusions and recommendations

---

time, in particular, can be a major cost component and should be included in calculations.

– *Effectiveness* – This refers to the potential to bring about real change. All actions should be considered for their direct impact, such as energy savings, and their indirect impacts, for example raising awareness.

– *Timespan* – The amount of time it takes before results become apparent is an extremely important political factor. A balance will need to be struck between short-term/small-scale and long-term/broad-scale actions. The immediate benefits are important, particularly as a demonstration of commitment, but should be viewed in the light of the more broad-ranging auditing aims.

DECISION MAKING

This is often viewed as the final stage in the process. In fact it is no more than a midway point, because it is only in the subsequent stages that tangible progress has begun to be made. In fact, decision making should realistically be viewed as a continuum, with different levels and a series of implicit points. Most obviously, the members and officers closest to the audit at several different stages in the process will need to make decisions on ways forward. Choice of aims, objectives, indicators, etc all refine the options open and therefore represent decision points. On another level, council staff and the wider public should have helped frame these choices and have thus also participated in decision making. Their feeling of 'ownership' for the process (and thereby their degree of involvement) will, as much as members' commitment and the level of resources, decide the ultimate effectiveness.

The issues involved in decision making, both internal and external, are essentially about institutional management. As such they will be addressed in the next chapter.

SPECIFY FORM AND FORMAT OF ACTIONS

Having arrived at the stage where a set of recommendations have been agreed on it is now extremely important that the process presses forward so that these are put into effect. The two components that will characterize an action plan are form and format.

Form

Form relates to the worked-through details of what each particular action proposal involves. It is basically a further development of the assessment but this time not focusing on what the authority would like to do, but on what it *can* and *will* do, and how it proposes to go about it. There are four basic elements:

1) **Prioritization:** This should be looked at again, but unless circumstances have changed it should be the same as in the assessment.
2) **Budgeting:** While actions requiring a resource input may have been previously costed, they now must be given a budget for implementation. It could either be a special 'green' budget or could involve drawing on existing departmental budgets. The latter is probably easier but allocations should be 'tagged' so that expenditures can be monitored.
3) **Delegation:** The responsibilities with regard to each action should be specified. It may be appropriate to write these into service plans or personal development plans.
3) **Timeframe:** Targets for what is to be achieved should also indicate when it is to be achieved by. A useful scale might be: ongoing; immediate; within budgetary year; within specified medium-term period; long-term.

Figures 14.11 and 14.12 show that over three-quarters of authorities had either included recommendations or were intending to, but that many less had specified the precise form for each action. This is not altogether surprising given the descriptive nature of many audits but it can do little to aid the successful implementation of actions.

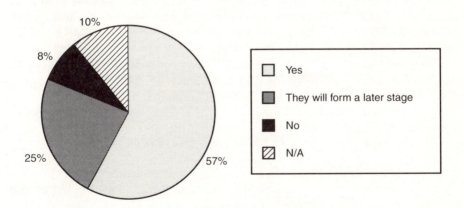

Figure 14.11 Were recommendations for action a part of the audit?

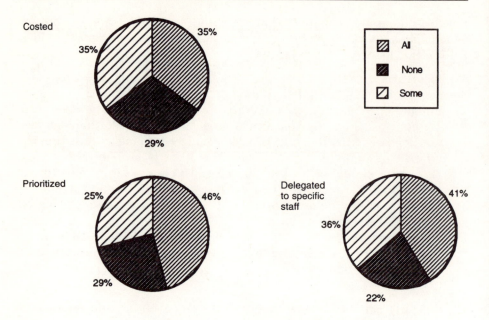

Figure 14.12 Form of recommendations

Format

The format for presenting recommendations might seem like a rather irrelevant point to comment on but there are in fact choices here that can very much help or hinder the EA process. The basic choices are to include the recommendations for action within the audit report (as required by EMAS) or to produce a free-standing action plan. The former allows easy reference between issues and proposed action, thus aiding understanding but allowing only brief details to be included. The latter allows for a comprehensive presentation but can delay the process and might not allow for sufficient justification of *why* particular actions are to be pursued. Combining both approaches could maximize the advantages and would also facilitate a public consultation exercise by getting comment on the preliminary audit report before producing the final action plan.

IMPLEMENT ACTIONS

Easy to say but not always easy to do! The important thing to bear in mind is that what really counts is outcome and not output. This highlights the need for a monitoring system but also for an implementation 'regime' which maximizes outcome. Both of these requirements will be discussed later. Figure 14.13 gives an indication of the range of actions which authorities

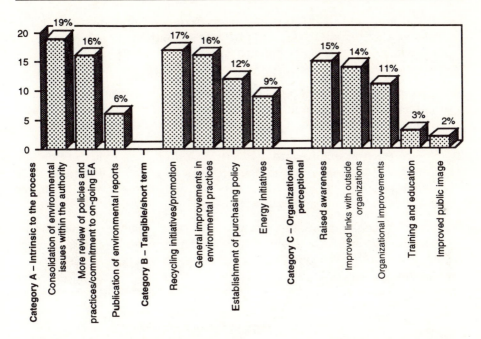

Figure 14.13 Significant actions/benefits to result from environmental audits

themselves have considered significant. They are grouped into three categories so that the areas of greatest progress can be seen.

There is a very interesting spread evident between the categories. It is not simply the tangible environmental improvements (recycling, purchasing, tree planting, etc) that are judged as important. The longer term institutional changes (either emanating from the EA process or as a result of training and awareness raising) are seen as significant benefits. It appears that a good balance is being struck between these different categories.

MONITORING

Strictly speaking, the monitoring task has begun much earlier in the process. Creating a suitable framework for monitoring should have been a consideration from at least the operational objectives stage when a set of measurable indicators are chosen. This framework should have then been integrated into the other stages of the process (eg while specifying form of actions and choosing a database).

The survey showed that despite the importance of monitoring, one-fifth of authorities had not given any thought to it and over half of the remainder admitted to having only a partial framework. However, it must be remembered that the survey was reporting on most councils' first attempt at EA. It is probable that the situation has improved since then.

As to what a monitoring framework should achieve, there are two main elements:

1) **Checks and balances:** Feedback into the process in order for standards and mechanisms to be improved. It therefore involves monitoring the implementation of actions, the performance of policies and the management systems.

2) **Environmental quality and awareness:** Although of a different nature these two components could be regarded as the standard against which progress is measured. This aspect of monitoring basically involves the continual updating of a SoE survey.

While some recommendations from an audit are relatively easy to monitor, for example the inclusion of environmental implications sections in committee reports, others can involve an intricate set of procedures, for example the myriad of elements in a community recycling policy. The monitoring framework must therefore be custom made to suit each particular issue.

REVIEW

The review represents the meeting point between two phases of the EA process. There are two basic ways to approach a review. Firstly, there is a **partial review**, which is most favoured by local authorities, whereby the performance of the process is reported on and in particular action implementation is evaluated and progress updated. Secondly, there is a **comprehensive review** where the original aims and principles are reexamined to accommodate major institutional changes and new knowledge. Examples of the former are new legislation and policy guidance, altered financial circumstances, a revised political agenda or management reorganization. Examples of the latter are new technologies, advances in scientific understanding of environmental capacities or impacts, developments in best practice or the realization of substantial gaps in the current process.

While the partial reviews should be reported on at least annually, a comprehensive review might only be needed every five years or so. The results of both should be widely disseminated and can play a major role in promoting environmental awareness by advertising the benefits of positive action.

CONCLUSION

This chapter has explained a staged and strategic process whereby an EA process can be given the time and resources to evolve within an authority.

It has been suggested that EA should not only be owned by a local authority but should be something in which the wider community becomes involved.

The series of stages discussed here should help maintain the coherence of a continually evolving environmental strategy. Chapter 15 will explore the elements in a complementary management system.

CHECKLIST

► An EA should be viewed as both an internal and external process. The tasks involved may be broadly distinguished as IA and SoE. Every audit will address both tasks, but with a varying degree of emphasis on each.

► Adopt a strategic approach to EA. Within a staged process, focus objectives and scope towards the achievement of tangible environmental improvements. At the same time maintain a corporate overview of the entire process.

► The principles and aims should be as 'strong' as is realistically possible (given resource constraints, levels of commitment expected, etc). A vision of sustainable development could be set out and expanded upon.

► The aspirations of the audit should be tempered by specifying realistic but achievable 'general' objectives. This will help fulfil the aims while keeping the process manageable.

► Clearly define the scope of the audit at an early stage. This should specify the issues to be addressed and the depth of analysis required. Choose the most reliable and challenging standards, targets and examples of best practice. Define issues in terms of measurable indicators.

► Clearly define the operational objectives before beginning information collection. Ensure the significance of data in terms of relevance and reliability. Investigate the potential of all useful sources. Establish a database (preferably computerized) at an early stage.

► The assessment should interact with all other stages in the EA process. Best practical methods should be used to aid objectivity but should not obscure the transparency and political choices.

► If EA is viewed as an interactive and political process, then decision making will benefit from participation and transparency. This implies addressing all levels and points at which decisions are made.

▶ A set of implementable actions must result from the process. Spend time specifying the appropriate form and format.

▶ Actions should be aimed at bringing about both short-term and long-term changes. Maximize outcome and not output.

▶ From the outset consider the elements in a monitoring framework. Later, after action recommendations have been made, elaborate on each of these elements in order to provide a sound basis for reporting progress.

▶ A system of partial and comprehensive reviews should continually update the process and report publicly on progress.

REFERENCES

ACC, ADC, AMA (1st edition) (1990) 'Environmental Practice in Local Government'
ACC, ADC, AMA, LGMB (2nd edition) (1992) 'Environmental Practice in Local Government'

15

MANAGEMENT OF THE EA PROCESS

Noel Bruder

INTRODUCTION

Issues of management have been referred to previously as being at the very core of an EA process. In many respects it is management, in terms of the organization, the individuals and the specific mechanisms which defines an audit rather than the scope, procedures or other aspects of the 'technical' policy process. To put this another way, there is a distinction in auditing between the techniques of environmental management and the political process (in the widest sense of the word) of decision making and institutional change. The previous chapter has focused on the former, while hopefully also drawing attention to the overriding importance of the institutional aspects. This Chapter aims to build on the discussion of process by examining how EA can (or can be made to) fit within the structures of a local authority and how it can promote participative decision making and positive change.

While obviously no two local authorities are the same, they all share certain characteristics defined by the political and legislative context. So, while it is true to say that there can be no definitive way to manage EA, it is equally the case that certain elements will be common to all. It is these communal elements that form the basis of this discussion.

Even more than in Chapter 14 the observations made here are based on personal observations in a number of authorities. In this sense the findings of the questionnaire survey are used more to test the validity of specific elements arising from the case studies. This should work to support the recommendations for good practice which are put forward by evaluating how widely applicable they may be.

THE POSSIBILITIES AND PROBLEMS OF A MODEL MANAGEMENT SYSTEM

There is always a danger when recommending approaches to management that the discussion becomes too prescriptive. The emphasis ceases being on workable elements and instead puts forward a definitive and one-dimensional 'model' of what a management system should look like. Just this type of approach is the basis for much management theory. The elements in a system are combined and sold as a 'recipe' for success which can be taken and applied anywhere. This approach to presenting a model management system is not pursued here. This chapter takes as a basic rationale that an EA process is inextricably linked to its organizational and situational environment. The degree of fit and the scope to evolve are therefore the prime determinants of a successful approach.

The model presented below (Figure 15.1) is not intended as a prescription for how to organize and manage an EA. It is more a description of a set of elements or mechanisms that have been found to work well in a number of situations and which should be replicable in most local authority contexts. Alongside the tangible management mechanisms it also illustrates some of the intangible elements which will be of equal, if not greater, importance in a successful EA process.

Each of the elements in the model will be elaborated on in the following sections. As in Chapter 14, a series of recommendations are made based on the evidence of what appears to work in a wide number of cases. Throughout the chapter the discussion will attempt to address some of the more intangible factors – such as values, perceptions, and feelings of ownership – which to a large extent will characterize an audit.

It should be kept in mind that although management issues may be couched in terms such as mechanisms, duties, procedures etc..., they are in fact about people. Ultimately it is the individuals involved who will determine the effectiveness of the process. Chapter 16 presents a few cameo performances.

CORPORATE COMMITMENT AND COMMITTEE STRUCTURE

It is at the member level that the decision to undertake an audit is ultimately taken, so the support and commitment of the members will obviously be crucial if the process is to have any chance of being successful. Just to illustrate this statement, Figure 15.2 shows those aspects which the questionnaire respondents thought most impeded progress with their audit.

Lack of direct member commitment and of the resources which would be one sign of evidence of this are cited as the two most common causes of failure in EA.

TANGIBLE ELEMENTS INTANGIBLE ELEMENTS

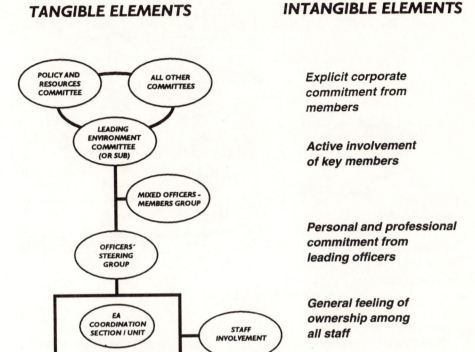

Explicit corporate commitment from members

Active involvement of key members

Personal and professional commitment from leading officers

General feeling of ownership among all staff

Cross-departmental coordination

Community involvement sought

Figure 15.1 Elements in an EA management system

The most visible manifestation of this commitment is in the committee which deals with the EA. Figure 15.3 shows the main mechanisms that have been chosen.

Increasingly Councils are establishing special environment or 'green' initiatives committees specifically to deal with the audit and other such corporate strategies. These committees have in most cases been shown to have a pivotal role in EA. They act as a forum for debate, an arena for

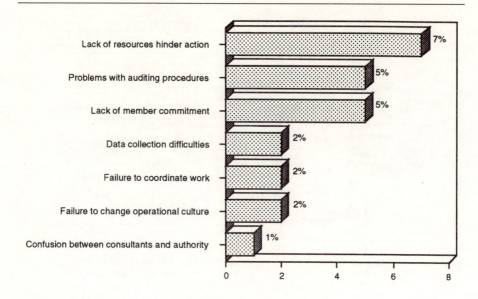

Figure 15.2   Areas of failure

progress to be monitored, a vital link to other council policy areas and to the corporate goals, a political expression of commitment and a mechanism to ensure objective assessment and effective implementation. They also help ensure that the audit is managed as a cross-authority initiative.

Where there is no environment committee the audit must be added to the remit of another committee. The danger with this is that the audit could receive low priority, being simply one additional matter added to their workload, or it could be marginalized within the authority by being viewed as the responsibility of one particular department.

The other level to policy direction is to inculcate the principles of the audit within all sections of the authority. This can be greatly facilitated by requiring all committees to have regard to the environment in decisions that they make. This will in any case be necessary because it is through the committees that recommendations must be passed for approval and resource allocations. The more involved these committees are, possibly through representatives on the environment committee, the more likely they will be supportive of the changes the audit seeks to bring about. A relatively simple mechanism which many authorities have found useful is to include a paragraph on the environmental implications of each decision within the committee reports. This is already a requirement with regard to financial and equal opportunity concerns and if undertaken in the correct spirit can be extremely effective. Another way to reinforce a corporate commitment is to include the broad aims of the audit within any statements

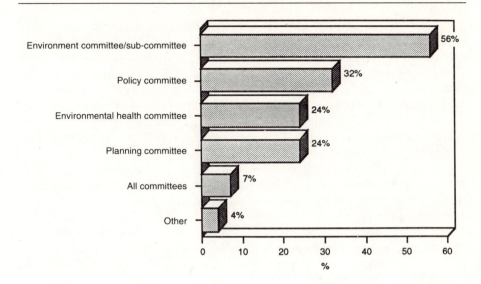

Figure 15.3 Members committee dealing with environmental initiatives

of overall policy. Many authorities now have such statements and it is important that the environment receives explicit recognition as a top priority council concern.

OFFICERS' STEERING GROUP

Three-quarters of authorities in the survey had created a steering (or working) group as the principal interdepartmental management mechanism. This certainly provides a clear control structure but in fact is much more than that. It acts as a forum for debate, direction and dissemination of information. More specifically, it performs the following functions:

- it enlists the participation of all departments and other interested parties in the management of the audit;
- in the absence of another coordinating mechanism, it provides a formal link between officers and members;
- it advises and manages those undertaking the day-to-day work on the audit;
- through its members, information and comment can be passed both to and from all levels and sections of the authority;
- important issues can be debated and reported on in a formal way;
- it oversees the work on all stages of the audit process;
- it monitors progress with implementing actions and facilitates updating and review.

The exact terms of reference and composition of a steering group vary widely. What *is* important is that the membership is drawn from throughout the authority. Preferably they should be high-ranking officers but more importantly they should approach the audit with a personal and professional commitment. Some authorities have benefited from having a more open steering group structure. Direct involvement by councillors obviously helps improve communication, while representatives drawn from local community and environmental organizations strengthen the public's participation. Occasionally a second working group is created comprising more junior officers, but also other staff and public representatives. This can relieve the main group of some of its duties while also building up a broader base of auditing expertise and generating wider involvement and ownership.

Finally, the steering group must be a permanent addition to management structures. This means staying in place even after the initial audit phase. During certain periods it may not need to meet as frequently but it has an ongoing role which needs to be performed.

MANAGING THE PROCESS – INTERNAL AND EXTERNAL EXPERTISE

The question of who should *do* the audit was discussed in Chapter 2. While there are no definitive answers, a combined approach using internal and external expertise would seem to be the most appropriate option. This section will examine the mechanisms for day-to-day management in more detail, specifically looking at the general in-house arrangements, the specific role of an environmental coordinator and the benefits to be gained from using consultants.

In-house arrangements

The benefits to be gained from conducting the audit predominantly in-house are very convincing. The central point is that a process must be managed by those involved in its formulation and most importantly its implementation. While theoretically it may be possible for a committee to formulate the aims, hire consultants to conduct an assessment and pass the results on to staff for implementation, this is not an EA *process* and for this reason will almost certainly be limited in its usefulness. The process is as much about how it is done as about what the outcome is. The change an audit seeks to bring about should be evidenced in the organization as much as in the wider environment. This means developing robust internal mechanisms from an early stage. Some of the advantages of this will be:

■ An on-going process requires that expertise and awareness are built up over time. The sooner the learning process starts the better.

■ Widespread involvement is essential, in the first place to overcome any resistance to what might be seen as outside prying and in the second place to begin generating a feeling of 'ownership' among all staff and hopefully the public.

■ By examining their own activities, individuals can learn the importance of their role and responsibilities in relation to the environment. This awareness is an essential prerequisite to achieving a change in values (and individual values are what organizational culture is made of).

■ More pragmatically, an in-house audit is probably the cheapest option and certainly the most flexible.

Naturally there are also disadvantages in this approach, but as I shall argue below, these can be compensated for by the limited employment of consultants.

Having decided to manage the audit in-house the next questions to arise are where and how.

Who should be involved in the in-house audit?

The greatest difficulty that has arisen is that an EA by its nature must be cross-departmental. It should therefore ideally not be done by one section but should be incorporated into the work of all departments and functional areas. Naturally this requirement is difficult to meet. Being a new process, EA must, at least to start with, fit into the existing administrative structures. Indeed, many would argue that this is the only viable approach to avoid the audit becoming marginalized as a process unconnected from the rest of the work of the authority. Figure 15.4 shows the responses of those authorities who said that the audit had been undertaken by a special EA 'unit'.

Obviously what is taken to constitute a unit varies considerably but it does indicate the areas of the authority where the management has concentrated. Of particular note is the split between the planning, environmental health and chief executive's functional areas. This same division is evident in Figure 15.3 which showed the committees dealing with EA (note: chief executive's office is considered to be responsible to the policy committee). While the chief executive's office operates on a corporate basis, the planning and environmental health functions are quite distinct and often professionally guarded interests. This can sometimes give rise to unhelpful tensions. In a particular authority that was surveyed, two totally contradictory responses were received, one from environmental health and the other from planning!

In the long run no doubt EA will find its place in the organization. The environment committee and the steering group are already established

263

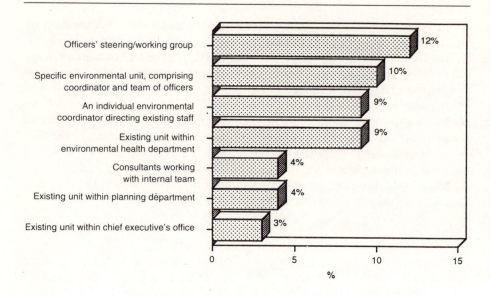

Figure 15.4 Nature and role of the EA unit

elements in an environmental management system. In addition to these, EMAS proposes a whole range of mechanisms for conducting and reporting on audit performance. Some authorities have already instigated major organizational changes in order to give greater prominence to environmental matters. Many of the new environment committees and environmental service departments are not just involved with EA but are the result of an amalgamation at both officer and councillor level of hitherto separated environmental functions. Typically this will include planning and environmental health, so the departmental tension may well resolve itself through a broadening of the remit of specialist sections and a growing realization of the interdisciplinary nature of environmental problems.

Managing the in-house audit

Figure 15.4 above gives a rough indication of the type of arrangements that have been used in managing an audit in-house. This re-emphasizes the important role that a steering group performs. Its members would appear in many cases to not only coordinate but also conduct a large part of the audit themselves. Indeed, given that only about half the authorities in the survey said that they had a special EA unit, there were clearly many more who must have managed the day-to-day work on a more informal basis. Experience would suggest that these informal mechanisms are a combination of members of the steering group carrying out a review of their own departments and chief officers (or their representatives) conducting their own review based on guidelines issued by and with the final information being evaluated by the steering group.

This informal type approach is much more prevalent than many in local government would care to admit. When asked how much time in total had been spent on the initial auditing phase, nearly three quarters of authorities could not even make an estimate of the number of hours. Optimistically this could be explained by saying that the tasks have simply been absorbed throughout the authority. However, what the case studies reveal is that the work is done in a very piecemeal way, with steering group members devoting what amounts to their spare time on performing many of the auditing tasks. Indeed in a number of cases there is a single, usually high ranking officer, who in effect ends up conducting the audit almost single-handedly with only minimal support from elsewhere.

This informal approach to management has certainly got its advantages, particularly where a highly committed individual has introduced EA into an otherwise disinterested authority. It is arguable, however, that the goals of auditing can never be achieved in this way. Participation and transparency are not fostered and the audit can therefore not be maintained in the long term.

One of the main steps in creating a more formal management system is to employ a specialist environmental coordinator.

The role of the environmental coordinator

Figure 15.4 has already shown the importance of having a specific environmental coordinator in order to conduct many of the EA tasks. Box 15.1 shows a typical job description for a coordinator post. Clearly the range of duties should more than justify the expense involved, and with Local Agenda 21 and EMAS soon to be added to these duties it is arguably an essential investment.

Particular care must be taken with regard to the location and rank of the coordinator's post. It should obviously be situated so that interdepartmental involvement is maximized and the greatest number of links are forged. With regard to the previous discussion, this would most likely be an amalgamated environmental services department or otherwise the chief executive's office as a relatively neutral point. With regards to rank, the post should be sufficiently senior so that the wide range of duties can be carried out with authority and without having to constantly seek authorization.

The emerging profession of environmental coordinators is qualitatively different from most other types of local authority professional groupings. They essentially perform a linking role between a whole range of natural and social scientist specialists. Their usefulness is therefore not in doing all the work on the audit themselves but in enabling others in the authority to effectively manage the process.

Box 15.1   Duties and responsibilities for Bristol City Council's
environmental coordinator

1)   To coordinate the monitoring, development and implementation
of the City Green Charter
2)   To develop and maintain a specialist knowledge of environmental
policy
3)   To coordinate the development of a Local Agenda 21
4)   To coordinate the development and implementation of an Eco-
Management System
5)   Prepare Green Charter Action Plans and monitor their implementation
6)   Prepare committee and management reports as appropriate
7)   Contribute generally to the operation of the development team
8)   Maintain records of action taken and conduct correspondence in
connection with the duties undertaken
9)   Provide such support and advice as from time to time the health
and green initiatives manager may require
10) Attend such committee or other meetings as may be required
from time to time and give reports and presentations as appropriate
11) Liaise with other directorates and external organizations as
appropriate
12) Observe the City Council's Equal Opportunities and all corporate
employment policies and the application of their principles in all
aspects of the service provided by the postholder
13) Be responsible for own safety and not endangering that of col-
leagues/others in workplace
14) Ensure that output and quality of work is of the highest possible
standard and accords with current legislation and City Council
policies
15) Carry out such other duties as may reasonably be required in
relation to a post of this nature, without prejudice to any grading
appeal rights

Many authorities who have already employed a single environmental
coordinator are now expanding into a small team to cater for the ever-
expanding EA related functions.

How to use consultants?

The two major potential pitfalls of in-house auditing are a lack of objectivity
and of expertise. While these can be lessened over time by developing the

internal management systems there will probably always be a role for consultants in these areas. In relation to objectivity, external auditors can bring a professional detachment and impartial attitude with them into the process. Indeed, one of the great advantages of EMAS is that it will require this external validation, thereby instilling more confidence in the level of assessment and the results. But the consultant's role should be limited in this respect to a review of what is otherwise an internal exercise. A deeper involvement in the management would not increase the level of objectivity but would certainly reduce the participation of council staff and thereby lessen the 'ownership' felt for the audit.

Expertise is essentially what the authority is buying when it hires a consultant. This will hopefully be of both substantive and procedural issues. If consultants are used judiciously, they can help supplement internal expertise and at the same time train local authority staff in the methods and procedures of auditing. This might for instance involve an initial training course for members and officers on defining the aims and tasks of EA appropriate to that authority. More broadly there could be awareness raising sessions at all levels, from subject specific best practice to the role of individuals as members of the community. This type of training could be a continuous part of staff development.

If any authority is still not convinced that EA should be managed internally, let Box 15.2 serve as a warning that you don't necessarily get what you pay for with consultants.

GENERATING CORPORATE OWNERSHIP

One of the goals of EA should be to create a strong sense of ownership for the process throughout the authority. Ownership is about values, perceptions and motivations, none of which are factors that lend themself to easy analysis. However, it is such an important issue that some attempt must be made to find out how it can be generated and maintained. This section is going to look at two factors, involvement and awareness, which are elements of ownership but which represent relatively tangible aspects which should be more amenable to influence by the auditors.

Involvement

Involvement is essentially a function of participation and manageability. While the participation of everyone in the process might be the ideal, this would be practically impossible because of problems of management, consultation and the need to maintain a degree of control. The previous sections have dealt with the mechanisms for involvement of members and some high ranking officers. While each of the groups performs an essential

---

Box 15.2   The value of consultants!

Authority X employed a consultant to carry out a joint SoE/IA on the basis of his widespread knowledge of the environment and the auditing process. The work was to take six months and lead to the production of a comprehensive report including recommendations. The audit actually ended up taking twice as long and the final report was criticized for not saying anything the authority did not already know and not recommending anything that would not have happened anyway.

Authority Y hired a group of consultants to do their IA. Because of the authority's lack of knowledge of auditing and the consultants' inexperience there were problems defining the terms of reference and the appropriate fee. In the end, the audit cost more and took longer than either the authority or consultants had expected. There was also a feeling that council employees ended up doing much of the work themselves because of all the information they had to collect to give to the consultants.

Finally, **Authority Z** chose a makeshift consultancy which could draw on a wide range of expertise to carry out an IA. Different expectations of the process led to complications which resulted in little use being made of the final report.

One of the conclusions to be drawn is that consultancies are on the same learning curve as local authorities. As experience in both the authorities and the consultancies increases there is less likelihood that these sort of problems will occur. There are moves currently underway to create a professional accreditation body which should guarantee standards of performance and make the choice of consultancy firms much easier for local authorities.

---

role, they obviously only represent a tiny proportion of the local authority numbers. The kind of mechanisms used to gain wider staff involvement are shown in Figure 15.5.

Most of these are fairly traditional, but still potentially effective and easy to use. Exactly what is meant by 'informal' involvement is not clear. It would appear that this covers such things as word of mouth dissemination of information, a general openness to staff suggestions, relying on managers to inform staff and in turn represent their views, and more broadly, persuading staff to examine their roles and responsibilities.

The benefits of having departmental 'green' representatives have obviously been seen by many authorities. Occasionally these are the same people as those on the steering group but in order to spread the workload it could be a good idea to involve other officers, chosen (or elected!) because

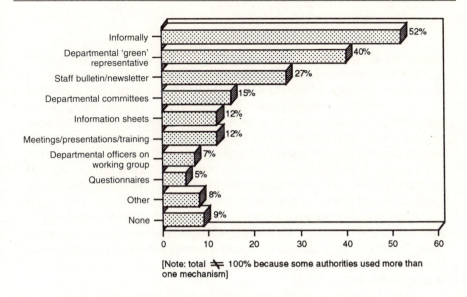

[Note: total ≠ 100% because some authorities used more than one mechanism]

Figure 15.5   Mechanisms to gain involvement of members of staff

of their high level of awareness and commitment to environmental issues. They could, for example, be a sub-group of the main steering group who deal specifically with matters of internal interest.

Finally, direct involvement of staff through meetings, presentations and training programmes probably offers the greatest, but as yet underutilized, potential. Box 15.3 gives examples of two useful approaches to training. A simple method to begin is to include an environmental element in staff induction courses, although obviously other methods are needed for existing staff.

These two examples of training programmes show that on one level they are aimed at building expertise but they have a much more important role in engendering awareness. Ultimately this is how values are changed and is therefore the route to achieving the broader goals of EA. As Figure 15.6 shows, this point is not lost on those authorities engaged in EA, with raised awareness considered to be the area where most progress has been made to date.

Individuals must be shown both the means and the rationale for taking action. All levels of staff will be responsible, in their different ways, for implementing the recommendations of an audit, so efforts must be made to gain their involvement and support. Figure 15.7 gives an idea of the level of success achieved so far in raising internal awareness. Although many authorities were still unsure of how much awareness had changed, there is a significant majority who felt that the EA process had helped.

Box 15.3   Examples of training programmes

Clwyd County Council believe that getting everyone involved, or gaining wide ownership, is a key factor in the success of their audit. At an early stage there was a training course for key officers and members which helped develop the audit methodology. Later, after the process had begun, a wider programme of staff training was initiated. The goal was to create internal awareness by stressing the importance of the environment. The method was to train a small number of staff, initially in two departments, and for these staff then to subsequently run training sessions with the materials provided. In this way, awareness and knowledge should 'cascade' throughout the whole authority.

LB of Sutton have organized two levels of training and awareness raising. In order to increase members' knowledge and commitment, a limited number of sessions on specific environmental topics have been held. A larger training programme was also run with the intention of training a large body of staff in the principles and techniques of EA. So far about 30 staff from all departments have been involved. With a nucleus of trained auditors they hope to be able to spread the workload and the range of participation. A large programme of awareness raising sessions is also planned.

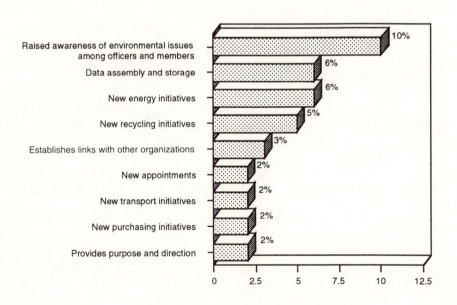

Figure 15.6   Areas of success

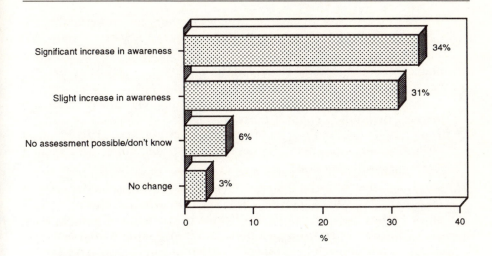

Figure 15.7   Change in environmental awareness within the authority

The final point on ownership and involvement refers back to the point made at the beginning of this section about needing to keep the process manageable. While it is unlikely to fall down due to over-involvement, the elements in the process must still be coordinated so that effort is not wasted and tasks duplicated. The management of change requires strong support structures. Most of these structures have already been mentioned – an environment committee, steering group, environmental coordinator (or team), 'green' representatives. The survey showed that only about half of the authorities were happy with the degree of coordination achieved. In general, steering groups had been very successful in this regard. Surprisingly, however, an environmental coordinator did not seem to greatly enhance corporate cooperation. This could be partly due to the post being often located within a single service department and partly because the employment of an expert makes others in the authority feel that they can then leave the work to the coordinator.

COMMUNITY INVOLVEMENT: EA FOR THE PEOPLE AND BY THE PEOPLE

Although it might sound strange to some authorities, *every* audit is done for the wider community. Even those authorities who see no role for the public in 'their' RIP are mistaken in thinking that it is not done for the community. There are at least four good reasons why this is:

1) A local authority represents the view of its community. On one level

this can be achieved through elected councillors but more fundamentally there should be direct means of expressing views on particular environmental issues.
2) Councils should lead by example. The public must therefore be kept informed of what the council is doing and why.
3) A local authority's mandate for action ultimately comes from the public. The public's support must be sought and maintained.
4) The ultimate goal of EA is to improve the environment. This involves raising public awareness, harnessing the community's energy and directing positive action.

These reasons should be enough to convince any authority of the need to gain the public's involvement. But, whatever the case, the days of EA as a voluntary activity with no mandatory requirement to involve the public are limited. Elements of PIA have already been incorporated within new regulations to appraise development plan policies, which of course includes a large element of consultation. Strategic Environmental Assessment (SEA), which is shortly to be the subject of an EU regulation, will require a new openness on the part of government agencies to inform and involve the public. The public have already gained access to a wide range of information held by public bodies as a result of the 'Freedom of Access to Environmental Information' regulation. EMAS contains requirements for public involvement. Under the scheme, the published 'Environmental Statement' is intended to be comprehensible and accessible to the public. It is not compulsory but is considered appropriate to produce a draft of this first for public consultation. Most fundamentally, the principles of EA, now also enshrined in Agenda 21 and the EU's fifth action programme, are based on the need for openness, honesty and participation. The concluding chapter will discuss what this might mean for EA in more detail but one thing is certain, the community's role in setting the agenda and managing the initiative is set to grow.

The different roles of the community were briefly mentioned in Chapters 2 and 14 and discussed in more detail in Chapter 13. These were basically as sources of information and advice and as implementors of change. Here we elaborate on these roles in the context of the management functions of the authority.

The public as informants and advisers

Referring back to pages 245–7 of the previous chapter, it was shown that local community and environmental organizations were a major source of information. Depending on the issues, there are a whole range of groups that should have useful information and advice to offer. In addition, the contacts that are made should help ensure that the audit addresses those issues considered to be of greatest importance and thereby helps defray potential criticism later in the process. Consultation with the wider public has also taken place, as shown in Figure 15.8.

Clearly this has not been as widespread as one would hope. The greatest area of involvement has been post-audit, when public opinion was sought on options for action and to verify findings. Surprisingly few authorities sought to find out what the public considered to be the most pertinent issues for the audit to address. What to the authority may be considered as a peripheral issue could for a large proportion of the public be of immediate importance. Not alone does the authority risk criticism for not addressing these issues but it could alienate large sections of the community. A simple opinion survey, like that shown in Table 15.1 would suffice, if done early enough and if the findings are really used to direct scope.

The public as implementors of change

An equally important role for the community is as partners with the council in implementing actions and monitoring progress. This role is reinforced by the first, because if the public do not feel that their involvement has been sought they will in turn be very reluctant to support the audit. This is once again an issue of 'ownership'. Apart from a limited RIP, most of the potential actions that can result from an audit will rely on the community for implementation. Authorities can make policy decisions to educate, enforce, encourage, etc, but their own actions will of necessity be limited. In a

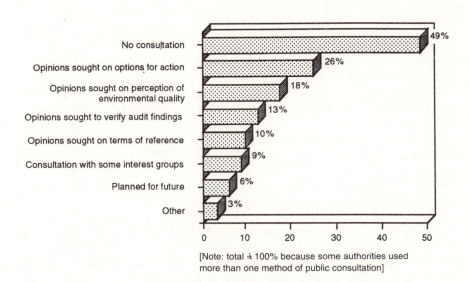

[Note: total ≑ 100% because some authorities used more than one method of public consultation]

Figure 15.8   Public consultation

Table 15.1 Avon County Council's public opinion survey

FOR EACH OF THE ENVIRONMENTAL ISSUES LISTED BELOW PLEASE INDICATE WHETHER
THE ISSUE IS IN YOUR VIEW: VERY IMPORTANT;   IMPORTANT;   NOT IMPORTANT.
(Please tick one box for each line)
Please also add in the left-hand column any other issues that should be given priority and also
star in the right-hand column those three issues which you think should have top priority in
any environmental action plan in the county.

	VERY IMPORTANT	*IMPORTANT*	*NOT IMPORTANT*	*Stars 3 only*
ENERGY CONSERVATION				
ENVIRONMENTAL EDUCATION				
GREEN BELT				
HISTORIC BUILDING CONSERVATION				
NATURE CONSERVATION				
OPEN SPACE PROTECTION				
POLLUTION CONTROL				
RECYCLING INITIATIVES				
TRANSPORT POLICIES				
WASTE MANAGEMENT				

Note: This pre-audit survey was only one part of a wider programme of consultation that involved public
meetings, exhibitions, workshops, comments on draft audit report and draft action plan and an
environmental forum

working partnership with the community the audit will become a much
more powerful force for change. The sort of networks this involves are
already in place and achieving great success. A few general examples are
shown in Box 15.4.

Another area where the community should be directly involved is in
monitoring and reviewing progress. Ultimately it is the public and not any
objective measures of performance which will decide whether the goals of
EA are being achieved. Two important aspects of this are **environmental
quality** and **levels of environmental awareness**. Both are directly related
to people's everyday lives and their cooperation in deciding whether

---

Box 15.4   Partnerships between councils and the community

- Wildlife groups throughout the country undertake a range of nature conservation tasks on behalf of and with the support of local authorities. This includes nature reserve management, ecological surveys, environmental monitoring, species protection and habitat creation
- Colleges and universities link up with authorities to provide education and training for staff, specialist advice and placement posts
- Recycling schemes run by voluntary groups often operate in cooperation with council waste disposal services and receive financial and logistical support
- Private enterprises, from industrial firms to farms, often enter into voluntary agreements to help protect and enhance the environment. This can range from negotiated arrangements with developers to improve landscaping or reduce pollution, to management agreements on farms to preserve a special site of interest
- Civic societies and residential groups often advise on and help finance the enhancement of urban areas

---

change has occurred or not is essential. Their views and perceptions should of course be balanced against more intangible and perhaps long-range factors but they should nevertheless be a major element in reviewing progress. More directly, specialist interest groups are often the most reliable and comprehensive sources of information on environmental trends. In addition, academic institutions, business organizations and public agencies all have data and expertise which can help monitor environmental quality and reflect progress in other areas.

Finally a sustainable community must be built on self-awareness and empowerment. Figure 15.9 shows that some success has already been achieved through EA in increasing environmental awareness among the public.

There is still much work to be done in translating awareness into positive action but, through community involvement, a local authority can help achieve change not just for the people but by the people.

The role of an environmental forum

Of the range of mechanisms that can be used to encourage community involvement (see Chapters 2 and 13), perhaps the most significant is the environmental forum. Most authorities engaged in EA now have such a forum (at the time of the survey nearly 40 per cent already had). Essentially

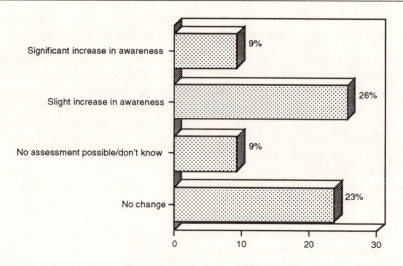

Figure 15.9 Change in environmental awareness in local authority's region

it is a mechanism for liaison between the local authority and its community and between different interests within the community. As such it is an excellent vehicle for achieving the information, advice and partnership roles outlined above. In some regions it has been the first opportunity that environmental interest groups have had to engage with each other, let alone with the authority. The potential is therefore immense. Networks of information and contacts can be established, new alliances forged and joint initiatives developed. Most importantly it provides an opportunity for debating issues and deciding agendas. This discursive and consensual approach must surely help dispel prejudices by creating greater under-standing of the limitations as well as the opportunities that there are for action. This could be particularly helpful for the local authority whose limitations on action, as dictated by mandate and finance, are not always appreciated by outside bodies. Having said this, the forum should not become a venue for the public to constantly criticize the authority on particular issues, nor one for the authority to simply explain away their inactivity or lack of success. The important characteristics to foster are open and free-ranging debate. There are plenty of models of successful environmental forums, for example in Leicester City and Lancashire County. Some useful tips are offered in Box 15.5.

A final point to make is that the authority should put great effort into persuading members of the public to get involved. An apparent lack of interest on the part of the community should not be taken at face value. Those authorities who have done well in EA have often had to spend time encouraging the public that their input will be truly valuable. Signs of inertia

---

Box 15.5   Tips for a successful environmental forum

■ Membership should be drawn from as wide a range of interests as possible. This should include: local conservation, environmental and amenity groups; the private sector; educational establishments; government agencies; other local authorities; individual members of the public with special interests; minority groups; relevant sections of the authority itself

■ If there is a high level of involvement, consider setting up sub-groups to focus on particular topics – for example: economy; wild-life; energy, etc. It is still essential to maintain the overview of the main forum

■ The council's role should not be one of leader but rather of facil-itator. The agenda should be set by the participants and if there is a chairperson it should be an elected post, or perhaps held on a rotating basis. The council should be careful not to over-represent itself. The facilitator role could include providing the meeting place, the secretariat and the promotion

■ The frequency of meetings should be decided jointly but should be often enough for participants to feel a real input and not so often to deter attendance. Flexibility is also important so that key stages of the audit and important issues can be dealt with as they arise

---

should be combated rather than blindly accepted. Thus begins the process of empowerment.

RESOURCES – MYTHS AND REALITIES!

The major barrier to the adoption of comprehensive audit procedures in local government is one of cost.

(Grayson, 1992)

This is undoubtedly a realistic assessment. Fear of resource implications is mentioned in the majority of texts on auditing and cited in Part II of the survey as the principal reason for not carrying out an audit. It is also not surprising, given the costs of some of the most well known audits – Lan-cashire County Council, for example, spent £200,000 on their SoE survey while Humberside County Council's pollution audit cost £300,000.

However this is essentially an issue about commitment. Resources are in effect tangible evidence of a real will to act on the part of those directing the audit. The myth about resources in EA is that it is an expensive process to manage. As explained below, the reality is that the process is relatively inexpensive to undertake and manage but will inevitably highlight the need for extra expenditure on environmental objectives.

Figure 15.10 shows the initial audit budgets for surveyed authorities and Figure 15.11 the implementation budgets. The major budgetary elements are shown in Figure 15.12.

Initial budget

The initial budget represents the costs involved in getting the EA process off the ground, that is, the surveying and reporting costs. It is significant that almost the same proportion of authorities said that the audit was financed from existing resources as said that there was a specified budget. This redirection of existing resources towards the audit raises questions as to where the money would have been spent if not on the audit. However, in effect the allocation of a special EA budget also involves a redirection of funds within an authority. This is the reality of auditing. It costs money! As with many other areas of environmental activity, such as recycling, tree planting and nature protection, the authority must decide if, on balance, the costs are justified. Where it differs from other areas of environmental activity is that the systems set up by an EA management system should help an authority coordinate its environmental expenditure. Thus, for example, the rationalization of recycling activities or the pursuit of multiple objectives through single activities can improve overall cost-effectiveness. For this reason clear knowledge of the costs is essential. Without this

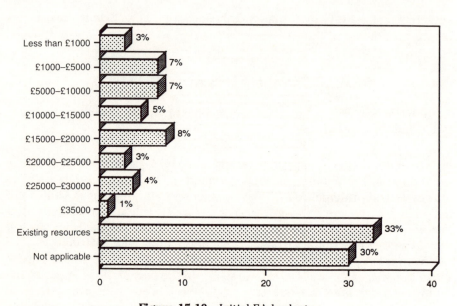

Figure 15.10 Initial EA budgets

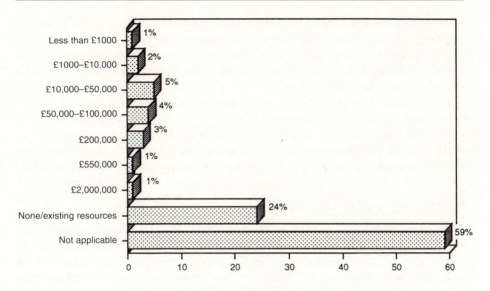

Figure 15.11 Implementation budgets

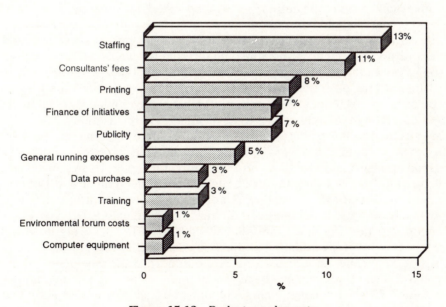

Figure 15.12 Budgetary elements

279

knowledge it will be very difficult to evaluate the cost effectiveness of the auditing process and to justify its continuance.

The amounts in Figure 15.10 clearly show that auditing need not be as resource consuming as is commonly thought. The majority of authorities spend between £10,000 and £15,000 on the initial audit. Figure 15.12 shows that by far the largest cost element is labour; staff and/or consultant's time. The other significant cost elements are printing, publicity and general operation expenses. These costs may be identified and clearly managed within the EA process. Given clear objectives for the audit and knowledge of available resources, the process can be made to fit within these parameters.

Implementation budget

As regards the implementation budget, much less data were supplied by the authorities. Many actions recommended by an audit will not involve cost implications. These may have to do with changes in policy and staff priorities or simply rationalization of activities. Other actions may incur minor costs but these are often only in the short term and are more than offset in the longer term. Recommended actions on energy efficiency, transport management and recycling are examples of areas where long-term cost savings are possible.

Inevitably though, long-term progress will require extra resources. For illustration, Table 15.2 shows some of the potential actions that can be taken to improve council practices, broken down by their cost implications.

An examination of the authorities who specified implementation budgets showed that the smaller amounts in Figure 15.11 represent very specific 'green' projects such as a new tree planting scheme, purchase of additional monitoring equipment, or establishing internal mechanisms for recycling. The larger amounts are a range of revenue and capital expenditures which will forward the objectives of EA but to a large extent represent costs which would have been incurred anyway. This usually includes community recycling, traffic calming, grants to environmental organizations, landscape improvements, litter abatement and so on. There is a distinction here between the audit as a vehicle for change and as a mechanism to coordinate existing policies and practices. More broadly, this could be perceived as a distinction between the pursuit of sustainable development and the continued improvement of existing (traditional) environmental areas. It is obviously realistic for an audit to attempt to coordinate existing environmental expenditures but it should not limit itself to this. This need not necessarily involve additional resources; more important is that policies are integrated and resources are used to pursue multiple objectives. Where resource savings are achieved, such as in those areas listed in column one of Table 15.2, the net benefit can be ploughed back into other EA activities. Some authorities have set up special funds for just this purpose.

Table 15.2 Potential actions to improve council practices

Savings	No cost	Low cost	High cost
Energy efficiency measures	Assess environmental impact of all policies and practices	Staff and public education and training	Redesign or relocate council buildings
Rationalize purchasing	Greater corporate commitment	Publicity of environmental issues and initiatives	New transport networks and modes
Community involvement in implementation	Generate staff 'ownership' of environmental initiatives	More environmental monitoring	Environment/ Ecology/Interpretive Centre
Switch to unleaded or diesel petrol	Cycle allowances. More incentives to use public transport – e.g. contributions to bus and rail passes	General environmental improvements – eg tree planting, pocket parks, wildlife meadows	Major environmental improvements – eg creation of country park, wildlife areas
Fuel efficiency measures	Greater dissemination of environmental information	Grants for voluntary organizations	Employment of environmental specialists
Reduced car allowances Reduced essential car users Reduced engine sizes Parking charges	Council land and buildings managed in an environmentally sensitive way	Support community initiatives	Invest in GIS for monitoring, education and information provision
Reuse and recycling of all appropriate materials	Include environmental specifications in contracts	Service on environmental forum	
Reduced material use – eg sending E-Mail rather than memos reduces energy and paper use	Inform business and the public of impacts and responsibilities	Purchase of environmentally friendly goods	
		Improve non-car access to council land and buildings	

Table 15.2 Continued

Savings	No cost	Low cost	High cost
		Traffic calming schemes	
		Support public transport – eg subsidize buses	
		Assess environmental impact of all developments	

Notes:
1) Cost is calculated on an aggregate basis. If, for example, short-term (1–3 years) minor costs are offset by greater long-term savings, this is considered a saving
2) Calculations exclude staff time while recognizing that this may be a large cost element
3) From left to right most of the actions could be placed in the next category with a proportionate increase in effectiveness and expenditure

A final point is that the non-response rate to questions on resources is very high, which indicates a possible lack of thought for the financial implication of EA and an apparent weakness in monitoring the management of the process. Together with data on the amount of staff time put into EA, this is an area which will have to receive more attention, particularly in the context of EMAS.

CONCLUSION

This chapter has discussed the elements in a management system for EA. These are illustrated in Figure 15.1. The tangible elements to the system are drawn from emerging best practice in a wide number of local authorities. The intangible elements cover a range of factors which have been demonstrated to be of fundamental importance in the conduct of an EA process. An authority undertaking an audit should assess the contribution that each element could make to their process but should only choose those that are appropriate to their circumstance.

CHECKLIST

▶ Members must demonstrate their commitment to EA. A special environment committee acts as an expression of priority and a mechanism to ensure progress. The audit should be a corporate initiative.

▶ Establish a permanent EA steering group. This should provide the focus for management. All functional areas of the authority, and other groups if appropriate, should be represented.

▶ If EA is to succeed it must be managed as an internal process of learning and change. To maintain this in the long term, the structures, experience and sense of 'ownership' must be built up.

▶ An environmental coordinator is an essential element in the management system. The post should be located so as to maximize interdepartmental cooperation.

▶ Consultants should be used in a supportive role, offering advice, training and objectivity.

▶ Generating a feeling of ownership throughout the authority is an essential task of EA. The management system should embrace all levels and all sectors, emphasizing the role and responsibility of each individual, through a programme of training and awareness raising.

▶ The public should not just be consulted on the audit but should be facilitated to participate as active members. They can provide valuable advice and information and become partners in implementing change.

▶ Resource efficiency should be a key goal of EA. Monitor the costs of maintaining the process and of implementing the output.

REFERENCES

Grayson, L (1992) *Environmental Auditing – A Guide to Best Practice in the UK and Europe* Technical Communications and British Library Science and Information Service, Letchworth

16

PROSPECTS FOR THE FUTURE

Noel Bruder

INTRODUCTION

This chapter serves a dual purpose. Firstly, it acts as a conclusion for Part III, reiterating some of the main points from Chapters 14 and 15. Two themes in particular are discussed, implementation mechanisms and the role of individuals, because they are illustrative of a number of fundamental issues.

Secondly, this chapter rounds off the discussion on EA in general and the role that the process can play in the search for sustainable development. It examines the prospects for EA within an evolving system of local environmental management and then explores the role of the EA process in the pursuit of sustainable development goals.

IMPLEMENTATION MECHANISMS

Implementation mechanisms are by right an element of all other management systems. However, they are of such importance that they deserve special mention. Examining these mechanisms also emphasizes the imperative of producing an implementable set of actions. This should be used as a principle to define the purpose and direction of auditing activities.

Some of the mechanisms were discussed previously in relation to form and format for action recommendations. Overriding these details, however, is the requirement for a high level commitment to action and the management mechanisms to deliver it.

On a very pragmatic level, the first real test for members is when verbal support is to be turned into financial backing. Many a far-reaching goal in EA has been circumscribed when it came to deciding between allocations for the audit and for another interest, like education or housing (though ideally many interests should coincide). Where real choices are concerned, it will be the personal and professional commitment on the part of members that decides whether EA is favoured.

In a different sense, the same is true for officers, other staff and the wider public. An involvement throughout the process will be crucial in generating ownership, which will in turn dictate the degree of progress possible. In most cases the changes called for in the audit will impact on either the general local authority staff or the wider public. It is also here that the responsibility for implementing most of the actions will lie, rather than with high ranking officers or members. It is therefore important that potential resistance to change is avoided through involvement and awareness raising. The public's role in implementation should also be explicitly addressed. Often a dual set of mechanisms will have to be set up; internally a regime will be established in order to make the action happen externally. So within the authority, service and personal development plans might need amending; new budget allocations made; a reporting structure put in place, etc.... These mechanisms are then used to facilitate a better relationship with the public, through for example cooperation, education and grant provision.

There are two final points on implementation mechanisms. Firstly they must be dispersed throughout the authority in order to encompass even those not directly involved in the earlier EA stages. Secondly, they have an external component, broadly defined as community involvement, which must be managed alongside the internal regime.

INDIVIDUALS IN ENVIRONMENTAL AUDITING

The discussion so far has been presented in a reasonably objective and rational way. The point was made in the introduction to Chapter 15, however, and is now reiterated, that in actual fact the EA process is neither totally objective nor totally rational. The reason for this is that individuals are involved, and this in turn means that values, perceptions, beliefs and feelings, together with the whole gambit of other human factors, influence the process. Despite many people's efforts these will never be comprehensively understood, either in relation to the environment or any other matter.

While human factors can not be entirely planned for, a realization of their significance is extremely important. This requires some angle from which they can be looked at; that is, a factor which reveals the underlying beliefs but is more open to examination. Commitment – the willingness to provide high level support on an on-going basis – is such a factor. The importance of commitment in all stages of the process lies in the fact that EA is not yet institutionalized within local government. While the legislative mandate, policy context, management structures and procedural methods are still developing, the institutional gap (as such) is being filled by the commitment of key councillors and officers. In practically every authority encountered, certainly those who have made significant progress, the influence of these key individuals has been profound. Box 16.1 presents two cameos to give an indication of the difference that personal commitment can make to the process.

The goal of EA should be to develop and spread this sense of commitment so that as the institutions supporting the process grow in strength so too does the level and depth of personal concern. This will simultaneously create the opportunity and the willingness to act.

Box 16.1 Personal commitment to EA

■ *Councillor 'Green'*
She sees her commitment as being both personal and political. She grew up in a rural area and now represents a rural constituency. This connection to the land, as she describes it, has made her more aware of the environment and of the problems that are faced. On being elected a Labour councillor she saw the opportunity, and indeed the responsibility, to take some positive action. This was supported by the ruling Labour Party who, as a result of the high profile of environmental issues in 1989, had included the environment as one of the council's corporate aims and begun an EA. She had a key influence in setting up an environmental strategy sub-committee and in pushing for the establishment of the post of environmental coordinator. Although the council has maintained ongoing support for EA she had to push very hard at times to get the resources and level of involvement that was necessary to drive the process forward. In this sense, her achievement has been in lobbying other councillors and in providing a high level of political support and encouragement to the officers.

■ *Assistant Chief Planning Officer, Herbert Layer*
Although a planning officer, he is part of the larger environmental services division and has therefore an interest in a wide range of issues. It has been said of him that without his knowledge and enthusiasm the audit would not have got as far as it did. He was instrumental in initiating EA and has had a dominant role throughout the process. As director of the internal 'green' team he is involved directly in implementing many of the auditing recommendations. EA is therefore integral to his daily work.

PROSPECTS FOR THE ENVIRONMENTAL AUDITING PROCESS

It has been emphasized throughout this book that EA is not a limited, one-off product but rather a strategic and evolutionary process. The elements in and management of the strategic process have been discussed at length. This section explores the prospects for the future development of EA. It should be read in conjunction with Appendix 4 which highlights some of the main contextual factors likely to influence local authority action.

The role of coordination

This book has attempted to define EA very broadly because it is apparent that the process has now become not just one, but a whole set of overlapping and interlinked activities. These were described initially in Chapter 1 as the tasks of MA, RIP, PIA and SoE. However, a whole set of related activities have also been touched on. These have included environmental management systems, strategic environmental assessment, Local Agenda 21, appraisal of development plans, and the identification of environmental capacities and indicators. These emerging activities are in one sense independent processes designed to fulfil their own sets of goals. From another perspective, however, they are all intimately connected within an extended system of environmental management. Ultimately they all set out to review environmental performance and to recommend ways whereby human impact can be reduced. This is exactly the rationale for EA. So, in theory there is much overlap between these activities. Exactly what is happening in the real local government setting is more difficult to say. Experience to date would appear to confirm a high degree of interrelatedness between the activities and perhaps more importantly between the management of the activities. A couple of examples of this are the expanding role of environmental coordinators, originally employed for EA but now also developing Local Agenda 21, and the use of PIA methodologies in the environmental appraisal of development plans (see Chapters 4 and 8 respectively).

Figure 16.1 shows the overlapping system of activities in this expanded view. The figure also demonstrates the pivotal role that EA has within this system. It forms the hub around which much of the activity circulates. Clearly, the problem that could easily arise from this conception is that so much is sucked into the centre of the system that it becomes impossible to manage and coordinate all the separate activities. While this is potentially a grave problem, the solution actually lies within EA. As originally conceived, an audit was not only designed to review environmental performance but also to coordinate the response to the problems that were found. The importance of this coordinating role has not exactly been lost along the way but it has equally not been highlighted in the majority of audits. Faced with

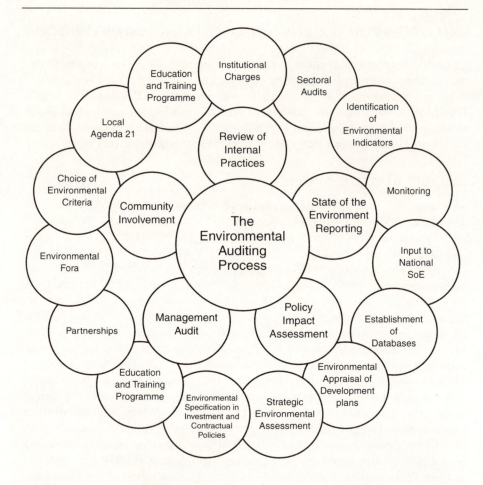

Figure 16.1 Environmental auditing at the centre of an overlapping system of environmental management

the realities of traditional bureaucratic systems, auditors have often had no choice but to assess issues separately and to pursue sectoral responses. The danger with this type of approach has always been that problems are shifted rather than solved and that the essential areas of overlap are forgotten. In the long run progress will no doubt be made but it will involve more time and effort than if a coordinated approach was followed.

The introduction of environmental management systems

A revival of the coordinating role of EA is no doubt set to come about with the introduction of environmental management systems. EMAS in particular lays great emphasis on this with not only an overall management system for each of the registered operational units but also a 'Corporate Overview and Coordination System' to ensure that the audit is the responsibility of the entire authority.

With a management system as a core element in an expanded view of the EA process, each of the activities would be tied together and brought forward as a unified whole. Each would also be working to achieve the principles and goals set out in an environmental statement. If this statement is based on a vision of sustainable development then the separate activities would be seeking to integrate different aspects of the vision. What this involves is a view of sustainable development which is both far-reaching and practically useful. Defining sustainable development in this way is the subject of the next section.

DEFINING SUSTAINABLE DEVELOPMENT IN PRACTICAL TERMS

While there has been a whole mass of information on what sustainable development means, many people are still totally perplexed as to how it can be applied in a UK local government setting. Some still see it as a global issue to do with halting rainforest destruction or controlling climate change. They recognize that local authorities have a role but do not consider it as being directly relevant to their everyday duties. Others readily admit the responsibility of local authorities but sometimes view *all* environmental issues as contributing to sustainable development. There is of course a valid case for this view, in that it is the cumulative impact of many minor activities that both cause the damage and lead to positive change. This stance does not, however, help very much in furthering the cause of sustainable development. If all environmentally damaging activities are unsustainable and all improvements are sustainable then the debate has not moved on very far. A more subtle approach is required which takes into account the scale of the problems and the degree of change which will be needed to bring about solutions.

A useful starting point is to identify the range of environmental issues which are dealt with by local authorities. Table 16.1 is a very broad attempt at this according to 'traditional', 'new' and 'sustainable development' perspectives.

The three columns are in no way conclusive but they do help to distinguish between different levels of impact and scales of concern. They also demonstrate how it is not just new issues that are taken on board but more usually the change in perspective is due to an expanding view of an existing issue.

Traditional environmental issues are those that have been built up since

Table 16.1 Local authority perspectives on environmental concerns

Traditional environmental perspective	*New/broad environmental perspective*	*Sustainable development perspective*
Health and safety Waste collection and disposal Pollution control – point source and single substance	Environmental risk assessment Waste management strategy – reduction and recycling Energy conservation Prevention of pollution	Environmental quality management Equity in access to environmental resources Closure of resource loops – pollution and waste avoidance – more efficient use of resources – multiple purpose and use
Land use control Heritage conservation Achieving balance and quality through development planning	Integration of land use planning and other policy goals Reduction of environmental impact	Strategic environmental assessment – hierarchy of policy, plan, programme and project Unbreachable environmental constraints Systems view of environment–economy–society relationship
Nature conservation – designated sites and endangered species Open space provision for amenity Landscape protection	Habitat enhancement Consideration of total natural resource	Contribution to global biodiversity Natural resource constraints Intrinsic value placed on other species
Single issue monitoring	Multiple issue monitoring and review	Monitoring, review and feedback within holistic environmental system
Public participation	Education, advocacy and awareness raising Access to information	Community involvement Access to agenda setting and decision making processes

the very inception of local government. The important thing to note about them is that they are essentially reactive; a system of control has arisen in response to environmental problems. Another feature is that issues of environment are traditionally treated separately from issues of society, economy, etc. Areas of overlap between, for example, the polluting impacts of transport and the land use planning system were not normally a priority. Finally, the area of concern was considered to be very localized with little or no effort put into collaborative efforts with neighbouring authorities, let alone a consideration of global or even national concerns. Traditional responses include such tools as sectoral based strategies (for waste, health etc) and single issue plans (eg development plans exclusively designed to control and direct development).

The last few years have seen a shift in perspective towards what is referred to in Table 16.1 as the 'new' environmental perspective. Clearly the issues themselves are not new but the way in which they are viewed often makes them qualitatively different. Generally they represent a development on the traditional view whereby the control of problems is replaced by a more proactive management approach. Thus waste is no longer only an issue of collection and disposal but also of reduction and recycling. Similarly pollution is not just about maintaining minimum standards and controlling point sources but is about prevention first and integrated management wherever it is allowed. The philosophy behind this new view is that 'prevention is better than cure' and demands that are made on the environment should be managed so as to maximize the benefits and minimize the negative impacts. The first set of audits were typical responses to these issues, as are nature conservation and recycling strategies. There are also signs that the boundaries of local authorities are beginning to break down both in terms of how they view their area of influence and the necessity for more cooperation with other agencies. Thus a local authority is just as likely to be drawing guidance from the EU or even the UN as it is from UK Central Government. Similarly, actions proposed by a local authority might easily be directed for implementation by a local amenity group or offered under contract to a private sector organization. This has led to the emergence of new networks, locally, nationally and internationally, which seek to coordinate effort and expand the local authorities' area of influence.

The leap from the 'new' environmental to the sustainable development perspective is taking place at this very moment. It has already been evidenced in some of the more recent auditing work. It is being encouraged by Agenda 21, the EU's fifth action programme and by the Government through the Sustainable Development Strategy. Table 16.1 tries to give some flavour of the issues involved. Like in the change from traditional to new environmental issues, the emergence of sustainable development is less about taking on board additional concerns and more about the change in perspective that is coming about. A useful way to look at this is as a change from a linear perspective to a systems view of the environment. A local authority's environment exists itself as a unified and dynamic system and overlaps with all other systems from a local to a global level. These connections are represented in Figure 16.2. This shows the vertical and horizontal integration between and within systems.

There are two important points to make. Firstly, all systems are connected, or to be more exact all systems are in fact one. Just like in the natural sciences where ecosystems are only abstractions from the biosphere (the global system), the boundaries in Figure 16.2 only exist for management convenience. Secondly, within each individually defined system all elements are also linked. This applies both between and within all aspects of society, economy and environment.

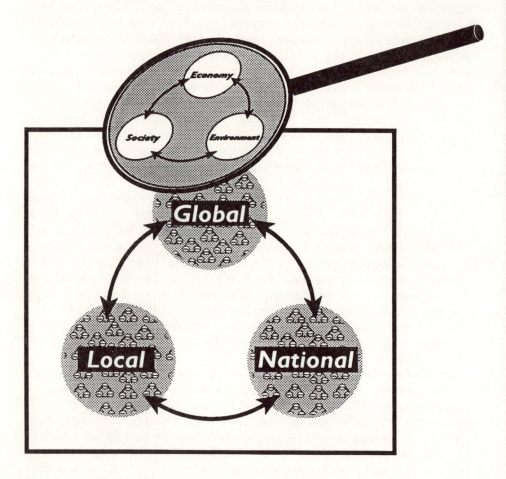

Figure 16.2 A systems view of environmental concerns

These two points have direct relevance for the management of sustainable development in a local authority setting. The first point implies that all levels of concern must be considered in any analysis. A good example of this is vehicle pollution. Whereas this was traditionally assessed from the point of view of local impact it is now increasingly being viewed in the context of global environmental change. The issue of scale was discussed previously in Chapter 14 in relation to defining a realistic scope for an audit. The recommendation was that the principle of 'thinking globally but acting locally' be followed. This can be added to by saying that local actions should be assessed for their contribution to both national and global change. It is therefore no longer sufficient to simply pay lip service to the higher level impacts. The authorities' influence on these must be proactively addressed. Local Agenda 21 and SEA will certainly figure prominently as tools for incorporating this wider brief.

The second point, to do with the connections within systems, involves the adoption of a number of principles for sustainable development, as shown in Box 16.2.

Most of these principles are well known and have been explained elsewhere in the book. The others, which relate to the systems view, should act as a bridge between the more conceptual principles and the definition of operational objectives for EA. For example, the principle of equity in sustainable development is often quoted but rarely translated into practice. This is because the requirements of inter- and intra-generational equity

---

Box 16.2 Principles for sustainable development

- Act locally to sustain the global environment
- The political process should be characterized by honesty, participation and transparency
- Prevention is better than cure;
  uncertainty should be managed through the political process;
  when in doubt pursue a precautionary approach
- Adopt a systems view of the human–environment relationship. This should emphasize integration, feedback and the closure of resource loops
- Environmental, social and economic efficiency should be striven for by applying the most 'elegant' solutions in order to gain the maximum benefit. This is a function of Best Practical Means (BPM) designed to meet multiple objectives
- Human impact should be managed according to a code of ethics. This should emphasize inter- and intra-generational equity and the intrinsic value of all living things

---

simply cannot be met by a single local authority, even if the mechanisms for doing so were known. However, applying the principle of environmental and social efficiency means that at least the resources consumed and the pollution caused within the local authority area have resulted in the greatest good for the least damage. In terms of carrying capacities this means that the burden placed on other societies (either in space or time) has been kept to a minimum. Using the same example, and applying the principle of systems, it should mean that the negative impacts resulting from development are reduced through feedback and the closure of resource loops. Any residual impact should be internalized and, according to the principle of honesty, participation and transparency in the political process, considered an acceptable impact in view of the benefits gained. This example shows that all the principles are interrelated and in a way serve as a series of filters through which decisions should be passed.

Applying the principle of honesty, participation and transparency in the political process is totally reliant on the society in question having a sense of ethical responsibility. In practical terms there is no other way for the views of future generations and other societies to be considered other than as a moral obligation expressed by individuals through the institutions of government. This is why the final principle listed in Box 16.2 is one of ethics. When defining sustainable development there is no escaping the conclusion that it is essentially an issue of values, responsibility and integrity. EA can serve to direct society in the right direction but it can never act as a substitute for a code of ethics held individually and collectively by society: these should be revealed directly through the political process. If they are not, it is unlikely that government will respond to the needs of sustainable development. The first task of EA is therefore to generate the awareness that all members of society need in order to make informed choices.

There is currently a good deal of effort at all levels of government being dedicated to establishing how sustainable development can be put into effect. This is supported by fundamental work on defining environmental capacities and indicators, and collecting the information necessary to make sound judgements. EA can usefully be pictured as the focal point where the principles and practicality of sustainable development come together. The second task of EA is therefore to manage the changes that will be required, on one level within the organization but more broadly within society as a whole.

MANAGING THE CHANGE TO SUSTAINABLE DEVELOPMENT

It would not be appropriate to finish this book without addressing some of the political realities of managing the change to sustainable development. The book has argued that environmental auditing provides a process whereby a local authority, with the support of its community, can effectively implement the desired changes. In this respect it has been demonstrated that EA is sufficiently synoptic to encompass the relevant issues, is realistic enough to be accommodated by local authority organizations and is capable of directing strategic action within a flexible, honest and transparent system.

While the intrinsic value of EA is hopefully no longer a question, there remains the outstanding issue of the value that society places on such tools of environmental management. On a broad political level this is an issue far beyond the scope of this book. It relates to the relative importance that governments and the international community place on environmental factors in the conduct of their affairs. It can be argued that while environmental issues are now receiving more attention than in the past they are still not a priority when compared to the more established concerns of economy, defence, health, education etc. Witness, for example, the almost total absence of environmental safeguards in the recent revisions to GATT or, more locally, the absence of environmental concerns in current debates about the national curriculum. Sustainable development has done much to align environmental issues alongside other interests but as yet has done little to shift the balance of interests. The intractability of established systems to change is therefore a factor which needs to receive special attention.

In the local government context there are two aspects of the established system that present a particular challenge: the domination of economic interests and the hierarchical mode of management. Box 14.4 (page 243) showed how most current EAs have to a large extent sidestepped the 'thorny' issues of economic development. On the same point, Figure 14.5 (page 240) demonstrated that the majority of local authorities choose not to explore the links between environmental quality and economic well-being. These findings suggest that despite the rhetoric of sustainable development, local government EA is still having trouble breaking out of the traditional perception of what constitutes a legitimate environmental concern. Ultimately, the solution to this is to focus on the symbiotic elements in the relationship between economy and environment. These are the elements which emphasize quality of life rather than gross quantity of outputs and efficiency rather than profligacy in the use of resources. There is currently a good deal of effort being put into examining the economy–environment relationship. In particular, the LGMB have recently produced a guide to local authority initiatives in this area which sets out approaches to making economic development more environmentally sustainable (LGMB, 1993). On a different level the science of environmental economics is continually evolving more useful techniques and concepts which demonstrate the interdependence of the two components. There are no easy answers when it comes to the 'greening' of economic development. It is however essential that EA asks the right questions.

The second challenge to EA comes from the system of hierarchical control which currently dominates the local government sector. Chapter 15 has shown how these control structures are of fundamental importance in the conduct of EA. The advice given in this book is designed to maximize the effectiveness of established systems while also seeking to incorporate alternative approaches. It does not, however, go so far as to suggest a new pattern of control. This would be unrealistic. It does not mean that existing systems should not be questioned. Within established systems there is still considerable scope to develop more participatory mechanisms which can act to overcome some of the more disempowering aspects of hierarchies. A desire to generate ownership through involvement should therefore be a fundamental goal of EA. As with economic issues, there are no ready-made solutions which a local authority can adopt to ensure that all staff and the wider community will feel a sense of ownership for the EA process. Encouraging active involvement through information dissemination, consultation and consensual decision making should certainly help by making the process more accessible.

CONCLUSION

Environmental auditing is ultimately about bringing about change. The starting point is to evaluate the current situation in order to understand the degree and the direction of change required. The final goal is not yet fully known but is generally agreed to be a realization of the requirements of sustainable development. Part I referred to this as the 'holy grail' of modern environmentalism. In between the starting point and the final goal is the murky area of institutional and individual perceptions, motivations and commitment. It is here that the 'quest' really lies. It is not solely a quest for something tangible but also for the factors that will influence widespread and elemental awareness. EA is therefore not just a tool for environmental management but has an equally important role as a process of awareness raising. Both the conduct and output of an audit should be designed to bring about fundamental changes in the outlook and understanding of a local authority and its community. In this way, the process of change will have begun.

REFERENCES

Local Government Management Board (1993) 'Greening Economic Development – how local authorities have integrated economic and environmental approaches' LGMP, Luton.

STATE OF THE ENVIRONMENT (SOE) REPORT: CHECKLIST

Appendix 6 discusses some of the current work that is attempting to provide a comprehensive list of environmental indicators for use by local authorities.

This appendix does not attempt to pull together all the current thinking but does suggest a basic structure to the SoE and some key indicators to consider in the assessment.

STRUCTURE OF THE SOE

Based on the elements of environmental stock listed in Table 3.1, the table below makes some suggestions as to the scope of issues to consider. Detailed commentary can be found under the specific topics in Part II.

Elements	*Commentary*
1) **Atmosphere and climate** *Reducing CO_2 emissions* ■ energy in buildings see Chapter 6	Across the whole LA area, this is currently difficult to monitor sources. The best sources are probably the energy utilities, identifying the level of gas and electricity sales by zone. This, however, will not distinguish individual users or separate out industrial processing energy.
■ energy in transport see Chapters 7 and 8	The level of traffic in an area is the simplest indicator since it relates reasonably directly to fuel use and CO_2 emissions, and is regularly collected by the local transport authority. Land use change drives the need to travel, so this, too needs monitoring.

Elements	*Commentary*
■ Renewable energy see Chapter 6	An inventory of potential renewable energy sources and projects has been carried out by some authorities (eg Cornwall County Council) and is being encouraged by the Energy Technology Support Unit (ETSU) of the DTI.
increase CO$_2$ absorption	Difficult to monitor precisely, but the level of tree cover provides one measure. This can be regularly monitored by analysis of aerial photographs of the area.
2) **Biodiversity** see Chapter 5	The level of biodiversity may be related to (i) the area and quality of different habitats; and (ii) to the range and number of different species. Lists of both are provided by English Nature, RSPB and others. Monitoring will necessarily have to be highly selective.
3) **Air quality** see Chapter 10	Air quality standards from the EU and the WHO in relation to levels of SO_2 NO_x, O_3, CO etc provide the starting point. The number and location of monitoring stations is critical. Supplemented by information on emissions from specific major pollution (eg factories). Bristol City Council provides a model of good practice.
4) **Water** see Chapters 10 and 11	Monitoring of river flows and water table levels, water quality and sources of pollutants may be undertaken by the National Rivers Authority but will need supplementing by Environmental Health information on specific industrial and agricultural polluters, and the seepage from refuse tips.
5) **Land and soils** see Chapter 10	Except in relation to contaminated land or specific/severe erosion problems, information is not currently collected on a systematic and comprehensive basis. Some indications may be available from MAFF.
6) **Mineral and energy Resources** see Chapter 3	Information on planning permissions and extraction rates from County Planning Departments should be related to criteria of resource sustainability.

Elements	Commentary
7) **Buildings** see Chapter 8	The stock of buildings, and their condition, in relation to identified levels of housing, commercial and institutional needs – currently monitored (mainly by planning departments) on a very partial basis except in respect of housing and industrial land available. The proportion of new development occurring on brownfield sites or through renewal of existing buildings is a key indicator.
8) **Infrastructure**	Information on utilities, transport and service facilities, their extent, quality and adequacy in relation to need (overload, underuse) and, in particular, assessment of the process of maintenance and renewal.
9) **Open space** see Chapter 8	Register of the quantity, quality, use, and upkeep of open/green spaces (parks, allotments, commons, playing fields and all public access open space) – related to measures of need and demand, as illustrated for example by Kirklees MDC.
10) **Aesthetic quality** see Chapter 9	Monitoring of changing townscape and landscape quality across the whole local authority area; both objective measures (ie specific features) and subjective assessment reflecting resident perceptions. Monitoring complaints about noise levels and fumes, and regularly surveying areas suffering excessive noise (eg near main roads).
11) **Cultural heritage** see Chapter 9	Monitoring the preservation, use and upkeep, quality of listed buildings, conservation areas, historic monuments, historic landscapes/gardens, and archaeological remains.
12) **Community awareness** see Chapter 13	Monitor (as part of Local Agenda 21 programme) the level of awareness of environmental issues, and changing behaviour patterns in relation to the environment, amongst schoolchildren, residents and businesses. This may best be undertaken by school and college groups, so the process of survey itself promotes desired change.

REVIEW OF INTERNAL PRACTICES: CHECKLIST

DEFINITION

The Review of Internal Practices evaluates the environmental impact of the agencies' own operations and practices, suggesting change where appropriate. See Chapters 1 and 2.

PURPOSE OF THIS SECTION

- To provide a guide to the scope on RIP
- To identify departments for involvement in the process
- To allow a quick overall assessment of the current state of authority

DECISION AREAS

The material is organized into a series of seven decision areas each related to a facet of local authority operations. Some are specific to a particular department while others require corporate action. Apart from the first two, which are general in nature, the rest of the decision areas can be treated separately. Good practice is readily identifiable, and is set out briefly in the matrix that follows.

THE RIP MATRIX

This provides a simple and effective means of summarizing the situation in the authority. For each of the decision areas assess which policy (or non-policy) is currently being followed.

Decision areas and cross reference	Good practice	Bad practice
RIP 1 Corporate Issues		
a) Environmental strategy Part 1, Part 3	A comprehensive auditing process, working within clear policy guidelines, leading to the production and implementation of a detailed action plan	No statement of overall environmental policy No on-going auditing process Lack of coordination between environmental initiatives An audit report, but no resulting action plan
b) Management systems Part 1, Part 3	Environment committee with high level support Officers' steering group with involvement from all service areas Environmental forum facilitated by the authority; participation sought from all sections of the community Environment coordinator/team with overall responsibility for implementing the strategy Clear communication lines between all parts of the management system Programme of monitoring and review	Lack of coordination between members and officers and between different service areas No mechanisms for the involvement of staff or the public Responsibility for audit production and implementation not properly defined
c) Environmental training and awareness Chapters 2 and 15	A programme of staff development and involvement aimed at cultivating appropriate environmental knowledge, skills and attitudes, in a context that encourages staff to review current practices and innovate A more focused training programme for officers and members charged with developing and implementing the environmental strategy	No systematic attempt to provide environmental information or training to staff Individual initiatives aimed at changing attitudes stifled
d) Research Chapters 2 and 14	A comprehensive and coordinated programme of information gathering, assessment and report production, leading to heightened awareness of the condition and needs of the environment and the environmental impacts of council policies and practices Information held on a continually updated computerized database	Environmental issues not adequately researched, or analysis based on limited information sources None, or an inadequate database of environmental information

Decision areas and cross reference	Good practice	Bad practice
RIP 2 Property Services and Purchasing		
a) Office equipment and supplies Chapter 12	Comprehensive corporate approach embracing purchasing, reduction of consumption, reuse, recycling and appropriate disposal. Scope to include: paper products; energy consuming products; products containing CFCs, lead, asbestos, bleaches, phosphates; water consuming products; products using materials from unsustainable sources; products that risk health hazards	Purchase and use left to individual sections or departments No systematic attempt to incorporate environmental criteria into purchasing, reduce consumption, reuse materials or recycle
b) Waste and recycling Chapters 11 and 12	Reuse is considered before recycle A coordinated recycling scheme covering all sites and as many products as possible The scheme is run centrally, preferably by a full-time recycling officer, with representatives in each section to ensure smooth operation and general awareness Disposal of residuals by most environmentally benign means in accordance with 'duty of care' provisions	No in-house recycling service or lack of coordination between separate initiatives Recycling and disposal not considered as part of purchasing policy No policy on disposal of own waste
c) Site services Chapter 12	The environmental impacts of all site services are considered corporately, in terms of energy saving equipment, operating practices and products Awareness raising information and training given to staff Where services are contracted, environmental specifications are included whenever possible	Catering, cleaning, printing and reprographic services operated with little or no regard to their environmental or health impacts No staff training or special provisions in contracts
RIP 3 Sites and Buildings		
a) Construction and maintenance Chapters 6 and 12	Energy resource and pollution issues integrated into building construction/rehabilitation/maintenance and into road/infrastructure construction and maintenance, especially in terms of: ■ energy intensity of materials ■ sources of materials ■ reuse and recycling ■ appropriate disposal (where essential) ■ energy intensity of construction operations ■ economy of design in terms of raw materials ■ energy-efficiency of buildings in use	Building construction and maintenance programmes geared to compliance with building regulations but not considered further in terms of resource conservation or energy-efficiency Road building and maintenance programmes fulfil basic standards but lack an environmental/conservation dimension

Decision areas and cross reference	Good practice	Bad practice
b) Energy management Chapter 6	Long term energy plan for new and existing buildings with targets aimed at progressively reducing consumption and heat loss Programme of capital investment based on cost-effective and best available technology Energy efficiency officer/team to coordinate management, provide training, raise awareness and monitor consumption and costs	*Ad hoc* energy management with no systematic and centrally coordinated programme of energy efficiency measures Energy consumption monitored on a purely cost-benefit basis
c) Housing management NB This decision area could be construed as falling within the Policy Impact Assessment rather than the Review of Internal Practice. It is included here because of its close relation to energy management Chapter 6	Establish a plan for the progressive upgrading of the energy efficiency of council homes integrated with other maintenance and improvement programmes Establishing priorities using the Home Energy Rating Scheme integrated with other maintenance and improvement programmes and fuel poverty criteria Supporting tenant initiative and responding to their needs through tenant energy services	See b)
d) Aesthetics Chapter 9	General policy of aesthetic enhancement applies to all sites/ buildings managed by the authority, and policed by qualified designer or other suitable person Internal environment, cleaning, maintenance and decoration staff involved in enhancement programme Building extension/adaptation programme aims to achieve high aesthetic quality and functional efficiency External environment, design and maintenance for convenience, beauty and delight Programme of staff awareness and involvement	No particular policy for the authorities' own sites and buildings Aesthetic quality considered a secondary matter, an afterthought

Decision areas and cross reference	Good practice	Bad practice
RIP 4 Countryside and Open Space		
a) Grounds, parks and verges Chapters 5 and 12	All land managed by the council is made subject to a conservation strategy based on ecological principles aimed at: ■ maximizing biodiversity and safeguarding wildlife habitats ■ composting and recycling organic wastes ■ avoiding the use of artificial fertilizers and pesticides ■ reducing the intensity of maintenance regimes ■ increasing planting of native species ■ promoting organic methods ■ improving access ■ increasing open spaces, particularly in the built environment and on derelict sites ■ incorporating energy planning (shelter belts, shade etc) into landscape design	Maintenance regimes and new planting proceed along traditional lines with chemical controls, artificial fertilizers and grass monoculture predominating
b) Countryside services Chapter 5	There should be a comprehensive strategy covering all aspects of nature and landscape conservation This should include: ■ the relationship with outside organizations (assistance, grants, volunteer management) and formal parks service ■ education, interpretation and recreation ■ register of sites of ecological importance ■ a system of country parks and wardening ■ special provisions for designated areas (SSSIs, AONBs etc) ■ relevant good practice from a)	Lack of a comprehensive management strategy No coordination with the 'formal' parks service

Decision areas and cross reference	Good practice	Bad practice
RIP 4 Transport		
This decision area concerns in-house transport: the movement of employees and visitors. Transport policy *per se* is included in the PIA	Corporate policy promoting energy-efficient movement	No clear policy promoting energy efficient movement
Chapter 7	Officers located in-centre, accessible by public transport from most of the local authority area	Officers located away from town/city/ depending for access mainly on car use/ limited accessibility by public transport
	Car and mileage allowance schemes favour the use of small cars, and substitution of bikes/bus where appropriate	Car and mileage allowances schemes benefit larger cars by relating to engine size
	Car sharing scheme for employees, reinforced by parking permits	No car sharing scheme for employees
	All LA vehicles adapted to unleaded, or diesel and purchasing policy favouring fuel economy	Unattractive/inconvenient circulation in and around site for cyclists/pedestrians
	Attractive and convenient pedestrian/bike circulation in and around site	
	Vehicles maintained in efficient working order	
	Advice and training offered to staff	
	Recycling of waste products from maintenance	
RIP 5 Financial Policy		
	Adopting a sustainable financial planning stance in relation to use, control and investment of money, with responsibility for pursuing it clearly defined, seeing the process as an opportunity for spreading environmental awareness	Environmental costs and benefits are not formally incorporated in decision-making procedures or budgeting, contracting, or pension fund investment
	Adopting a policy for the letting of property that favours environmentally-conscious organizations and penalize firms which persist in polluting or desecrating the environment	
	Incorporating appropriate environmental clauses in all privatized service agreements, and ensuring contract-compliance, so that contracting out does not mean a *lower* quality of environment than if the authority were to undertake the operation itself	
	Reviewing investment policies of the pension fund to stress environmentally sound investments, and to involve superannuation contribution in the process	
	Grants and financial assistance to outside organizations should, in part, be based on environmental criteria and should promote environmental protection	

Decision areas and cross reference	Good practice	Bad practice
RIP 6 Personnel		
a) Recruitment	Environmentally damaging specifications are withdrawn from job descriptions (eg car allowances) and replaced with environmentally beneficial ones (eg a stated interest and awareness for the environment) Recruitment material and induction courses should have environmental component	No environmental aspects included in job specifications
b) Health and safety	There should be a comprehensive and well supported health and safety strategy which ties in with other policy areas (eg transport, pollution) and relates working practices with the hazards of environmental disbenefits Particular initiatives should cover – healthy eating, no smoking policy, hazards of VDUs, pollution and awareness raising	Only the minimum requirements are met and no links are made with related decision areas
RIP 7 Information Services and Advice		
Note: There is overlap between the internal (RIP) and external (PIA) functions of this decision area	Coordination between all the internal and external information and advice services, thus rationalizing resources and ensuring a higher profile for environmental issues A proactive approach to information provision particularly in relation to the new regulations concerning public access to environmental information Production of in-house booklets on issues such as energy-efficiency, pollution, office recycling, etc A programme of ongoing information dissemination to all levels of staff and council members	Internal and external information services run separately No programme of environmental awareness raising and insufficient resources for literature, exhibitions etc

POLICY IMPACT ANALYSIS: CHECKLIST

DEFINITION

■ An agency-based PIA evaluates the environmental impact of the agency's (eg local authority's) regulatory, policy and service activities.
■ A community PIA goes a stage further and evaluates the impact of all public or quasi-public sector agencies active in the area.

PURPOSE OF THIS SECTION

■ to provide a guide to the potential scope of a PIA;
■ to identify good practice in each main decision area;
■ to allow a quick general review of the current performance of the local authority.

DECISION AREAS

The material is organized in a series of decision areas related to broad elements of environmental stock, ranging from global ecology to local environmental quality. These do not necessarily coincide neatly with particular departmental or agency responsibilities. In each decision area, good practice is contrasted with poor practice. The latter often represents, unfortunately, *common* practice as well.

The decision areas relate as closely as possible to discussion in a particular chapter and are cross-referenced to the relevant sections.

CUMULATIVE AND INTERACTIVE EFFECTS

There is often not a simple linear relationship between policy and impact. For discussion of this, and techniques for dealing with it, see Chapter 2, page 28. The implication of cumulative and interactive effects is that the following list has a **caution** tag. It provides a starting point for analysis, but needs to be used with discretion, recognizing local conditions.

MEASURING SUCCESS

As discussion in Chapter 2 makes clear, there are several ways of evaluating policy, and success/failure is best measured by assessing *actual* impact, using SoE information. The list of good practice provided here has the advantage, however, of being simple, quick and clear, with recommendations for improvement built in to the process: particularly useful for councillors, community groups, environmental groups.

USING THE CHECKLIST

The statements of 'poor' practice and 'good' practice represent either end of a policy spectrum. Where does your authority fall on the spectrum?

Performance levels:

- **POOR:**   Stuck at the level of poor practice. Little real change in prospect.
- **IMPROVING:**   Innovative plans and some commitment to change.
- **PROMISING:**   Proven ability to achieve good practice, though in limited spheres, as yet.
- **GOOD:**   General and significant real progress implementing good practice.

Decision areas and cross reference	Poor practice	Good practice
PIA 1 Biodiversity *Significance: a global priority reinforced by local concern for habitats and species* Reference Chapter 5		
a) Forward planning for nature conservation	Wildlife not a significant issue in devising forward plans, beyond normal consultation with voluntary groups and official bodies	Comprehensive and implementable wildlife policies incorporated in development plans, with distinct habitats noted and retained, corridors planned, and habitat enhancement recognized in all development policies
b) Countryside management	Absence of effective wildlife management agreements with land owners or land lessees	Wildlife management agreements for all threatened or fragile habitats
c) In-house expertise in wildlife and ecology	Inadequate expertise available in-house to assess wildlife implications or applications or evaluate relevant environmental impact assessments	Effective nature conservation policies operated, with expertise available, and proper protection for SSSIs, other valuable habitats, trees and woodlands and fragile environments
PIA 2 Energy *Significance: global commitment to reduce greenhouse emissions; national concerns over non-renewable energy resources and problems of fuel poverty*		
a) Collaborative energy programmes Reference Chapter 6	No involvement in this field beyond the management of energy in the LA's own buildings and housing stock (see page 102)	Active participation in a joint working party (an 'energy action trust or campaign') with energy supply industries, Energy Efficiency Office, voluntary groups and key industrial consumers to: ■ coordinate an energy awareness campaign ■ tackle the problems of fuel poverty, debt and disconnections ■ promote an energy conservation strategy for the area

Decision areas and cross reference	Poor practice	Good practice
b) Energy supply planning	No involvement in this field, except responding to planning applications on an *ad hoc* basis	Clear environmental policy for response to external initiatives, eg solar buildings, earth-sheltered dwellings, wind generators, nuclear power stations etc thus reducing the uncertainties for developers Wide-ranging energy plan, linked with other agencies, including, for example: ■ survey of potential renewable energy sources ■ policy encouraging the development of small-scale CHP and renewable sources ■ promotion of CHP through 'joint public/private ventures'
c) Energy efficient building	Normal building regulation standards being applied in new build and rehab projects	Building design guidance aimed at Scandinavian levels of insulation, maximum solar gain, use of recycled or low-energy-intensity materials, etc
d) Energy efficient urban design	No explicit requirements in the siting, layout and planting of development sites	Adoption in local plan of explicit requirements on the siting, orientation, layout and planting pattern in new development to reduce heat loss and maximize passive solar gain Implementation of such policies with development briefs and effective negotiation over planning applications

PIA 3 Transport
Significance: global commitment to reduce greenhouse emissions; national concerns over non-renewable energy resources; local concerns to maximize accessibility; reduce transport poverty, and improve local environmental quality

Reference Chapter 8

a) Overall transport investment	TPP and DTp capital programme dominated by highway improvement and new construction with <10% expressly for pt and low energy modes	Integrated transport strategy aimed at reducing the need to travel and reducing car dependence Capital programmes increasingly dominated by pt investment linked to complementary land use policies

310

Decision areas and cross reference	Poor practice	Good practice
b) Traffic capacities	Increased traffic capacity through free-flow traffic management and new road construction and improvement	Traffic capacity reduced in most areas where pt priority, bike and pedestrian movement are prioritized Road improvements only for pt or environmental reasons, not car travel time Traffic calming principles applied in suburban and rural areas as well as inner urban
c) Walking and cycling	Limited action beyond ensuring minimum pedestrian standards are achieved in new development, and sporadic provision of pedestrianized areas and recreational cycle routes	Comprehensive pedestrian network being implemented, designed for convenience, safety and beauty, linked to land use policy Comprehensive hierarchical bike network planned and being implemented, for maximum convenience and safety
d) Public transport priority	Occasional, sporadic, pt priority measures; few or no segregated routes planned	Extensive priority on the core urban network (bus, tram or train) being implemented New or renewed areas being designed around public transport spine routes
e) Car restraint	Parking provision in-town and out-of-town to cope with expected demand	Parking provision severely restricted in-town and out-of-town where alternative means of travel are available Road-rationing techniques being evaluated
f) Transport interchange	Limited provision of interchange facilities except for major stations and/or selected peripheral park and ride	Comprehensive bike/bus/rail transfer facilities being provided, plus park and ride facilities in commuter settlements rather than edge-of-town
g) Freight movement	Lorry routes being planned and implemented	Freight transfer warehouse facilities being developed in appropriate locations related to rail and motorways

Decision areas and cross reference	Poor practice	Good practice
PIA 4 Urban Land Use *Significance: as for energy and transport* Reference Chapter 8		
a) Energy-integrated planning	Energy-efficient criteria are used in assessing development proposals, and policies are in place which generally welcome the development of renewable energy Energy planning is integrated with land use/transport planning at the town/city/country level, resulting in a coherent strategy for energy supply and energy demand management	Energy and land use treated largely as separate issues except where energy development applications are needed
b) Land use/transport integration	Accessibility by foot, pedal and public transport are important criteria determining individual commercial and residential development applications and the layout of new area The overall shape, locational pattern, and degree of concentration of settlements are being planned to enhance energy-efficient transport, and inappropriate dispersed or low density development resisted	Separate agencies working largely to specific remits effectively inhibit integrated land use and transport, particularly public transport, planning except for normal consultation procedures
c) Density of development	Housing, commercial and institutional densities largely determined by market conditions Housing densities in rural and suburban locations restricted to 'prevailing' levels in the interests of 'amenity'	General encouragement to modestly higher average net densities Variations in density levels explicitly related to level of access to public transport stops and local facilities
d) Housing location	Large proportion of new housing on a few major greenfield sites	Majority of new housing on brownfield sites Most new housing (brown or greenfield) dispersed widely around the urban areas to maximize choice

Decision areas and cross reference	Poor practice	Good practice
e) Location of jobs and facilities	Progressive dispersal of employment, retail, leisure, educational, health and social facilities into edge-of-town locations, local centres or single use sites, increasingly geared to car use	Reinforcement of multi-use town centres and major sub-centres which maximize public transport accessibility Town or sub-regional facilities prevented from expanding in local centres, car-based locations or single use locations Local facilities clustered in local high streets at the heart of residential areas, well served by walking, cycling and bus networks
f) Open space and landscape	Provision of open space on a disaggregated and opportunistic basis, with no general strategy Landscaping normally considered late in the planning process	General strategy being progressively implemented to create a network of open space linking between facilities, providing overlapping functions of recreation, wildlife corridors, energy and microclimate management, pollution/noise absolution and visual amenity
Urban form and settlement pattern	Stated policies of 'concentration', with peripheral growth around main settlements; but in fact in most areas a continuing decentralization of growth into suburban towns and villages	Integrated strategy designed to minimize the need to travel. It is not possible to generalize, each area is distinctive, but a pattern of dispersal would in all cases be inappropriate

PIA 5 Earth, Air and Water

Significance: national and local concern for the quantity and quality of key natural resources

Reference Chapter 10

a) Air quality	Statutory environmental health monitoring and enforcement duties being adequately fulfilled	Progressive strategy in place to upgrade all areas where local air quality poor, through smoke control zones, traffic management etc General strategy for reducing the level of global emissions to sustainable levels – and involving collaboration with other departments (and agencies) in a joint programme, incorporating the progressive local strategy

313

Decision areas and cross reference	Poor practice	Good practice
b) Water quality	A reaction approach, ie specific monitoring of water quality in response to complaints or problems	Effective and comprehensive monitoring of private water supplied and close liaison with National Rivers Authority on water course quality and mains, linked in to development control policies for town and country Strategy for moderating water demand growth and maximizing opportunity for local collection and treatment (eg reed-bed sewage systems, composting toilets) increasing local water and compost self-sufficiency
c) Ground quality	Contaminated land duly being registered, but monitoring/enforcement inadequately policed, and reclamation dependent on market-led initiative	Comprehensive approach to contaminated land including programmes to counteract land degradation/erosion as well as resistance to contaminated and derelict land
PIA 6 Non-Renewable Resources *Significance: general concern for the longevity or sustainability of raw materials and energy sources, and local concern to reduce the impact of mineral workings on the environment*		
a) Mineral conservation See Chapter 2	Environmental impact of mineral development properly considered, but the longevity or sustainability of supply in a given region not considered	Overall strategy for consumption of minerals, attempting to maintain or increase the longevity of proven recoverable reserves, in part by exploration, in part by reducing the rate of exploitation by efficiency and substitution
b) Waste minimization See Chapter 11	Respond to demand for waste collection services with no attempt to manage demand	Campaigning to persuade households/firms/institutions to minimize waste Providing a range of facilities and/or other incentives (eg local composting schemes, differential charging) to facilitate waste minimization
c) Recycling See Chapter 11	Recycling provision limited (eg to bottle banks) or non existent	Separation of recyclable materials by domestic and commercial consumers, plus effective reprocessing channels

314

Decision areas and cross reference	Poor practice	Good practice
d) Energy from waste See Chapter 11	Waste disposal reliant on conventional land fill and/or incineration	Comprehensive strategy for capturing energy from waste, including heat from incineration and methane from landfill
PIA 7 Local Environmental Quality		
a) Aesthetic quality See Chapter 9	A largely *laissez faire* approach to aesthetics, letting the market decide except in conservation areas	A general aesthetic policy being implemented, recognizing the distinctive character of different areas, geared to non-visual senses as well as the visual, encompassing imageability and the development of public awareness
b) Noise and odours See Chapter 10	Reactive approach, responding to complaints and problems as they arise	Effective strategy for reducing noise levels (esp traffic) and bad neighbour effects through planning policy and close liaison between Environmental Health and Planning on applications
c) Conservation of the built environment See Chapter 9	Listed building designation and conservation areas largely used as negative devices for forestalling undesirable change	Conservation strategy in place, with a budget, aimed at the progressive enhancement of valued areas and buildings, including plans for reuse of local materials and improving the energy efficiency of listed buildings
d) Landscape conservation	Landscape designations (AONB, protected coastline, high landscape value) used negatively to deter unsympathetic development	Comprehensive rural land use and landscape zoning, with management agencies in plan to achieve implementation

THE CONTEXT FOR LOCAL GOVERNMENT ENVIRONMENTAL ACTION

This appendix is designed to highlight the major policy and legislative developments that are likely to influence EA in the future. It has been strongly argued throughout the book that EA acts as an expression of both the role and responsibility of local government with regard to promoting sustainable development. In this context, the influences on the process will come not alone from local or even national policy levels but equally from the international community. The discussion is therefore in four parts; it begins with the global context, then reviews the role of the EU and the UK Government, and ends with a more specific look at how these other policy levels are likely to impact on UK local government.

THE GLOBAL POLICY CONTEXT

The most notable of the global level initiatives must be the Rio Earth Summit of 1992. Although it has been criticized on many counts it did produce a number of positive outputs. These included a declaration of sustainability principles, treaties on bio-diversity and climate change, a statement of forestry principles, and most importantly Agenda 21, an action plan for the 21st century. Most of these agreements are not legally binding and are therefore more statements of interest rather than strategies for action. It was left up to nation states to respond. It is now over two years since the summit and some results are beginning to show. In the UK the Government has produced action plans in response to all the agreements, the most notable of which is the Strategy for Sustainable Development. Many local authorities have also begun work on local sustainable development plans, called Local Agenda 21s. These will all be discussed later but what is important is that the UK, along with other countries, has begun to take steps towards implementing the principles arrived at in Rio.

A Commission for Sustainable Development (CSD) has been set up under the auspices of the UN to collect together reports on the progress that is being made at national level and to follow up on the Rio agreements.

Apart from the Earth Summit, the other main feature of the global context is the formation of networks. These are sometimes directed towards agreeing common action on a particular issue, such as the Montreal Protocol on ozone-depleting substances and the UN sponsored Intergovernmental Panel on Climate Change (IPCC) which aims to stabilize greenhouse gas emissions. More often, however, these are networks of organizations which seek to promote a common aim by sharing experience and by combining to produce a more powerful force. The International Union of Local Authorities (IULA) and the International Council for Local Environmental Initiatives (ICLEI) are good examples. A more informal exchange of information also takes place, particularly on a bilateral basis. Canada, Denmark and the Netherlands have been very fruitful sources of information and best practice for UK local authorities.

Global policies and initiatives have begun to have a direct influence on the environmental agenda of local government, most notably through Agenda 21. More usually, however, the influence is first filtered through other levels of government. These are examined next.

THE INFLUENCE OF THE EUROPEAN UNION

There can be no doubt that as far as the UK is concerned, the EU has been the main source of environmental policy development in the last twenty years. The fifth, and latest, action programme – *Towards Sustainability* – is a more explicit and strategic vision of sustainable development than even the UK Government's more recent Sustainable Development Strategy. But *Towards Sustainability* is only the centre-piece in a veritable banquet of initiatives that have come out of Europe in the last few years. Some of these, such as EIA, Eco-Management and Audit, draft proposals on SEA, ecolabelling, and the Directive on Freedom of Access to Environmental Information have already been discussed in the book with relation to their influence on EA. The real effect of some other initiatives has yet to be felt.

The Green Paper on the Urban Environment, published in 1990, has more recently been followed by a draft report on 'Sustainable Cities'. Both advocate an holistic view of the environment, with the adoption of EA-related tasks at the local and regional level as one of the main mechanisms for integrating policies. They also work to define operational principles for putting sustainable development into effect. Most of these principles are reflected in Box 16.2 (page 293).

Another major publication which has to date received little attention is the White Paper on 'Growth, Competitiveness, Employment' (known as the Delors report). This suggests some profound changes in the direction of European economic policy, in particular by taxing the use of natural rather than human resources. This has clearly got immense implications for sustainable development and the formulation of local economic strategies. At the June 1994 summit of EU leaders it was agreed to press forward with implementing the recommendations in the report.

One area of EA which has been rather neglected in the UK is SoE reporting. Within the EU, however, this has been a particular focus of attention. There are plans to further develop the CORINE network of environmental information and to coordinate the collection of standardized data from all member states. SoE reports have been published for 1992 and 1993 and the only thing holding up an expansion of the system is a delay in establishing the European Environment Agency.

Despite their success, the institutions of Europe still suffer from the same sectoral divisions as any other level of government. This is clearly evident in such areas as agriculture and transport, with one part of the EU advocating the environmental cause while another singlemindedly pursues economic growth policies. The situation is gradually changing and more policies, plans and programmes are being assessed for their environmental impact.

For UK local government, the EU has often been seen as a route whereby authorities could bypass the apparent inertia of central government by tapping straight into the policies and funds in Europe. The EU's support for regional level government and for the principle of subsidiarity will surely encourage a more dynamic role for local authorities as community based environmental protection agencies.

THE UK GOVERNMENT POLICY DIMENSION

Many of the important central government policy factors have already been mentioned in Parts I and II. This section will therefore be very brief and focus on two things: the support that is given to local authority EA and the emergence of SD onto the national policy agenda.

EA support

One of the most interesting things about EA is how it has flourished in the almost total absence of high level support from central government. It has been very much a locally led initiative which has drawn more from within and from forces beyond Central Government than it has from explicit national level backing. This must be in part a reflection of the lack of a coherent national policy framework on the environment.

This Common Inheritance, published in 1990, was the first White Paper on the environment for twenty years. It is more notable for its *lack* of vision and initiative than for its contribution to developing a strategic approach. Together with three follow-up review reports, it has helped raise the profile of environmental issues but has arguably not provided the guidance, mechanisms nor the political commitment necessary to translate the aspirations into actions. On a more positive note it did indirectly inspire confidence among local authorities that they would at least have implicit Government support to pursue their EAs. It was one of the documents most referred to by those in the survey reported in Part III.

Perhaps more important than the White Paper itself were the institutional changes that began to be brought about at the same time. Some of these were a direct result of proposals in the White Paper. This included the formation of two standing committees of ministers, one chaired by the Prime Minister and the other by Mr Heseltine, to coordinate activities between departments and to ensure that commitments were being honoured. In addition, every government department was required to nominate a minister to take responsibility for assessing their environmental impact and to produce a 'Green Housekeeping' strategy to report on progress in this regard. Additional efforts were proposed for building partnerships and developing networks between all levels of government and other agencies. The 'Central and Local Government Environment Forum' is one such initiative. A series of publications have also appeared which address aspects of EA. These include the 1993 SoE report, 'The UK Environment'; a manual on 'Policy Appraisal and the Environment', and another on 'Environmental Appraisal of Development Plans' which both relate to aspects of PIA; a series of 'Environmental Action Guides' for government departments to assess the impact of their internal practices.

Emerging from the same institutional context as *This Common Inheritance* were some major pieces of legislation and policy guidance. The early 1990s saw the introduction of the Environment Protection Act and the Planning and Compensation Act. Both served to strengthen the position of the environment on the political agenda. They also introduced new powers relating to pollution management and development control. A new set of Planning Policy Guidance notes (particularly nos 1, 12 and 13) have sought to provide local authorities with a working definition of sustainable development and a range of instruments for giving greater weight to environmental concerns in decision making.

Needless to say, these institutional changes have not met with unanimous approval. Within Government, some economic interests would appear to be doing their best to ignore them while outside of Government there has been much criticism of the lack of overall progress and the poor performance of some of the new mechanisms. There is still a general feeling that, although more is being said about the environment, the commitment to actually achieving real change is not yet widespread.

SD on the national policy agenda

Hopes were raised after the high priority given by the Government to the Earth Summit that this might represent a landmark in the way the environment was treated. These hopes were partly realized in the Biodiversity Action Plan and the Climate Change Strategy, but the key Sustainable Development Strategy was a disappointment to most people. Instead of building on Agenda 21, to which it was the Government's response, it mostly only reiterated the principles of sustainable development while proposing little new by way of targets or mechanisms. In particular, it was criticized for relying too heavily on the use of economic instruments which to date have achieved very little by way of advancing towards sustainable development. It also lacked a basic timetable for implementing its proposals and failed to adequately integrate the environment into other policy areas, most notably transport and agriculture.

Once again, the positive attributes of the Sustainable Development Strategy are less in what it says and more in the institutional changes which it proposes. The process of participation and consultation leading up to the strategy was itself a major step forward, while some of the proposals with the greatest long-term potential deal with new organizational mechanisms and means to generate wider community involvement. Box A4.1 lists the major proposals for creating a more conducive national context to help achieve progress in implementing sustainable development goals.

The slow but fundamental changes coming about in the way Government treats environmental concerns can only be to the benefit of local authorities. More support both politically and financially is certainly needed if the potential of EA is to be fully realized.

Box A4.1 Institutional mechanisms proposed in the sustainable development strategy

■ Annual progress report to the UN Commission on Sustainable Development (CSD)

■ *Government Panel on Sustainable Development*
   Expert representatives from all sectors to meet about four times a year. Role to provide authoritative and independent advice on issues of sustainability and to prioritize goals. To be consulted on issues of major importance and to have access to all ministers

■ *Round table on Sustainable Development*
   Representatives from main agencies and groups to meet about twice a year with ministers, under the chairmanship of the SoS for the Environment. To build consensus and exchange ideas

■ *Citizens' Environmental Initiative*
   To bring the message of sustainable development to the community and encourage public interest. Year of activities planned, beginning on World Environment Day in June 1994

■ To develop the measures arising out of *This Common Inheritance*
   – 'Green Ministers'
   – Ministerial committee on the environment
   – Environmental appraisal of new policies
   – Departmental 'Green Housekeeping' strategies

■ Further measures to develop the role of voluntary groups, business organizations and the public
   Including:
   – Environmental Action Fund
   – Encouragement and consultation with the Voluntary Sector Environment Forum, the Advisory Committee on Business and the Environment, local Green Business clubs etc
   – The 'Green Brigade'
   – Campaigns and awareness raising programmes

■ New national, regional and minerals Guidance Notes to help secure the objectives of sustainable development

■ Working group to produce preliminary environmental indicators by 1996

THE CHANGING CONTEXT OF LOCAL GOVERNMENT ENVIRONMENTAL ACTION

In stark contrast to the inability of central government to get to grips with the implications of sustainable development, UK local government has been at the very cutting edge of international efforts. Evidence for this has been supplied throughout the book – in relation to the enthusiastic commitment to pursue environmental strategies, the rapid development and dissemination of good practice, innovation in all areas of environmental policy, and most recently in building the Local Agenda 21 initiative. Indeed, there is so much going on in local government that it is often quite difficult to simply keep up with new developments.

Two aspects of the environmental context deserve special note. The first is environmental management systems. Both BS7750 and the adapted Eco-Management and Audit Scheme (EMAS) are now operational. The two schemes are very similar and it is planned to bring them even closer together after some practical experience is gained. For the moment however, EMAS has been specifically adapted for use in local government whereas BS7750 is still undergoing trials. It seems more likely therefore that EMAS will, at least to start with, provide the kind of framework that suits councils. This issue, together with an outline of the elements in and benefits to be gained from the scheme, is addressed in Appendix 5.

The second major development in local government is in formulating responses to Agenda 21. By the end of 1996 it is hoped that most authorities will have developed a Local Agenda 21 which aims to harness the energies of its community in the pursuit of sustainable development. The key themes in Local Agenda 21 are consensus building, empowerment and the development of robust environmental strategies. The emphasis is very much on the process by which these themes are addressed rather than on any formal outputs. Advice on how this process should be developed is being coordinated in the UK by the LGMB, under the direction of a steering group representing local government and other interested sectors. So far they have produced a range of publications (see Bibliography), promoted national and international networks, and facilitated cross-sectoral roundtables addressing different aspects of sustainable development. A number of research projects have also been launched dealing with such issues as indicators for sustainable development, programmes to raise awareness, and design guidance for use by local authorities and developers.

Although the exact look of Local Agenda 21 will not be clear until more practical experience is gained, there is a consensus emerging as to what elements will be included. These closely reflect the elements in the expanded view of EA outlined in Chapter 16. In a very real sense, therefore, the two processes are developing in parallel and will most likely merge into one in the near future. This will allow them to gain full benefit from each other's strengths. EA can offer the experience gained over a number of years in developing procedures and methodologies for assessing impacts and managing these both internally and in partnership with the community. Local Agenda 21 offers an expanded view of the role of local environmental strategies and, most importantly, provides for the involvement of all stakeholders in framing what these strategies should aim to achieve.

Local government has committed itself to the active pursuit of sustainable development. As the level of government closest to the citizen, their role is absolutely crucial. This has been recognized in Agenda 21, in the EU's Fifth Action Programme and in the Government's environmental policy. EA and Local Agenda 21 can provide the means to make the most of the opportunity that local authorities now have.

THE ECO-MANAGEMENT AND AUDIT SCHEME

BACKGROUND

The Eco-Management and Audit Scheme (EMAS) is an EU initiative to help industrial companies improve their environmental management and performance. It was adopted in June 1993 and is due to come into force in April 1995. The potential offered by the scheme lies in its formalized procedures for assessing the environmental impact of an organization's policies and practices and developing and publicizing a programme of actions for achieving corporate progress on these issues.

Other sectors have been quick to spot the benefits offered by the scheme. The DoE and the Local Government Management Board set up a pilot project in March 1992 to see how the scheme might be adapted for use by local authorities. This has led to the publication of an adapted EMAS (HMSO, 1993) which also became operational in mid-1995.

EMAS is closely allied to a new British Standard, BS7750, on Environmental Management Systems. Both have been developed in tandem and it is thought that those accredited under one will be well placed to fulfil the requirements of the other.

At the moment EMAS looks more likely to be adopted by local authorities, for the following reasons:

- It has been specifically tested for its applicability to local authorities while BS7750 is still undergoing trials.
- There is more of an emphasis in EMAS on actual and continual environmental improvements rather that on merely building better management systems.
- EMAS requires the publication and validation of a statement while BS7750 only requires the publication of the Environmental Policy. As explained below, the statement is a much more comprehensive document than the policy and its publication therefore allows for more public consultation and greater openness in the process.

ADVANTAGES

The principle benefit to be gained from using EMAS is that it is a formal framework for carrying out EA tasks. It therefore legitimizes the work that has been on-going in local authorities. More specifically, the advantages are:

- Improvements in the environmental performance of the organization.
- Improvements in the quality of services that the organization provides.
- Financial savings through more efficient use of resources.
- A more effective management system.
- A corporate approach to addressing environmental impact.
- External validation of the organization's 'green' credentials.
- Assurance of compliance with legal obligations and corporate policy.
- A demonstration to the community of care for the local environment.

OVERVIEW OF THE SCHEME

Table A5.1 presents the basic elements in EMAS and shows their comparability with the tasks of EA.

Apart from the fact that SoE reporting is not explicitly addressed, the two processes are otherwise overwhelmingly compatible. The new scheme should therefore consolidate current auditing activities while adding the extra benefit of independent validation.

It is intended that filling in the worksheets included in the guide will to a large extent represent completion of each of the requirements. A full set of completed worksheets will provide most of the information needed for presentation to the verifier.

An important feature of the original EMAS is that individual sites within a company can seek registration. The whole company need only adopt an environmental policy and commit itself to eventual corporate registration. Applying this to local authorities, it means that individual 'operational units' (departments, service units or other functional entity) can register in advance of the entire authority deciding to do so.

Another distinguishing feature of the adapted EMAS is that local authorities must consider the impact of their 'service effects' (through the role of planner, regulator, enforcer, educator etc) in addition to their 'direct effects' (resulting from internal activities). This is accommodated in the scheme by building separate review and management systems for service and direct effects.

The final point to note is that the elements of the scheme can be used simply as tools for better management without the requirement for formal registration. Some authorities may wish to test their own effectiveness before submitting themselves to public scrutiny.

Table A5.1 Comparison between EMAS elements and EA tasks

EMAs	*EA*
Environmental policy Overall aims and commitment to achieving continuous improvement Broad list of issues and responsibilities Must be corporate statement, adopted by whole authority	Environmental Charter or Environmental Statement
Environmental review Evaluation of environmental performance in relation to the regulatory and policy context Addressing actual effects and potential effects Scoping of issues followed by detailed review	The assessment component of RIP and PIA
Environmental programme Specify actions to translate the aims of the policy into detailed objectives for improvement To include: indicators, targets, timetables, delegated duties, resource implications	EA action plan or strategy
Management system Organizational responsibilities and mechanisms for implementing the programme Should fit with existing systems rather than duplicate them To include corporate overview and coordination system	MA and implementation aspects of an action plan
Environmental audit To assess the achievements of the programme and the adequacy of the management system Every activity at least every 3 years	Follow-up to an initial EA
Environmental statement A published report on environmental performance To be concise, comprehensible and accessible to the public	Environmental strategy/audit/ report
Validation All of the above are subjected to external verification which will lend to formal validation and the right to publicize participation and to use a special logo	No direct comparison but similar to the informal 'public' validation of published EA documents

ENVIRONMENTAL INDICATORS

INTRODUCTION

This appendix builds on the discussions elsewhere in the book which have examined the role of indicators in relation to the different tasks of EA (Chapter 2), in defining carrying capacities (Chapter 3) and helping to provide operational objectives for EA (Chapter 14). It also aims to put into context the range of indicators suggested for tackling the different issues in Part II.

This is an issue which is often approached with dread by practitioners and academics alike. The contention here is that much of the reason for this is not an inherent difficulty in understanding indicators but more due to misunderstandings over terminology and the perceived vagueness of the issue. Nevertheless, there is still an enormous amount of interest in indicators at all levels of government and their use in defining sustainable development objectives is certainly set to grow.

In the UK, there are two major initiatives underway which will raise the profile and help define the practical application of environmental quality and performance indicators:

1) A Local Agenda 21 Steering Group research project has recently reported progress on developing a set of sustainability indicators which should help measure key goals and thereby enable progress towards sustainable development to be monitored (LGMB, 1994). The project has now entered phase two which involves testing the indicators in selected local authorities in order to assess their applicability and usefulness.

2) The second initiative is part of an Audit Commission ongoing project to develop indicators on the performance of local authorities (see for example, Audit Commission, 1988). The mandatory publication of these indicators is seen by the Government as one means to ensure quality of service provision in line with 'The Citizens Charter' and the 'Local Government Environmental Charter'. Although this initiative is not addressing environmental indicators as explicitly as the Local Agenda 21 Steering Group work, it is just as likely to influence the application of indicators in local authorities. The DoE is also reported to be establishing a working group to develop a set of preliminary national indicators by 1996 (DoE, 1994).

WHAT ARE ENVIRONMENTAL INDICATORS?

Indicators are the means whereby carrying capacities (or thresholds) are translated into measurable terms which can be pursued through a range of targets. They are therefore basically measures of performance which help to quantitatively describe environmental quality and thereby allow progress to be monitored and success/ effectiveness to be judged. Their usefulness is usually in providing a summary of the mass of environmental (and socio-economic) information that is often required to understand an issue. As such they are a direct aid to decision makers and also facilitate public participation in political processes.

THE USEFULNESS OF ENVIRONMENTAL INDICATORS

The origins of environmental indicators lie in the usefulness (and limitations) that have been found from the use of indicators in other sectors; principally economic but also social. Economically, the key indicator in western society is growth measured in terms of Gross National Product (GNP). This, together with other economic indicators such as cost of living and level of unemployment, has provided the focus for development and planning. While the limitations of GNP as an indicator have for a very long time been recognized it has not been until recently that serious efforts have been made to overcome them. Very briefly, these limitations centre upon the fact that GNP does not adequately measure environmental degradation and in some cases actually includes it as an economic benefit (expenditure on pollution control being one example). Efforts to rectify this situation have been of two types:

1) This attempts to include environmental costs and benefits in measures of economic growth by putting a monetary valuation on the environment. The result would be an 'environmentally adjusted GNP'.
2) To replace GNP altogether or to parallel it with non-monetary indicators of environmental quality. France and Norway, for example, are developing environmental accounts based on physical indicators which measure the maintenance of environmental capacities.

The development of environmental indicators is therefore partly a recognition of the benefit that has been gained from economic indicators and partly in response to the inability of economic indicators (epitomized by GNP) to take sufficient account of environmental quality. More specifically, the advantages of indicators are:

■ making information accessible to decision-makers and the public;
■ allowing for comparison over time and space;
■ directing information collection;
■ allowing effectiveness to be measured and progress to be assessed;
■ if combined into indices, providing a convenient summary of data;
■ enabling the assessment of environmental components which cannot be measured directly but instead measuring variables which *indicate* the presence or condition of that component.

List derived from Thomas (1972)

A final point to make about the origin of environmental indicators relates specifically to public sector organizations. Traditionally, effectiveness or success in the public sector has been measured using a range of organizational performance targets, largely derived from the fulfilment of statutory duties and corporate goals. Recent changes such as Compulsory Competitive Tendering (CCT) and the contracting of service provision (through direct labour organizations) have led to the demand for new measures of performance. Environmental indicators, such as those being developed by the Audit Commission, could be one of these new measures.

TYPES OF ENVIRONMENTAL INDICATORS

The first thing to note when discussing types of indicators is that they are synthetic: they have no meaning other than that defined by the purpose for which they have been selected. There is therefore no universal set of indicators and they can be chosen and combined in any form that most suits the conceptual purposes involved. In relation to local government environmental auditing, indicators will be defined in relation to goals and objectives in a plan or strategy. At national level they could be defined by government policies and international agreements.

Broadly speaking indicators can be divided into two types: environmental quality indicators and environmental performance indicators.

Environmental quality indicators

Often referred to as primary indicators, these are used to measure the condition of key environmental features. The features chosen should either be significant in terms of level of impact or scarcity *or* they could be indicative in that they represent an overall measure of quality or basic trends. Examples of the former are mass of gases like CO_2 and SO_2 and of the latter, chemical oxygen demand (COD) in water and quantity of waste generated.

Environmental performance indicators

These do not measure the condition of the environment directly but rather the influence of human activities on the environment. They include both secondary indicators which measure basic quality by proxy and the general effectiveness of policy and tertiary indicators which assess the direct effect of particular policies. Examples include the level of economic activity, public opinion, number of protected areas and amount of energy generated.

In environmental auditing terms, an SoE study will generally attempt to measure environmental quality indicators while an IA will set its objectives in terms of environmental performance indicators. The targets set for the latter will have the objective of achieving goals defined in terms of the former. Reducing CO_2 emissions from transport, for example, will be designed to achieve a predetermined target so as to contribute towards the control of global warming.

Another important point to note is the difference between **direct** and **indirect performance indicators**. A local authority's practices, over which there is direct control, can be measured using objective and clearly defined indicators. The amount of energy consumed or waste produced are examples of such direct performance indicators.

In the case of policies, the local authority can establish indicators and set targets but do not have direct control over the activities of others. A more indirect performance indicator is therefore required, one which measures the activities of the authority but recognizes that these only influence the actions of others. An example of this would be the number of management agreements entered into with farmers in order to promote nature conservation. This is the basis of the advice given in EMAS, in relation to what they call 'service' effects.

Environmental accounting indicators

Another type of indicator which is related to the two already mentioned but of a different order, concerns the integration of environmental concerns in economic policies. For the want of a convenient title, these may be called **environmental accounting indicators**. This type of indicator was mentioned previously in relation to the requirement to amend or replace conventional economic indicators such as GNP. The two broad forms that these indicators could take were also mentioned. Putting an economic valuation on environmental costs and benefits is a means to measure performance while a system of natural resource accounts can be used to measure quality. Environmental accounting indicators are therefore not intrinsically different from the other two but are used for a fundamentally different purpose.

A final distinction that may be applied to indicators is between those which are for purely **internal use** in an organization and those which are for **external use**. This is an important distinction because the two sets need not correspond to each other. Internal indicators are designed to review policies and practices and thereby provide information and feedback to decision-makers. They should therefore be chosen for their ease, reliability and representativeness in measuring operational procedures, outcomes, levels of satisfaction, achievement against standards etc. External indicators should be derived from those used internally but have an overriding requirement of providing information in a digestible form. Essential qualities are therefore accessibility, clarity and brevity. Clearly, internal and external indicators perform different tasks and it would be a mistake to misuse them.

CONCLUSION

This discussion has explicitly recognized some important uses for environmental indicators, while also emphasizing the need for caution in their application. The usefulness centres around the ability to summarize complex issues and comprehensive sets of information. In doing so they help both decision-makers and the public in understanding what are often all-embracing environmental issues. The corollary of this position is that no simple set of indicators can be useful to measure performance of human impact. That is to say, reducing the complex environment to a few abstract and summarized statistics can obscure rather than clarify the issues. The answer to this vexed problem lies in the amount of authority that is placed in the indicators. If one accepts that they are indicative rather than in any way conclusive, then they become a useful 'tool' to help set and judge objectives. This is exactly the view that has been expressed by the OECD in their preliminary set of indicators (OECD, 1991) and by the current local authority research (LGMB, 1994). Both emphasize the point that there is no universal set of indicators but that a selection chosen for their relevance to the particular circumstance and policy context can aid decision-making and participation in a non-prescriptive fashion.

A final point is simply that all indicators represent a compromise between time and resources on the one hand and relevance and reliability on the other. Just as there are no universal indicators there are equally no perfect ones. There are only those that are optimum within their given context.

INTERNATIONAL EXPERIENCE

The discussion so far should serve to demonstrate that there are no definitive sets of environmental indicators. Indeed, such an idea is probably unrealistic given the scientific uncertainties, and unhelpful given the political exigencies. There is, however, a wealth of international experience that can be drawn on and learnt from to help inform the UK debate. This section will first provide an overview of some of the main international developments, and then to illustrate the potential for indicators, will look in more detail at the Canadian Federal system where some very real progress has been made.

Overview

The foremost international efforts are being made by the OECD. In response to an OECD council decision in May 1989, later supported by the Heads of State of the G7 countries, meeting in Paris in July 1989, the organization set about developing environmental indicators:

> The work carried out by the OECD focuses on sets of indicators to be used for the integration of environmental and economic decision-making, at national and international level.
>
> (OECD, 1991a)

Three different sets of indicators are under development:

1) In the longer term they hope to be able to develop sector indicators which will indicate environmental efficiency and the linkages between different sectors, economic policies and environmental trends.
2) They also hope to develop environmental accounting indicators, integrating environmental concerns into economic policies through satellite accounts and natural resource accounts.
3) Initially, however, they have concentrated on producing a generalized set of indicators which present a summary of environmental performance and quality. A preliminary set, published in 1991 (OECD, 1991a), together with the OECD 'Report on the State of the Environment' (OECD, 1991b), uses these indicators to present a summary of the key trends.

The indicators report describes its scope as follows:

> It comprises 18 environmental indicators *per se*, followed by 7 key indicators reflecting economic and population changes of environmental significance. It includes indicators of environmental performance, some relating to environmental quality itself (eg river quality, nature protection), some to natural environmental goals (eg sustainable use of the water resources, controlling waste generation), and some to international environmental agreements and issues (eg SO_x emissions, trade in forest products).
>
> OECD, 1991a, p 9

While further work is planned and the results to date are encouraging, the development of indicators at the international level can do little more than offer encouragement to individual nation states. This is recognized by the OECD and is also a key concern for the UN, who themselves have now set about work on indicators. The UN work will build on their long-standing monitoring networks which have produced the Annual Environmental Data Reports, presenting reliable national and international information in a uniform format.

Indicators are an aid to decision making by enabling progress towards the achievement of goals to be measured and reporting on this progress in an accessible and informative way. They are thus of little use if disassociated from the centres of power and the implementation forums. Until such a time as a more powerful international agency arises, with real legislative force, it is at national government level and below that indicators will need to be employed. Canada is one country that has made a degree of progress.

Canadian environmental indicators

The development of environmental indicators began in response to a commitment in the national 'Green Plan' (1990), which arose out of the decision of the G7 Paris Economic Summit in July 1989 (mentioned earlier in relation to the OECD indicators). In a forward to a preliminary report on indicators (Government of Canada, 1991) the Minister of the Environment stated that

> the government is further committed to developing and releasing, on a regular basis, a comprehensive set of environmental indicators by 1993. Our ultimate goal is to develop a comprehensive state of the environment index equivalent to the GNP.

Neither the comprehensive set of indicators nor the composite index have yet been finalized but the preliminary report on progress and a regular series of bulletins have been produced.

The work on indicators is being undertaken by a special Task Force within Environment Canada (the Government environment department), linked to a specialist SoE reporting group. Through a limited process of consultation, the preliminary set of indicators was published in 1991. This consisted of 43 separate indicators in 18 'issue' areas (arranged according to environmental categories and important natural resources). The intention was to set the process in motion by drawing on existing information and monitoring sources and then to use the preliminary set of indicators as a basis for wider consultation and debate. The 'trial run' was also to help test their relevance and usefulness. Eventually it is hoped that a comprehensive set of indicators will be available to measure progress in reaching targets and ultimately to assess whether sustainable development is being achieved.[1] In addition to measuring progress against targets it is hoped that the indicators will provide an early warning of potential environmental problems and signify the ability to manage human impacts so as to reduce stress and resolve problems.

The process of developing and implementing the indicators is relatively simple but is highly instructive. There are five steps in the process which are set out in the preliminary report[2]:

1) **Identify societal goals to which the indicators relate:** The overriding goal which defines the context of the indicators is sustainable development. This is defined as 'to assure the viability of the ecosystem; the protection, maintenance, and sustainability of natural resources; and the protection and enhancement of human health and well-being' (p 3).

2) **Devise a framework within which the indicators operate:** This sets the conceptual bounds of the investigation and ensures the technical feasibility and orderly development of the indicators. The basic method is to start with a consideration of what the potential users wanted and then, through a workshop and meetings of the key participants, a matrix of the proposed framework emerges. This matrix, summarized in Table A6.1, is designed to ensure that indicators are identified in a systematic and comprehensive way. It is stressed, however, that complex elements of the environment can seldom be traced in a direct cause and effect relationship, so the matrix is an aid and not a rigid mechanism.

3) **Identify selection criteria by which to judge potential indicators:** The criteria are: scientific validity; the availability of data to show trends over time; responsiveness to environmental changes; representativeness; understandability; relevance to goals, objectives and issues of concern; comparability with targets and thresholds; applicability to issues of national concern.

    The subjectivity of the criteria is recognized but it is felt that the selection process would inevitably entail value judgements.

4) **Consult with data holders, experts and potential users:** The development of preliminary indicators entailed an extensive consultation and review process. Their publication is intended to test their applicability and usefulness and thereby generate continual feedback.

5) **Verify that the indicators communicate the message effectively to the intended audiences:** The process should continually validate and evaluate the effectiveness of the indicators.

The preliminary set of indicators have now been on trial for nearly three years. Progress has been slower than expected but the process is still ongoing. A number of environmental indicator bulletins have been published, the most recent in February 1994 covering urban water. There has also been much work put into improving existing data gathering and reporting networks, and where necessary devising new information systems. There is no indication yet as to when the comprehensive set of indicators will be completed.

A parallel initiative to Environment Canada's indicators project is work ongoing

---

1 Government of Canada, 1991, p 2.
2 ibid.

Table A6.1 Framework matrix for developing environmental indicators

	Types of indicators (reflecting the OECD types)		
Categories of environmental resources (drawn from the goal of sustainable development)	*Measures of environmental condition (exposure/response)*	*Measures of human activity stresses*	*Measures of management responses*
Environment component/ecosystem state (air, water, biota, land)			
Environment-related human health (eg drinking water, waste management)			
Natural economic resources (eg energy, forestry)			

Source: Derived from Government of Canada, 1991, p 97

by Statistics Canada to develop environmental resource accounts. The ultimate goal of environmental indicators, according to the Minister of the Environment, is to develop a state of the environment index equivalent to GNP (see page 331). Although this goal still appears far off, there has been some success in developing individual resource accounts (eg for oil and gas, and energy use).

It is still far too early to evaluate the success of the Canadian environmental indicators. Other countries, such as the US and Australia, have also been making progress but with less success at the national level than in Canada. With work on these areas only having just begun in the UK, there is certainly much that can be learnt from the Canadian experience.

REFERENCES FOR ENVIRONMENTAL INDICATORS

Audit Commission (1988) *Performance Review in Local Government: a handbook for auditors and local authorities* HMSO, London

Department of the Environment (1994) *Sustainable Development: The UK Strategy* p 220, HMSO, London

Government of Canada (1990) *Canada's Green Plan for a Healthy Environment* Minister of Supply and Services, Canada

Government of Canada (1991) *A Report on Canada's Progress Towards a National Set of Environmental Indicators* Minister of Supply and Services, Canada

Local Government Management Board (1994) *Sustainability Indicators Research Project: Report of Phase One* a report prepared for the Local Agenda 21 Steering Group, LGMB, Luton

Organisation for Economic Co-operation and Development (OECD)(1991a) *Environmental Indicators – A Preliminary Set* OECD, Paris

Organisation for Economic Co-operation and Development (OECD) (1991b) *The State of the Environment* OECD, Paris

Thomas, W (ed)(1972) *Indicators of Environmental Quality* Plenum Press, London

ENVIRONMENTAL AUDITING QUESTIONNAIRE

(Distributed to all English and Welsh local authorities)

Bristol Polytechnic

St Matthias, Oldbury Court Road
Fishponds, Bristol BS16 2JP
Telephone Bristol (0272) 655384 Ext
Fax (0272) 585422

Department of Town and Country Planning
Head of Department and
Dean of Faculty of Environmental Management
Professor Peter Fidler

Dear Sir / Madam,

The enclosed questionnaire has been compiled to find out more about the process of environmental auditing in local authorities.

As I'm sure you are aware, the last few years have seen a growing interest in the benefits to be gained from environmental auditing. There is, however, a lot of research still to be carried-out in order to improve procedures and to assist in establishing models of good auditing practice.

This questionnaire is intended as a survey of local authorities' experience to-date. It will cover all local authorities in England and Wales. Part 1 is for those authorities who have carried-out an audit or are in the process of carrying one out and Part 2 is for those authorities who have not yet undertaken an audit. To be successful responses are required from all participants in the survey.

Because there is a lot of confusion over what constitutes an audit, I have adopted the definition used by the Local Government Management Board (LGMB). An environmental audit can therefore be an Internal Audit (IA), a State of the Environment Report (SoE) or a combination of the two (IA/SoE). IA is defined as " a systematic and objective evaluation of the environmental performance of a local authority." SoE is defined as " a comprehensive appraisal of the condition of the overall environment within the area covered by a local authority."

I look forward to receiving your completed questionnaire.

        Thank you.

        Noel Bruder

Polytechnic Director A C Morris MA FCA FSS FRSA

335

Part 1 <u>Local Authorities who have undertaken, or are in the process of undertaking, an environmental audit</u>

Identification

i.   Name of Local Authority   :

ii. Name of Respondent   :

iii. Department/Section/Post held   :

iv. Date   :

The purpose of the audit

1) Bearing in mind the definition of an audit outlined in the covering letter, with which type of audit has the local authority been involved?

Tick

one

box

1. State of the Environment Report (SoE)

2. Internal Audit (IA)

3. Full/Comprehensive Audit (SoE/IA)

4. Other - please specify

2) What stage has the audit process reached?

Tick

one

box

1. Completed

2. In progress

3. Being planned

3) What were the stated objectives of the audit?

1. Heightening awareness about the condition and needs of the environment

2. Enabling the authority to raise the profile of environmental issues

Tick

as

appro-

priate

3. Helping the authority to play an enhanced role in resolving environmental problems

4. Increasing public access to environmental information

5. Widening public participation in environmental decision making

6. Providing a baseline of environmental data in order to monitor progress and change

336

Codes
(Office
use only)

7. Identifying gaps in environmental data

8. Encouraging and co-ordinating co-operation between the many agencies - public, private, and voluntary, which have an environmental role

9. Enabling the authority to assess the environmental impact of their policies and practices

10. Producing an action plan, charter, or strategy for the environment

11. Providing a resource for educational use

12. Engendering the concept that environmental quality and economic well-being are complimentary

13. Providing information to assist the authority in their enabling/advisory role

14. Improving the image of the authority as an environmental role-model

15. Other - please specify

4) Who set the objectives of the audit?

1. Chief Executive or his/her office

2. Environmental Forum

Tick

one   3. Policy Committee

or   4. Environment Committee/Sub-committee

more   5. Officers working group

6. Other - please specify

5. None of the above

Codes
(Office
use only)

5) Before the audit was undertaken, did the authority have any of the following?

1. A general environmental policy ☐

2. An environmental or 'Green' charter ☐

Tick

3. A strategy for the environment ☐

one

4. Any other specific environmental policies - please specify ☐

or

more

☐

5. None of the above ☐

6) Have you referred to any of the following documents while preparing the audit?

1. 'Environmental Charter for Local Government' - Friends of the Earth ☐

2. 'Environmental Practice in Local Government' - ACC, ADC, AMA ☐

Tick

3. 'Managing the Environment - local authorities in action' -
Local Government Training Board ☐

one

4. 'The Environmental Role of Local Government' -
Local Government Training Board ☐

or

5. Other local authority audits ☐

more

6. Canadian or U.S. work on auditing ☐

7. 'Our Common Inheritance' - Department of Environment ☐

8. 'Environmental Auditing in Local Government' - Local Government
Management Board ☐

9. Other - please specify ☐

10. None of the above ☐

The Management of the Audit

7) Which of the following procedures were employed while carrying out the audit:

SoE   IA

1. Policies and practice of the authority listed, with general comments

2. Collection and analysis of secondary data about the local environment

Tick

one

3. Primary surveys on the state of the environment

or

4. Data for each environmental subject area assessed against pre-determined indicators or standards; eg. Friends of the Earth Charter

more

5. Use of a comparative matrix assessing the impact of each of the authorities policies and practices against each environmental subject area

6. Other - please specify

8a) Is there a unit or section within the local authority which has dealt specifically with the audit?

Tick
one
box

1. Yes   (go to Question 8b)

2. No   (go to Question 9)

8b) Briefly explain the nature and role of this unit

Codes
(Office
use only)

9) Which members committee deals with environmental initiatives?

    1. Policy Committee ☐

Tick   2. Environment Committee/Sub-committee ☐

one   3. Planning Committee ☐

box   4. Environmental Health Committee ☐

    5. Other - please specify ☐

Tick
one
box

10) Was an inter-departmental officers' working group established with responsibility for the audit?

    1. Yes ☐

    2. No ☐

11) Have any of the following staff appointments been made or planned in connection with the audit?

    1. Environmental Co-ordinator ☐

    2. Environmental Scientist ☐

    3. Researcher ☐

Tick   4. Database Manager ☐

one   5. Other - please specify ☐

or

more

    6. No new appointments ☐

<table>
<tr><td></td><td align="right">Codes
(Office
use only)</td></tr>
</table>

12) What mechanism has been used to link officers and councillors?

Tick

one

or

more

1. Officers - members co-ordinating group ☐

2. Environmental co-ordinator ☐

3. Representatives from officers on the principal environment committee ☐

4. Informal contacts ☐

5. Other - please specify ☐

13) Were outside consultants employed at any stage of the audit?

1. To help set the aims and scope of the audit ☐

Tick

one

box

2. To undertake the audit ☐

3. To assist internal staff in carrying-out the audit ☐

4. To review an internal audit ☐

5. Other - please specify ☐

14a) What was the budget for the audit?

Enter
amounts

| Initial budget | £ |
| For implementation of actions | £ |

14b) What are the main budgetary elements?

15) How many person- hours has the audit taken to complete?

Enter
number
of hours
or tick
box

1. Specify number of hours: ☐

2. Estimate of number of hours ☐

3. No estimate possible ☐

4. Not applicable ☐

Codes
(Office
use only)

Consultation Process

16) Were the public consulted as part of the audit?

Tick
one
or
more

1. Opinions sought to set terms of reference

2. Opinions sought on perception of environmental quality

3. Opinions sought to verify audit findings

4. Opinions sought on options for action

5. Other - please specify

6. No survey of public opinion carried out

17) Was an environmental forum established to represent the views of other agencies - public, private and voluntary?

Tick

one

box

1. Yes

2. Already in existence

3. No

18) How was the commitment and involvement of members of staff gained?

1. Staff bulletin/newsletter

Tick

one

or

more

2. Special information sheets

3. Departmental committees

4. Departmental 'Green' representatives

5. Informally

6. Other - please specify

7. None of the above

Tick
one
box

19) How important, in the context of the audit, is the influence a local authority can have on other groups' policies and practices through its role as regulator, advisor, educator and enabler.

Very
important

Not important
at all

Scope of the Audit

20) What subject areas/ issues have been covered in the audit?

Environmental Category   Areas of assessment

(Tick boxes as appropriate)	State of the environment	Impact of local authorities own <u>practices</u>	Impact of local authorities <u>policies</u> on the environment
Geology & Soils			
Air Quality			
Water Quality			
Waste & recycling			
Noise			
Energy			
Urban land use			
Rural land use			
Landscape & townscape			
Wildlife			
Open space			
Transport			
Food & agriculture			
Economy & work			
Purchasing policy			
Estate management			
Consumer advice & protection			
Environmental education			
Investment policy			
Other - please specify			

21) What sources of information have been used for the audit?

1. Primary surveying ☐

2. Data already existing within the local authority ☐

3. Central government ☐

4. Local voluntary organisations and community groups ☐

Tick

one

or

more

5. National voluntary environmental groups
   (eg Greenpeace, CPRE, FoE) ☐

6. Environmental Protection Agencies
   (eg National Rivers Authority, English Nature) ☐

7. Private industry ☐

8. Academic institutions ☐

9. Other local authorities ☐

10. Local authority associations ☐

11. Other - please specify ☐

22) Was a database used to compile the data?

Tick

one

box

1. Geographic Information System (GIS) ☐

2. Other computer system ☐

3. Manual database ☐

4. None ☐

23) How was the local authority's position on each issue assessed?

	SoE	IA
1. Predominantly U.K. limits or values	☐	☐
2. Predominantly E.C. limits or values	☐	☐
3. Best practice, nationally	☐	☐
4. Where possible best practice, internationally	☐	☐
5. Targets set in an environmental strategy or charter	☐	☐
6. Other - please specify	☐	☐
7. No attempt at assessment	☐	☐

Tick

one

or

more

344

Achievements of the Audit

24) How successful has the audit been at co-ordinating the activities of different departments within the local authority?

Tick one box

Very successful   ☐☐☐☐☐   Very unsuccessful

25a) How closely has the final audit report matched the stated objectives?

Very closely   ☐☐☐☐☐   Not at all

Tick one box

25b) Can you identify some areas of success and failure?

26) How effective was the chosen methodology found to be in meeting the objectives set for the audit?

Tick one box

Very effective   ☐☐☐☐☐   Not at all effective

27) How would you assess the contribution the audit has made to raising environmental awareness within the local authority and in the area as a whole?

(Tick as appropriate)

	Within local authority	Within area
1. Significant increase in awareness	☐	☐
2. Slight increase in awareness	☐	☐
3. No change	☐	☐
4. No assessment possible/ Don't know	☐	☐

28) What publications have resulted, or will result, from the audit?

	Public documents	Items for sale	Internal
1. State of the Environment(SoE) report	☐	☐	☐
2. State of the Environment summary	☐	☐	☐
3. Internal audit(IA) report	☐	☐	☐
4. Internal audit summary	☐	☐	☐
5. Joint SoE/IA report	☐	☐	☐
6. Joint SoE/IA summary	☐	☐	☐
7. Strategy for the environment	☐	☐	☐
8. Environmental action plan	☐	☐	☐
9. Information bulletins/newsletters	☐	☐	☐
10. Other - please specify	☐	☐	☐
11. No publications	☐	☐	☐

Tick

one

or

more

29a) Were recommendations for action a part of the audit?

1. Yes ☐

2. No ☐

3. They will form a later stage of the auditing process ☐

Tick

one

box

Tick as

appro-

priate

29b) Were these recommendations:

	Yes	No	Some
1. Costed	☐	☐	☐
2. Prioritised	☐	☐	☐
3. Delegated to specific staff	☐	☐	☐

The Next Step

30) What is the next stage in your auditing process?

1. Produce an IA report

2. Produce a SoE report

Tick   3. Produce a SoE/ IA report

one   4. Formulate an action plan

or   5. Implement recommended actions

more   6. Public consultation on findings

7. Internal debate of findings

8. Other - please specify

31) Have procedures been established to monitor performance on issues raised in the audit?

Tick   1. Yes

one   2. No

box   3. Partially

32) Can you list the 3 most significant actions which have taken place as a result of the audit?

1.

2.

3.

347

Codes
(Office
use only)

33) How often will reviews of the audit take place?

(tick as appropriate) Full Review Partial Review

1. Every year

2. Every 2 years

3. Every 3 years

4. Every 4 years

5. Every 5 years

6. More than 5 year intervals

7. No review planned

Thank you very much for helping with this survey. Please have a quick look back through the questionnaire to ensure that all questions are answered in full. A prompt return of the questionnaire, in the envelope provided, would be much appreciated.

Finally, I would be grateful to receive any documents your authority have produced relating to environmental auditing, or details of those available for purchase.

Thank you for your assistance.

Noel Bruder

Bristol Polytechnic,
Faculty of the Built Environment,
School of Town and Country Planning,
St. Matthias,
Oldbury Court Road,
Fishponds
Bristol BS16 2JP

Telephone (0272) 655384 Extension 262

Part 2 <u>Local Authorities who have not yet undertaken an environmental audit</u>

Identification

i.   Name of Local Authority   :

ii.   Name of Respondent   :

iii.   Department/Section/Post held   :

iv.   Date   :

A possible future audit

1a)   Do you intend to carry out an audit in the future?

Tick   1. Yes   (go to Question 2)

one   2. Undecided   (go to Question 2)

box   3. No   (go to Question 1b)

1b)   If you have decided not to carry out an audit, briefly explain why not

2)   Bearing in mind the definition of an audit outlined in the covering letter, what type of audit would be most appropriate for your authority?

        1. State of the Environment Report (SoE)

Tick   2. Internal Audit (IA)

one   3. Full/Comprehensive Audit (SoE/IA)

box   4. Other - please specify

        5. Don't know

Codes
(Office
use only)

3) Which of the following objectives do you think an audit should fulfill?

1. Heightening awareness about the condition and needs of the environment ☐

2. Enabling the authority to raise the profile of environmental issues ☐

3. Helping the authority to play an enhanced role in resolving environmental problems ☐

4. Increasing public access to environmental information ☐

5. Widening public participation in environmental decision making ☐

6. Providing a baseline of environmental data in order to monitor progress and change ☐

Tick 7. Identifying gaps in environmental data ☐

as

appro- 8. Encouraging and co-ordinating co-operation between the many agencies - public, private, and voluntary, which have an environmental role ☐

priate 9. Enabling the authority to assess the environmental impact of their policies and practices ☐

10. Producing an action plan, charter, or strategy for the environment ☐

11. Providing a resource for educational use ☐

12. Engendering the concept that environmental quality and economic well-being are complimentary ☐

13. Providing information to assist the authority in their enabling/advisory role ☐

14. Improving the image of the authority as an environmental role-model ☐

15. Other - please specify ☐

4) Do you think audits should be conducted using -?

Tick 1. In-house team (existing staff) ☐

one 2. In-house team (new specialist staff) ☐

box 3. External consultants ☐

4. A combination of the above ☐

		Codes (Office use only)

5) Have any of the following documents been brought to your attention?

1. 'Environmental Charter for Local Government' - Friends of the Earth

2. 'Environmental Practice in Local Government' - ACC, ADC, AMA

3. 'Managing the Environment - local authorities in action' - Local Government Training Board

Tick

one

or

more

4. 'The Environmental Role of Local Government' - Local Government Training Board

5. Other local authority audits

6. Canadian or U.S. work on auditing

7. 'This Common Inheritance' - Department of Environment

8. 'Environmental Auditing in Local Government' - Local Government Management Board

9. None of the above

The Local Authority and the Environment

6a) At present, does any evaluation of environmental policies and practices take place? (financial, quality, achievements etc)

Tick
one
box

1. Yes   (go to Question 6b)

2. Partially (go to Question 6b)

2. No   (go to Question 7)

6b) Briefly explain what form this evaluation takes

7) Does the local authority have any of the following?

Tick

one

or

more

1. A general environment policy

2. A strategy for the environment

3. A 'green'/environmental charter

4. None of the above

351

Codes
(Office
use only)

8) Which parts of the authority are responsible for environmental initiatives?
(ie. the development of new policies and programmes, monitoring strategies etc)
Mark with an asterix the lead agent(s) for environmental initiatives

1. Policy Committee

2. Environment Committee/Sub-committee

3. Planning Committee

Tick   4. Environmental Health Committee

one   5. Environmental Co-ordinator

or   6. Planning Department

more   7. Environmental Health Department

8. Inter-departmental Officers Working Group

9. Officers - Members Co-ordinating Group

10. Other - please specify

9a) Is there a separate budget for environmental initiatives?

Tick
one   1. Yes (go to Question 9b)
box
    2. No (go to Question 10)

9b) How much is this budget, annually?

Enter
amount £

10a) Has a public opinion survey on environmental issues been carried out in the area?

Tick
one   1. Yes (go to Question 10b)
box
    2. No (go to Question 11)

10b) How have the results of this survey been utilised?

11) Should the local authority be aware of environmental impacts at the following scales?

Tick as appro-priate

1. Globally

2. Nationally

3. Regionally

4. Locally

12) Briefly describe the three most recent environmental initiatives undertaken by the authority?

1.

2.

3.

13) Does an environmental forum exist to represent the views of other agencies - public, private and voluntary?

Tick

one

box

1. Yes

2. Being considered

3. No

Thank you very much for helping with this survey. Please have a quick look back through the questionnaire to ensure that all questions are answered in full. A prompt return of the questionnaire, in the envelope provided, would be much appreciated. Finally, I would be grateful to receive any documents your authority have produced relating to environmental policies and plans, or details of those available for purchase.

Thank you for your assistance.

Noel Bruder

Bristol Polytechnic
Faculty of the Built Environment
School of Town and Country Planning
St Matthias
Oldbury Court Road
Fishponds
Bristol BS16 2JP

Telephone (0272) 655384 Extension 262

BIBLIOGRAPHY

PART I: ENVIRONMENTAL AUDITING AND SUSTAINABILITY

Auditing

Association of Metropolitan Authorities (1989) *Action for the Future: Priorities for the Environment* AMA, London

Association of County Councils (1990) *County Councils and the Environment* ACC, London

Baskeyfield, A and Bardon, K (1991) *Local Authorities and the Environment: the position of the environmental audit within the public sector* Hatfield Polytechnic, Occasional Papers in Environmental Studies No 13, Hatfield

Brooke, R (1990) *The Environmental Role of Local Government* Local Government Training Board, Luton

Department of the Environment (1991) *Policy Appraisal and the Environment: a Guide for Government Departments* HMSO, London

Department of the Environment and Local Government Management Board (1993) *A Guide to the Eco-Management and Audit Scheme for UK Local Government* HMSO, London

Elkington, J (1990) *Environmental Auditing: A Green Filter for Company Policies, Plants, Processes and Productions* Conference Proceedings, IBC Technical Services Ltd, London

Friends of the Earth (1989) *Environmental Charter for Local Government* FoE, London

Friends of the Earth (1989) *An Introduction to the Environmental Charter for Local Government* FoE, London

Jacobs, M (1991) *Environmental Audit in Local Government: a guide* Local Government Management Board, Luton

Local Government Training Board (1990) *Managing the Environment: Local Authorities in Action* LGTB, Luton

Hillary, R (1993) *The Eco-Management and Audit Scheme: a Practical Guide* Technical Communications, Hertfordshire

McLaren, D and Bosworth, T (1990) *Environmental Audits of Local Authorities: terms of reference* Friends of the Earth, London

355

Mann, J (1991) 'Environmental Audits: the key to success' *Environmental Policy and Practice*, Summer 1991, 1(2), pp33–43

Morphet, J (1991) 'Environmental Auditing – an emerging role for green guardians' *Town and Country Planning*, June 1991, pp177–79

Morphet, J (1992) 'Gearing Up for the Eco-Audit' *Town and Country Planning*, February 1992, pp35–6

Planning News Journal *Environmental Assessment and Audit: A Users Guide 1992–1993*, Trio, Gloucester

Raemakers, J and Wilson, E (1992) (2nd ed) *Index of Local Authority Green Plans* Research Paper No 44, Edinburgh College of Art, Heriot-Watt University, Department of Planning and Housing

Raemakers, J (ed) (1992) *Local Authority Green Plans: A Practical Guide* Research Paper No 39, Proceedings of a Seminar held at Edinburgh School of Planning and Housing, 22 May 1992, Edinburgh College of Art, Heriot-Watt University, Department of Planning and Housing

Richards, L (1991) 'Environmental Auditing of Local Authorities' *European Environment,* Vol 1, Part 6, December 1991, pp22–6

Street, P (1992) *Approaches to Environmental Auditing in Local Authorities: Key Factors in an Effective Audit* unpublished MSc Thesis, Wye College, Kent

Taylor, D (1994) 'Piloting the EC EMA Regulation in Local Authorities' Proceedings of 3rd Annual Conference of the Institute of Environmental Assessment, London, September

Sustainability

Blowers, A (ed) (1993) *Planning for a Sustainable Environment* report from the Town and Country Planning Association, Earthscan, London

Department of the Environment (1990) *This Common Inheritance: Britain's Environmental Strategy* HMSO, London

Department of the Environment (1994) *Sustainable Development: The UK Strategy* HMSO, London

Department of the Environment (1994) *Climate Change: The UK Strategy* HMSO, London

European Commission (1990) *Green Paper on the Urban Environment* EU, Luxembourg

Gore, A (1992) *Earth in the Balance: Forging a New Common Purpose* Earthscan, London

Jacobs, M (1991) *The Green Economy* Pluto Press, London

Levett, R (1992) *Earth Summit: Rio 92, Supplement No 2: Agenda 21 A Guide for Local Authorities in the UK* Local Government Management Board, Luton

Local Government Management Board (1993) *A Framework for Local Sustainability: A response by UK Local Government to the UK Government's first strategy for sustainable development*, LGMB, Luton

Local Government Management Board (1993) *Towards Sustainability - The EC's Fifth Action Programme on the Environment: A guide for local authorities* LGMB, Luton

McClaren, D and Bosworth, T (1994) *Planning for the Planet* Friends of the Earth, London

Meadows, D H; Meadows, D L and Randers, J (1992) *Beyond the Limits: confronting global collapse, envisioning a sustainable future* Chelsea Green, Vermont

Pearce, D; Markandya, A and Barbier, E B (1989) *Blueprint for a Green Economy* Earthscan, London

Pearce, D (1990) *Sustainable Development* Earthscan, London

United Nations Environment Programme (UNEP) (1993) *Agenda 21: Programme of Action for Sustainable Development* UNEP

World Commission on Environment and Development (1987) *Our Common Future* (The Bruntland Report), Oxford University Press, Oxford

PART II: AUDITING KEY POLICY AREAS

Chapter 5: Nature Conservation

Further Reading

Countryside Commission (1993) *The National Forest Strategy* Countryside Commission, Northampton

Countryside Commission, English Heritage, English Nature (1993) *Conservation Issues in Strategic Plans* Countryside Commission, Northampton

Department of the Environment (1992) *Planning Policy Guidance Note 20: Coastal Planning* HMSO, London

Department of the Environment (1993) *Countryside Survey 1990 Main Report* Countryside Series vol 2, HMSO, London

Department of the Environment (1993) *Trees in Towns* HMSO, London

Department of the Environment (1994) *Planning Policy Guidance Note No 9: Nature Conservation* HMSO, London

Department of the Environment (1994) *Sustainable Forestry: The UK Programme* HMSO, London

Department of the Environment (annual) *Land Use Change in England* HMSO, London

English Nature (1991) *Site Management Plans for Nature Conservation* English Nature, Peterborough

Goldsmith, F B and Warren, A (1993) *Conservation in Progress* Wiley, Chichester

Nature Conservancy Council (1990) *Handbook for Phase 1 Habitat Survey: a Technique for Environmental Audit* NCC, Peterborough

Smith, R and Pritchard, D (1994) *Strategies for Wildlife: a study of local authority nature conservation strategies in the United Kingdom* RSPB, Sandy, Bedfordshire

Journals

ECOS – British Association of Nature Conservationists

English Nature and Enact – Managing Land for Wildlife (both English Nature)

Natural World – Royal Society for Nature Conservation (RSNC)

Conservation Planner – RSPB

Chapter 6: Energy

Further reading

CORE Conference (1990) *The Green Ultimatum for Building Design* Centre for Organisations Relating to the Environment (CORE), Bristol, March 1990

Curwell, S R; March, C and Venables, R (1991) *Buildings and Health: the Rosehaugh Guide to the Design, Construction, Use and Management of Buildings* RIBA Publications, London

Department of the Environment (1994) *Energy Efficiency in Council Housing – Guidance for Local Authorities* HMSO, London

Littler, J and Thomas, R (1984) *Design with Energy: the conservation and use of energy in buildings* Cambridge University Press, Cambridge

Olivier, D (1992) *Energy Efficiency and Renewables: Recent Experience on Mainland Europe* Energy Advisory Associates, Credenhill, Herefordshire

Sadler, R and Spencer, L (1983) *The Marketability of Passive Solar House Designs* London Business School, London

Smyth, A (1991) *Seasonal Affective Disorder* Unwin Hyman, London

Yannas, S (1989) *Passive Solar Energy Efficient House Design Handbook* Architectural Association, London

Chapter 7: Transport

Further reading

Association of County Councils (1991) *Towards a Sustainable Transport Strategy* ACC Publications, London

Barton, H and Stead, D (1993) 'Bristol Energy and Environment Plan: Sustainable Transport for Bristol' University of the West of England, Bristol. Faculty of the Build Environment Working Paper 3

Commission of the European Communities (1992) *Green Paper on the Impact of Traffic on the Environment* Brussels

Department of the Environment (1993) *Planning Policy Guidance Note 13: Transport* HMSO, London

Ecotec Research and Consultancy Ltd (1993) *Reducing Transport Emissions Through Planning* HMSO, London

ERR (1989) *Atmospheric Emissions from the use of Transport in the UK* vol 1, The Estimation of Current and Future Emissions, Earth Resources Research (ERR) and World Wide Fund for Nature (WWF), London

ERR (1990) *Atmospheric Emissions from the use of Transport in the UK* vol 2, The Effect of Alternative Policies, Earth Resources Research (ERR) and World Wide Fund for Nature (WWF), London

Holman, C (1991) *Transport and Climate Change: Cutting Carbon Dioxide Emissions from Cars* Friends of the Earth, London

Hughes, P (1991) 'The role of passenger transport in CO_2 reduction strategies' *Energy Policy,* 19(2), pp149–60

MVA Consultants (1991) *Bristol Integrated Transport and Environment Study (BRITES)* final report, Avon County Council, Bristol

OECD (1988) *Transport and the Environment* OECD, Paris

Roberts, J et al (1992) *Travel Sickness: the need for a sustainable transport policy for Britain* Lawrence and Wishart, London

Simpson, B (1994) *Urban Public Transport Today* E and F N Spon, London

TEST (1991) *Wrong Side of the Tracks: impacts of road and rail transport on the environment – a basis for discussion* Transport and Environment Studies, London

Tolley, R (ed) (1990) *The Greening of Urban Transport: planning for walking and cycling in Western cities* Belhaven, London

Whitelegg, J (1993) *Transport for a Sustainable Future* Belhaven Press, London

Chapter 8: Land Use Planning

Further reading

Barton, H, Davies G and Guise, R (1995) *Sustainable Settlements: a Guide for Planners, Designers and Developers* Univeristy of the West of England, Bristol, Local Government Management Board, Luton

Breheny, M (ed) (1992) *Sustainable Development and Urban Form* Pion, London

Elkin, T; McLaren, D and Hillman, M (1991) *Reviving the City: Towards Sustainable Urban Development* Friends of the Earth, London

Commission of the European Communities (1991) *Green Paper on the Urban Environment* Brussels

Department of the Environment (1993) *Planning Policy Guidance Note 22: Renewable Energy* HMSO, London

Department of the Environment (1993) *Environmental Appraisal of Development Plans: A Good Practice Guide* HMSO, London

English Nature (1992) *Strategic Planning and Sustainable Development* EN, Peterborough

Jacobs, M (1993) *Sense and Sustainability: Land Use Planning and Environmentally Sustainable Development* CPRE, London

Owens, S (1986) *Energy, Planning and Urban Form* Pion, London

Owens, S (1991) *Energy Conscious Planning: the case for action* Council for the Protection of Rural England, London

Transnet (1990) *Energy Transport and the Environment* Transnet, London

Chapter 9: Conservation and Aesthetics

Further reading

Cantaenzino, S (1993) *What Makes a Good Building?* Royal Fine Art Commission, London

Department of the Environment (1994) *Quality in Town and Country – A Discussion Document* HMSO, London

English Heritage Towns Forum (1992) *Townscape in Trouble: Conservation Areas, the Case for Change* Butterworths Law, London

HRH Prince of Wales (1989) *A Vision of Britain* Doubleday, London

Percival, A (1979) *Understanding our Surroundings* Civic Trust, London

RTPI (1993) *The Character of Conservation Areas* Royal Town Planning Institute, London

Worskett, R (1969) *The Character of Towns* Architectural Press, London

Chapter 10: Pollution

Further reading

Department of the Environment (1974–) *Central Directorate on Environmental Protection* Pollution Papers (ongoing), HMSO, London

Department of the Environment (1978–) *Digest of Environmental Protection Statistics* (ongoing), HMSO, London

Department of the Environment (1978–) *Interdepartmental Committee on the Redevelopment of Contaminated Land* (ICRCL) (ongoing), HMSO, London

Department of the Environment (1990) *This Common Inheritance: Britain's Environmental Strategy* HMSO, London

Department of the Environment (1991) *This Common Inheritance: Britain's Environmental Strategy* first year report, HMSO, London

Department of the Environment (1992) *This Common Inheritance: Britain's Environmental Strategy* second year report, HMSO, London

Department of the Environment (1993) *Urban Air Quality in the United Kingdom* first report of the Quality of Urban Air Review Group, HMSO, London

Department of the Environment (1994) *Paying for our Past* Consultation Paper on The arrangements for controlling contaminated land and meeting the costs of remedying the damage to the environment, HMSO, London

Department of the Environment (1994) *Planning Policy Guidance Note 23: Planning and Pollution Control* HMSO, London

Harrison, R M and Perry, R (1986) *Handbook of Air Pollution Analysis* Chapman and Hall, London

Hellawell, J (1986) *Biological Indicators of Freshwater Pollution and Environmental Management* Elsevier Science, Oxford

Hester, R E (1986) *Understanding our Environment* Royal Society of Chemistry, London

Her Majesty's Inspectorate of Pollution (1994) *Environmental, Economic and BPEO Assessment Principles for Integrated Pollution Control* Consultation Document, HMSO, London

Institute of Environmental Health Officers (1990) *Air Pollution Injury to Vegetation* IEHO, London

National Society for Clean Air (1994) *National Society for Clean Air and Environmental Protection Pollution Handbook* NSCA, Brighton

Purcell, R Y et al (1988) *Handbook of Control Technologies for Hazardous Air Pollutants* Taylor and Francis, Basingstoke

Royal Commission on Environmental Pollution (1971) *Pollution Reports* (ongoing), RCEP, HMSO, London

Journals

Acoustics Bulletin
Chemistry and Industry
Clean Air
ENDS
Environment and Business
Environmental Pollution
European Environment
Journal of Epidemiology and Community Health

Journal of Hazardous Materials
Journal of the Air Pollution Control Association
Journal of the Institution of Environmental Health Officers
Journal of the Royal Society of Health
Water and Environment Manager

Chapter 11: Waste and Recycling

British Plastics Federation (1993) *Directory of Plastics Recycling Companies* BPF, London

Cointreau, S M et al (1994) *Integrated Resource Recovery: Recycling Municipal Refuse* World Bank Technical Paper No 30, Washington

Confederation of British Industry (1990) *Environmental Auditing Guidelines for British Industry* CBI, London

Freshfields (ed) (1994) *Tolley's Environmental Handbook* Tolley, Surrey

Friends of the Earth (1991) *Recycling Officer's Handbook: FoE Guide for Local Authority Recycling Officers* FoE, London (Additional publications available on similar topics)

Local Authority Recycling Advisory Committee (1992) *Local Authorities Composting* WRA, London

Local Government Management Board (1992) *Local Authorities and the Environment* LGMB, Luton

New, R (1986) *Plastic Waste Recycling in the UK* Warren Spring, Stevenage

Royal Commission on Environmental Pollution (1985) *Resource Recovery* RCEP, London

Seymour, J and Giradet, H (1990) *Blueprint for a Green Planet* Dorling Kindersley, London

Tron, R (1987) *Recycling: A Practical Guide for Local Groups* Warren Spring, Stevenage

Waste Watch (1991) *Recycling: A Practical Guide for Local Groups* Waste Watch, London (Additional publications available on similar topics)

Woodfield M (1987) *Environmental Impact of Refuse Generation in the UK* Warren Spring, Stevenage

Periodicals and abstracts
Environmental Health News
Environment & Business
ENDS
Journal of the Institute of Waste Management
Hazardous Waste & Hazardous Materials
Recycling & Resource Management Magazine
Waste Management Research
Water & Waste Treatment
Warmer Bulletin

Chapter 12: Purchasing

Further reading

Elkington, J and Hailes, J (1988) *The Green Consumer Guide* Gollancz, London

Elkington J and Hailes, J (1989) *The Universal Green Office Guide* Universal, London

Local Government Management Board (1992) *Environmental Practice in Local Government* LGMB, Luton

Local Government Management Board (1994) *Green Purchasing and CCT* LGMB, Luton

Chapter 13: Community Awareness

Further reading

ACRE (1991) *Village Appraisals* Action with Communities in Rural England (ACRE), Cirencester

Bedford Square Press *How Green is Your City? Pioneering approaches to environmental action* available from Plymbridge Distributors Ltd, Plymouth

Calouste Gulbenkian Foundation *Meanwhile Gardens* Calouste Gulbenkian Foundation, 98 Portland Place, London W1N 4ET

Davidson, J (1988) *How Green Is Your City?* Bedford Square Press of NCVO, London

Department of the Environment (1993) *Your Council and the Environment – The Model Local Government Charter* DoE, London

Shell Better Britain Campaign (1994), Guide, Shell UK, Birmingham

INDEX